LEARNING
SUBMISSION

LEARNING
SUBMISSION

Joshua Tenpenny

Alfred Press
Hubbardston, Massachusetts

Alfred Press
12 Simonds Hill Road
Hubbardston, MA 01452

Learning Submission
© 2022 Joshua Tenpenny
ISBN 978-0-9905441-9-7

Second Printing

Printed in cooperation with
Lulu Enterprises, Inc.
Morrisville, NC 27560

Dedicated to the s-types of MAsT Massachusetts, the organizers of MsC, and (of course) to my master.

Contents

Introduction: The Rocky Road of Submission

A few years ago, at a Master/slave event (a gathering for people to discuss having a mutually fulfilling power imbalance in intimate relationships) I went to a slave-only discussion group. The room was packed with people from all over the country, some very new to this and some with decades of experience. At one point, one of the slaves said that she feared she was the wrong type of person to be a slave, because she was too assertive and opinionated, and she knew "real" slaves were supposed to be quiet and deferential.

A slave sitting next to her nervously raised her hand, and said, "Well, I *am* quiet and deferential, and I worry *I'm* doing it wrong, because I hear people saying that slaves should be powerful and assertive people, not passive doormats. I am pretty passive. Maybe I *am* a doormat?"

The facilitator then asked the group, "How many of you have felt like you are the wrong type of person to be a good slave, or that you don't fit the 'real slave' model?" He raised his own hand, and so did about three-quarters of the slaves in the room. Some hesitantly, some confidently. Nearly all of the more experienced people raised their hands.

For many of us, Master/slave relationships bring out some of the most vulnerable parts of ourselves—and that goes for masters as well as slaves—and most of us spent years ashamed of (or afraid of) our desires. So when a few of us have the willingness to stand up and say "I have these desires, and here is how I express them in a healthy, mutually fulfilling way," then they can become an inspiration to a whole lot of people who are relieved to have *any* remotely reasonable model.

It is not surprising that the model takes on so much power with us. But since we are looking to the model for reassurance that who we are and what we want is OK, when we see those parts of ourselves which fall outside of that model, that can bring back the feelings of shame and doubt. So, we redefine ourselves to fit the model, or we hide the parts that don't fit.

In an ideal world, when we are brave enough to share our concerns, we get the reassurance that our struggles and insecurities are part of the process, and then by sharing our own path, we are that model and inspiration for others like us.

Unfortunately, it doesn't always work out like that.

Sometimes when we are brave enough to be open about these things that fall outside the model, we are told that we are "Doing It Wrong." Maybe that message is subtle, maybe it is explicit. Maybe it isn't you who has been singled out, but it's someone like you, and that is enough.

In travelling around the country and teaching about M/s, my master Raven and I have met a lot of people with strong (and often differing) opinions on how to do M/s "right". I believe they, like us, genuinely want other people's Master/slave relationships to succeed and want our communities to thrive.

These relationships aren't easy. Even under the best circumstances, with the best intentions, this is dangerous territory we walk. When people have fought their way through this jungle and mapped the hazardous terrain, they want to share what they have learned—and when they see people veering off the marked trail, careening recklessly towards quicksand, they are likely to say, "What the hell are you doing? That's not the right way!"

In their eagerness to help, they may forget that there is more than one path through this jungle, and that some obstacles we need to face for ourselves. But for each person who is mindfully and intentionally heading for the quicksand, aware of and prepared for the risks, there are probably a hundred who are blindly heading that way because they read *Fifty Shades of Gray* or something like that, and only ten of them have any idea of the challenges ahead. While the advice is not *universally* applicable, in most cases it is solid advice.

This is the second reason to speak up when we fear we are doing things the "wrong way". Maybe we are. Maybe there are hazards in our path we aren't aware of, and even if we are pretty sure this is the right choice for us, we can at least try to find out *why* our chosen path is considered such a bad idea.

Our communities should be places where we can feel comfortable saying "Hey, I'm not sure if I'm doing this right. Can you help?" rather than being shamed or remaining silent. They should also be places where we can—kindly, compassionately, and *effectively*—talk to people who seem to be heading the wrong way.

So, when you notice that someone does things in a way that breaks the "rules" you know of how to be Master and slave, or when you feel like you are failing to live up to the standards of your community, let that be the start of a conversation, not the end of the conversation. We've only been mapping this territory for a short time in the grand scheme of things, and we can use all the field reports we can get.

Learning Submission was created by many hands. The people who wrote for it and were interviewed for it are real people, dealing with real lives while following, in part or wholly, the guiding orders of another person whom they trust. The style of relationship varies as much as the terms they use. Some are part-time and some are full-time. I tend to refer to anyone on my side of the slash as an "s-type", short for "submissive or slave", but there are so many terms used, and we know that people have differing definitions of all those terms, and there's no central authority to tell anyone that they can't use a certain word unless they do or don't do this set of things. We have let the various contributors use whatever terminology they use for themselves and for their "M-type" (whether Master, Mistress, Dominant, Daddy, Leader, Owner, or some other title). We were more interested in the reality of their situation than in their choice of terminology. We've also retained the capitalization preferences of our authors.

Every one of our contributors admits that the way to "mastering submission" wasn't easy, wasn't at all like an erotic novel. They struggled, they fell, but they got back up again—and they learned. Now we are passing at least some of their accumulated wisdom to you. If you've dreamed of being the follower to a strong and trustworthy leader, regardless of what others might say, this is our gift to your future. If you are already the s-type in a relationship, this is our gift to your present, to let you know that you're not alone.

This book is divided into two sections. The first section is for s-types who are seeking the right M-type, and it's all about how to prepare yourself and what to watch out for. The second section is all about the bumps in the road once you're ensconced as the follower in the relationship, because the difficulties don't all stop once the collar is on. Submission is hard work, and there's no shame in struggling with it—every follower does at some point.

This book contains a wide range of advice, opinions, and personal experiences. Any contradictions between the pieces are a reflection of the varied perspectives. It is our hope that among these essays, you will find advice relevant to you, and some reflection of your own joys and struggles.

Good luck,

Joshua Tenpenny
July 2022

Joshua Tenpenny (a.k.a. Raven's Boy) is a wholly owned subsidiary of the vast enterprise that is Raven Kaldera. He has spent 18 years as Raven's devoted assistant, partner, and slave for life. With Raven, he travels worldwide to talk about how to have healthy and mutually fulfilling authority-based relationships. Formerly a computer engineer and sex worker, in Raven's service Joshua has become a massage therapist, Shiatsu practitioner, and yoga teacher; an all-purpose farm hand and handyman; a devout polytheist and church secretary; and the computer tech behind Raven's various projects. Joshua is proud to have served as the 2014 Northeast Slave titleholder, and is a loyal member of MAsT Massachusetts. Joshua is the author of "Real Service" and the creator of the Service Notebook. He is polymorphously perverse, and strives to find spiritual fulfillment through any act of worthy service.

Part 1
Preparations

Myths, Lies, and Stupidities About Submission and Slavery

Raven Kaldera and Joshua Tenpenny

People often come into the world of power dynamic relationships with stars in their eyes, engorged genitals, and pornography spinning in their heads. (Or perhaps romantic bodice-ripper fantasies.) If they manage to find a partner, their dreams of how it "should be" get quickly smashed, and they may blame it on the partner and keep looking for the dream instead of adapting to reality. We've made a list of the most common assumptions people have about this role in power exchange, and we're here to throw cold water on those fantasies ... and maybe, just maybe, some real flowers will grow from that soil. If you read nothing else in this book, at least read this article. It will give you a basic idea of the different kinds of submission and slavery, and help you to figure out where you are on the map.

Myth #1: Being a submissive or (especially) a slave means that you live every day as if it were a porn fantasy—beatings, bondage, depraved sex acts, rubber clothing, etc.

Here's where we must throw our first bucket of cold water, and it's a big one. Most people find that managing the equivalent of a full-on BDSM scene every day is too much work, and it doesn't make room for all the necessary parts of life such as working, making a living, dealing with family members and friends, raising children, having hobbies, caring for elderly parents, doing paperwork, negotiating with roommates, etc. In the porn, masters are usually independently wealthy and never seem to do anything but play with their slaves and have dinner parties, and thus the "slaves" have a few domestic duties and are mostly playthings. In real life, only the tiniest percentage of humans would be able to live in that world.

Instead, relationships must compromise with reality. Some couples choose to have ordinary relationships with the occasional long weekend of fun and depraved BDSM play—and may not actually see each other in between—and some simply have an authority exchange where the dominant partner can tell the submissive partner what to do in their real, ordinary life, but that part isn't particularly sexy. Instead, it gives the s-types in question a sense of being cared for and a good leader to follow.

That doesn't mean that a more extensive power exchange relationship can't be kinky. It's possible to salt everyday life with small and subtly hot reminder of unequal roles. But in general, with very few exceptions, the sort of activities that go on in porn and in a scene can only be kept up for short periods of time. This means that the more full-time the power exchange may be—or the relationship itself, for that matter—the more time is spent "doing reality", if perhaps with a constant awareness that you're not the one making the decisions, and you have agreed to do it the way your dominant partner wants.

Some would-be slaves search desperately for the perfect permanent porn scene, over and over, only to find multiple failures. It might be more useful for them to just have an ongoing relationship where they have intense scenes with someone who enjoys their kink, and then go back to real life in between those periods.

This myth has a corollary, which we'll refer to as Myth # 1A, which says, "Full-time Master/slave relationships are actually impossible." The trumpeters of this myth are assuming, just like the porn-soaked searchers, that it means a daily BDSM scene which takes over your whole life. Yes, they are correct that it isn't sustainable. But no, that isn't what Master/slave relationships are generally about. Taking the unrealistic assumptions out of the picture shows that these relationships are quite feasible, when they are centered around a particular choice of relationship structure rather than a particular choice of kinks.

Myth #2: *These relationships are centered around sex and kink; nobody chooses this except for reasons of fetish.*

It's true that many (although not all) D/s and M/s couples do come out of the BDSM demographic, but we generally find that most long-term power dynamic relationships are far less about sex and far more about feeling that this is just a comfortable structure for the two (or more) of you to navigate the world together. While there are many happy kinky relationships between BDSM practitioners that last until both parties are old and gray, the relationships which are centered entirely around kinky sex, with little room for anything else, tend not to last very long (unless they consist only of part-time liaisons over a long period, with little to no contact in between). We've found that the less they are centered on kink (although matching sexual kinks can be an important part of compatibility) the more likely they are to work long-term.

Some couples who have a full-time complete authority transfer aren't even kinky (gasp!) and may not show up to BDSM events much, because they feel that they don't belong there. Vocabulary has sprung up around power exchange relationships for the non-kinky, including the terms Leader/follower and Leading/supporting.

Myth #3: "Real" power exchange relationships are full-time, 24/7, live-in situations.

Not at all. These are custom-built relationships, and the boundaries can be drawn anywhere. Some dominant partners hold sway part-time—such as when the s-type is in their presence—but not when the s-type goes home. Some have been given authority over some areas of the s-type's life, but not others—such as career, finances, voting, political views, friendships, family connection, religion, and children from former marriages. That does not make their relationship any less valid a power exchange. As we've said before, to claim that every power dynamic should go to the furthest extreme is the equivalent of saying that every believing Catholic should become a monk or a nun. Owner/property relationships, however sexy-looking from a distance, are not the cool kids' club.

Your relationship can be created any way that you want, and you don't have to follow someone else's template, be that the porn writer, the community you stumble into, or the couple you met last week. Designing a relationship that will work for both parties plus reality takes some time and thought and communication, but it's worth every minute you spend on planning it out and working it through.

Myth #4: *People want to become submissives or slaves because they have low self-esteem or are mentally damaged.*

Most of the slaves we know don't fit that mold at all—they are competent, worthy people who just want to be in these sorts of relationships. Some have figured out that they are better at being followers than leaders. Some want a venue for personal service, with someone trustworthy who will value them and their efforts. Some find that riding someone else's will helps them to motivate better. Some enjoy a highly structured relationship where they know exactly what to do and never have to guess because the rules are laid out. Some are highly assertive Type A people with hard-driving careers who want a safe place to relax and be carried along by someone else.

A percentage of s-types, of course, do come into these relationships with self-esteem problems, or any number of other mental diagnoses. Some have found that having the right M-type definitely helped their self-esteem over time if the M-type made a concerted effort to build it up. Many who have long-term relationships say that they are much saner in their power dynamic than they were out of it. Studies of couples in power exchange do not show a higher ratio of mental ill health than that of the general population.

This isn't to deny that some people with mental health problems do seek out power dynamics, hoping they will fix their problems, but most s-types we've met in relationships aren't those people.

Myth #5: *You should jump straight into a total power dynamic, handing over authority for everything in your life, from Day 1.*

We know some people who learned to drive a car by stealing their parents' vehicle in the middle of the night at the age of 14 and careening about town, desperately trying not to wreck up or get arrested. They survived it, but I doubt that anyone would ever recommend this as a reasonable way to learn to handle a car. Similarly, we know a small number of M/s couples who leaped straight into a dynamic without having known each other for very long, or negotiated particularly well. Every one of those couples has said to beginners, "Don't do it the way we did it. Take your time."

The surer way to handle it is to start slow. Give over a few areas of your life which won't ruin your life if they are mismanaged, and see how it goes for some weeks. If you can bring yourself to obey, and the M-type is able to manage those areas effectively and in a way that doesn't give you qualms, hand over another area and get used to that. Over time, trust will be built, and you can hand over more serious areas. If you want a list of suggestions, broken down by life area, we recommend the book *Negotiating Your Power Dynamic Relationship*, available at Alfred Press. It's good for both parties to look at, and for the cautious s-type, the potential M-type's willingness to go through the (rather slim) book with them can be a sign that they are willing to negotiate from a place of reality.

Myth #6: *Slaves have no limits.*

First, we want to make a distinction between limits and limitations. Limitations are things you can't physically or emotionally do, like flap your arms and fly, or stab someone on the street to get money for your master. Limits are *I will not do that.* It's perfectly OK to start out with lots of limits—and indeed, being able to say No shows that your Yes actually means something. Beware the dominant who pushes you to abandon your limits. A good one will respect them, and either be OK with you keeping those forever, or be willing to wait and earn your trust before working with you to let go of ones you could ditch if you really trusted the person.

For nearly all the slaves we know in long-term, healthy relationships, *I have no limits* is shorthand for *I inspected my M-type's limits and found them as good or better than mine, and I agreed to live under those.* That process of really seeing someone's values and honor takes time, and cannot be rushed. If the above isn't true for you, keep your limits.

The corollary to this is *Slaves have no rights,* or perhaps that ought to be phrased *Slaves should have no rights.* Except as we've said before, there is no "should" here. Any given consensual slave has as many rights as has been comfortably negotiated with their Authority. The majority of consensual slaves are going to be able to walk out if the relationship becomes too problematic, even if it is sad and painful and hard to break their promises.

Myth#7: *Slaves are not allowed to question orders.*

It would be great if masters were all perfect people who never gave a confusing order, or forgot to include important details, or made mistakes, or did not have all the information needed to make a good decision. We hate to tell you this, but that master doesn't exist in the world of human beings. The master you will end up with (assuming that you find the right person) will be a fallible human who will probably evidence all of the above—plus their own unique set of mental boners—at various points in the relationship. If you are to follow orders correctly, sometimes you will need to ask for clarification.

Beware the M-type who can't deal with you asking for that clarification. That's often a sign of insecurity. They may believe that questioning them is a sign of disrespect, and they haven't thought through how they will handle all the above-listed imperfections in their communications … and they are not self-aware or sensible enough to want to look at the gaps in their thought process, so they shut you down and cover it up. Then, of course, when you make the inevitable error which they set you up for, it will all be your fault. Hopefully that's a red flag you'll only need to go through once, if at all.

If you are dealing with an inexperienced dominant partner who lacks leadership skills but is willing to listen and communicate, you can point out that giving you maximum rather than minimum information will get them a better result, and that respect can be shown by the way you ask for information, rather than not asking at all. This can be followed up by suggesting that they think about how they would want you to ask for more information, in a way that will make them feel good about giving it rather than challenged or threatened. It's their job to tell you how to respectfully ask in a way they like. It's your job to learn to do it that way.

Some inexperienced M-types worry that too much questioning is a way of arguing with the order, or showing your dislike of the order. It's your job to search yourself and your motivations and honestly check to see if you're doing that. If you tend to be argumentative in the rest of your life, it may take a while to get over that habit, but the more you do it, the less you M-type can trust you to not be wasting their time or challenging their authority. If you can talk to them about it, and tell them that you're trying your best not to do that (or that you've examined your interactions and you're honestly sure that's not what you're doing) then they may feel better about you asking questions.

Also, unless the M-type has a great deal of experience giving (or at least receiving) orders in a context where the subordinate is not allowed to speak freely—such as military service—they are extremely unlikely to be skilled at giving clear orders and establishing that the subordinate understands them. In a power exchange context, many M-types find this to be more trouble than it's worth.

Regardless, don't let the flow of information be cut off, and don't put up with a partner who requires that.

Myth #8: The master sets the rules at the beginning of the relationship, and the slave gets no say. If there is a contract, the master writes it, and the slave must obey it.

Another unrealistic porn rule! All the good, long-lasting power dynamics we know involved mutual negotiation, over a period of time. Every s-type is different and has different needs, and the M-type can't just trot out a boilerplate system and expect it to apply to any random s-type indiscriminately. Instead, a good master will get to know you well, even getting into your head, and create the structure to fit both your needs and desires, with your aid and collusion. Beware of dominants who buy the porn rules. The two of you both need to have a say in how the system will work, or at the very least the M-type needs to take everything you are into consideration, or this bird won't fly for long.

Of course, a dominant has the right to say, "My way or the highway." And the s-type has the right to say, "No, we're not compatible. The right person would take the person I am into account." (Or, possibly, "Actually, I like everything about your way. Sounds like a plan.") The problem is when would-be masters try to fool inexperienced would-be slaves into believing that this is the way it should be done, or even the way it's usually done. It's not. Mutual negotiation is the more usual routine for the relationships which last.

Another version of this one is:

Myth #9: *If you are looking for an M-type, you can't set limits around what sort of M-type you want, because that would be unslavey. You must adapt to whatever M-type you talk to who is even vaguely not a psycho, and they get to say how the relationship goes from the beginning, without your input.*

Absolutely wrong. You need to choose just as wisely as you would for an egalitarian relationship—perhaps more so, because you will have less recourse. Do not settle. It's OK to regretfully inform a potential M-type that you don't think they're compatible enough with what you want. If they react in a surly manner, telling you that you're not a real slave, then you know you just dodged a bullet.

We always advise that seeking s-types don't settle for someone who, when you name your limits, says that they will hold off because they love you, or because they are merciful. Look for someone who says, "I don't do that. That's not who I am."

Myth #10: *Being a submissive or slave means that you never have to take responsibility for anything, including your own behavior. You dominant or master will be there to make you do the right thing, so you can revert to being a child with no responsibilities.*

We've had a lot of would-be slaves come to us with this fantasy. Being an adult is a difficult struggle for them, or they have trouble motivating themselves to manage their lives well, or they make bad decisions, or they suffer from emotional deregulation or mental illness, and they have some idea that becoming a slave would make it all better. The master would issue orders in their magical dominant master-voice, and they would find themselves automatically obeying even in the face of all their internal resistance.

That's setting both parties up for failure. Taking on the supporting role—even to the extent of being property—is not a way out of being an adult and taking responsibility for your behavior. Sure, you can have periods where you play at being a "little", if your dominant partner is into being your "Big", but you still have one big responsibility: You must be able to control yourself and obey orders. If you can't do that—without excessive arguing, fighting, or resentment—this isn't going to work. If you can't make yourself obey, even on the worst days, then your master is not in control—your own head problems are the master.

Of course, you can claim that a "True Master" would somehow be able to control you despite all your resistance, but we've not found that to work well. Generally, the obedience lasts until the s-type is having a bad day or really doesn't want to do the thing, and then the magic master-voice doesn't work, and they blame the M-type for not being able to "master them properly". After a few repeats of this, the whole thing falls apart and the s-type is off again, looking for that "True Master" who doesn't actually exist.

On the more dangerous side, the whole "Force me to obey!" can sometimes encourage inexperienced dominants who are at a loss—or unethical ones who want an excuse—to resort to physical violence in order to enforce obedience, which does not lead to any kind of a good situation.

Most honorable and reasonably competent dominant people aren't usually interested in the amount of work needed to force someone to obey, anyway. Having a partner who agrees to do something and then angrily rebels can make them feel like the s-type doesn't really want to be in that relationship after all. It's also a pain in the ass, and most won't put up with it. In addition, few dominants either want or are qualified to be a life coach. (Generally, the few who want to aren't qualified, and the few who are qualified don't want to do it in their personal life.) So, if you're looking for a power dynamic to fix your problems ... don't do it. Get some objective therapy instead.

Every crack that you fix before you come to the negotiation table will be a gift to your future dominant partner.

Myth #11: *No matter how difficult or unreasonable the order is, you are responsible for making yourself do it, and your dominant partner shouldn't have to think about how much an order costs you.*

You'll notice that this myth is the exact opposite of the one we just debunked. Both are untrue, and both are spouted out of the mouths of inexperienced people. The reality is somewhere in the middle of these two extremes.

It is your job to make yourself obey, yes. But if you're having trouble, you have the right to go to your M-type and tell them that, and ask for help, and get it. It's your job to be honest and transparent and not keep the information from them, because they need to know how you react to different situations. But it's their job to help you in your struggle with that order, and to make the best decision possible about how to handle it. Maybe that means rescinding, if they feel it's not worth the trouble. Maybe that means sitting down with you and figuring out how to make it easier, either be changing the parameters in some way, or reframing the painful parts, or something else.

The healthy process should look like this:

1) The M-type issues an order.
2) If the s-type is really struggling with it, they have the *obligation* to tell the M-type about their struggle.
3) The s-type has the *right* to ask for help with the order. (Unless they signed away that right, but any M-type who demands they give up their right to ask for help is pretty stupid in our book, and shooting themselves in the foot.)
4) The M-type has the *obligation* to help them get through the struggle.
5) The s-type has the *obligation* to work with the M-type in this process, and give it their best effort.

6) If all efforts fail after everyone has tried their hardest, the M-type has the *obligation* to rethink the situation. (Getting outside help or advice is perfectly reasonable here.)

These relationships may be unequal in status, but they are equal in responsibility. Each side of the slash has their own jobs, and they interlock with each other to make a complicated situation work in a healthy way. Which brings us to:

Myth #12: *Slaves should keep their feelings and problems to themselves; good slaves don't complain about anything.*

This is the exact opposite of what an s-type should be doing. Contrary to popular belief, M-types are not telepathic and cannot magically figure out what's going wrong in your head, especially if you deliberately hide it from them. Also contrary to popular belief, leadership and management of another human being is not easy, and withholding information from them makes it harder. The more transparent you are about your mental state, your concerns, your struggles, the more information they have in order to make good decisions about it. In fact, when you withhold that information, you make it impossible for them to do their job well. You are sabotaging them.

That's what you must tell yourself, over and over, if you're the sort of s-type who desperately wants to be seen as the "perfect slave", and you are ashamed to admit that you might be less than perfect and need some help. Remind yourself that *I am sabotaging my M when I hold this back.*

Beware the opposite side of the coin—the M-type who doesn't want to hear your concerns, who blows you off or does not take you seriously when you bring them to the table. This is not someone who sees who you are, or is interested in seeing who you are, and they will be unable to make good decisions for you.

Myth #13: *Men are naturally masters and women are naturally slaves.*

There are still a small percentage of people around who believe that nonsense, and they generally stick to very homogenous communities, because if they don't, they might encounter the thousands of female dominants with male submissives, gay and lesbian M/s couples, and the transgender and non-binary folks of all stripes who appear randomly on either side of the slash. Looking at the diversity of most such communities—all but the ones who specifically restrict their membership to a more monolithic whole—it's impossible to believe such antiquated foolishness. No matter what your gender, there are many people who also check that box who are on either side of power dynamics. In addition, as younger people are coming into this relationship style, the diversity only flourishes.

This is not to say that cultural stereotypes don't affect people, because they do. In fact, one could say that some people fetishize them. They find them sexy and/or romantic, so those stereotypes are the costumes, the drag, with which they "dress up" the relationship style. There's nothing wrong with saying, "This is who we are with each other," so long as that's followed up with "…even if that's not true for anyone else." It's generalizing outside of one's relationship that becomes ridiculous.

Myth #14: *All dominant/master-type people are SM sadists, and all submissive/slave-type people are SM masochists, and never the lines shall cross.*

Again, absolutely not true. Some people are dominant or submissive in their relationships but don't do SM at all, or are SM switches but don't switch their power exchange role. In addition, some folks are submissive sadists or dominant masochists. Some slaves happily give their masters the sensation play the masters want, exactly the way they want it, as a service. And … some SM switches also do power exchange switching in various ways.

Generally, the thing to remember is that activities are not dominant or submissive—people are. The sex people like doesn't line up neatly with their preferred role. One rule tends to be present in most power dynamics, though—the master gets the kind of sex they want, and the slave's job is to go along with it, whatever it may be.

Myth #15: *Masters can't love their slaves because they won't be able to discipline them OR masters must love their slaves or there will be abuse.*

Neither of these completely opposed myths are true. Some masters and slaves are romantically involved; some aren't and have service-centered relationships. Again, these are custom-built relationships and couples can work them out however they like.

Generally, the people going around saying that masters oughtn't to fall in love with their slaves are people who have never been the primary caretaker of a young child. They've never experienced a situation where you are required to spend eighteen years passionately loving another creature and still laying down the law about running in the street, sticking fingers in light sockets, beating up siblings, doing one's homework, etc., and dole out consequences without cutting off love. It's actually a lot easier with an adult.

The folks spouting the opposite myth usually think that love prevents abuse … but people are capable of loving each other and still treating each other badly. It's honor, good judgment, and self-control that prevents abuse.

Some masters—and some slaves, but that's rarer—prefer non-intimate relationships, and that works well for them. The majority seem to want romantic love into the mix, or else experiencing the intimacy of power exchange stimulates romantic love even if they didn't intend that. As long as both parties are on the same page, it's all good.

Myth #16: *Power dynamics, and especially Master/slave relationships, are very formal and have a lot of high protocol.*

Some do, some don't. You get to figure out what you want and pick a dominant partner who wants that as well. However, we have one caveat about high protocol: Beginning s-types often fetishize it, and then when they have to live it day in and day out, they find it repressive or stultifying or unsustainable over the long haul, in a chaotic real life. Be prepared to make changes—and to pick a dominant partner who is willing to make changes—if it wasn't the sexy ride you thought it would be.

The other half of that warning is that most M-types aren't really all that thrilled with high protocol. In fact, sometimes it seems like there are far more s-types who desire high protocol than there are M-types who are willing to go along with it. Formal, high-protocol relationships are a lot of work for the M-type, and they must be passionate about it or they won't bother.

Myth #17: *The sub has all the real power in the relationship because they can just walk away.*

That ... strongly depends on the relationship in question, and the agreements set up by both people, and how long it's been going on. If the authority transfer is limited only to certain areas of life which do not include jobs, money, major life decisions, etc., that may be true. If there is no agreement that the s-type is in for life and may not leave without the M-type's permission—or the agreement exists but both parties know on some level that it would not hold the s-type in the face of them becoming desperate—then that may be true to some extent. If the M-type is honestly concerned that the s-type will probably leave if the relationship goes in a way they don't like, then it may be true.

However, if there's an agreement that the slave (and at this point, they will probably be a slave) is not allowed to disobey their master, or leave without permission, and both parties are sure that this agreement will hold even in the face of difficulties, then the slave may have limited effective ability to resist their master. (We assume that's what they wanted, and we hope that the master is worthy of holding that power for them.) Even without a formal agreement, it can be extremely difficult to walk away from someone who has established any real measure of control over you. The conditioning can be very strong, even when that is not intentional.

This is on top of practical considerations such as employment opportunities, financial independence, etc. The closer the power exchange is to a total power exchange, the less effective power they have, by definition. There's a spectrum of transfer of authority, power, and control, from "only a little, and not in big important areas" to "everything in your life, plus some conditioning and internal enslavement".

We also want to stress that no place on that continuum is more "right" or "proper" than any other. The ideal is whatever works well for both parties, not any particularly point on the spectrum. Don't believe people who say that everyone should strive for any given level of power exchange. Work out what is right for you—and don't let a partner push you to a point you aren't comfortable with, either.

Myth #18: All relationships need safe words, or bad things will happen. OR Real Master/slave relationships don't use safe words.

Again ... it depends. Safe words were invented for BDSM play, which ends with the scene, and specifically for those who like to yell "No! Stop! Don't!" as part of roleplay and have it ignored. Power exchange couples who do BDSM as part of their sex play (and not all do) might or might not use safe words during kinky play, but very few couples ever use safe words to get out of the dynamic. (Unless "I'm upset and I don't want to do this anymore," is a safe word.)

Even with BDSM play, some non-PE couples might eliminate safe words because A) they never do dramatic resistance scenes where the bottom wants to pretend to want it to stop, and B) they have played together for so long that they intimately know each other's bodies and responses, and can easily tell when the partner is in distress.

The safe word argument is usually brought up by people who lack understanding of what a 24/7 power dynamic actually looks like, and are still stuck on Myth #1, thinking it's like a scene, but all the time.

*Myth #19: The term **submissive** refers to bedroom-only submission and obedience, while the term **slave** refers to outside-the-bedroom submission. OR The term **submissive** refers to a limited authority transfer,* *while the term **slave** refers to a more total authority transfer. OR pretty much any other way of dividing up those words, including defining **property**.*

Sadly, as of right now, there is not only no single accepted definition in general circulation, but also also a great deal of white-hot-angry infighting over which definitions ought to be the correct ones. Many people will insist that their definition is the right one, whether it's one of the above or something else. Don't believe anyone who says that their definition is the accepted one "in the community". What they're not telling you is that there is no one "community". There are a whole lot of small communities with different subcultures who don't all agree with each other, so the truest that statement can be is "That's what the people in my small subcommunity use as a definition, and we're pretending the rest don't exist." (And everything we said above goes for Master/Mistress/Dom/Domme/Dominant as well.)

Part of the problem is that people fetishize these terms. They conjure very strong imagery in people's minds, and emotions in their hearts. The fall in love with them, but at the same time they don't want to have relationship boundaries which don't make them happy. They get caught between having the relationships they want and perhaps losing those beloved titles if they go with someone else's definitions, so they decide that they are a whatever, and that the definition extends to the way they organize their relationship regardless of where the boundaries are. At the same time, other people may have strong negative reactions to those terms for historical/cultural reasons, and not use them even if their relationship boundaries look a lot like many others who do.

This makes it very difficult for the beginner to decide what label to take. "Am I a S---? Or not?" All that we can suggest right now is to not get hung up on labels. Decide what you want your relationship to look like first. Then, if one of those labels appeals strongly to you, use it. Understand that whichever label you take, someone will probably argue with you. Don't let it stop you.

We should also note that some folks have decided to throw out those terms altogether, and may use the terms "Leader/follower" or "Leader/supporter". Some refer to their s-types as their servant, or bondservant, or "charge". We look forward to seeing how this all settles out in a few years.

Doing Your Due Diligence
slave sherry

Getting into a power dynamic with a partner can be dangerous. Even if they aren't violent, there's always the possibility of emotional damage, and as submissives and slaves we are vulnerable. We're supposed to be vulnerable—that's part of the job! And allowing yourself to be open and vulnerable can be wonderful when it's with someone who has earned your trust, but that trust must be earned, not just given away indiscriminately.

Especially if you want to be a slave, the most important decision you make will be about the person you choose to submit to. If you use good judgment about choosing the person to whom you will eventually give your choices, you can relax and be comfortable and not have to yank them back. But you can't make that kind of judgment in a few days, or even a few weeks. You need to learn everything you can about them before you make a commitment where you agree to give up your rights.

Notice that I said, "agree to give up your rights", not "give up your rights"! On the one hand, you can't legally give up your rights to someone else, even if you think it's a hot fantasy. But we all know that this has nothing to do with the law—it's about two people making a personal agreement. The law doesn't legally require married people to love, honor, and cherish each other. Almost all slaves can, theoretically, break that agreement and walk away from it if they realize the relationship is not good for them. However, sometimes that walking-away bit isn't so easy.

Reasons Why It's Hard For Slaves To Walk Away

1) **Falling in love with the dynamic.** This is a phrase I first heard spoken by the editors of this book, and I resonated with it, because I've done that before. If you've been dreaming about being a slave to a wonderful master for years, you can end up falling in love with being a slave as much or more as you are with the human master. Sometimes those feelings are confused—it's hard to sort out what/who you love more, the

master themselves or the slavery. Sometimes falling in love with the slavery makes you think you've fallen in love with the master when that's not really what's going on. When you love the condition of slavery that much, you may be far more willing to put up with the wrong master to get it. Remember that there are other places in the world where you can get that. This unsatisfying situation is not the only one.

2) *Falling in love with the Master.* Even in an egalitarian relationship, it's hard to leave someone you love. Remember that love doesn't automatically mean compatibility, nor does it mean that people won't hurt each other. These kinds of relationships require a very high level of compatibility, and if you don't have that, love is not enough to make a power dynamic work out. A more egalitarian relationship, maybe, but not M/s.

3) *Your sense of honor.* Some slaves are strongly bound to their sense of honor. Their bond is their breath, and breaking it would make them feel like horrible people. "I promised, so I stay, no matter how hard it gets!" Except someone once said that "Death Before Dishonor" mostly sorts people into two piles: the dead and the dishonored. You need to make a promise to yourself as well, to care about and protect yourself as you would the most important person in your life. You may be thinking, "But slaves shouldn't think of themselves as the most important person in their life!" You'd be wrong. A slave who knows they have an excellent situation with a good master who can be trusted to care for them as well or better than they would care for themselves ... well, that slave has the safety to not think of themselves first. A slave who isn't in that situation—they are unpartnered, or their partner has not proven themselves trustworthy to take that burden— does not have the privilege (yes, privilege!) of laying down the burden of self-care-first. That must be your first promise. Any future promise that ends up contradicting it must be abandoned, and you learn the lesson not to make promises that will mess you up.

4) **Practical Limitations.** In some power exchange relationships, the s-type—especially if they are a slave—may not have access to their own money, or be allowed to hold a job, or own property, or drive a car, etc. (That's not true across the board, but some agree to these or other restrictions.) Some live in their master's home rather than having their own place. Some lose contact with their friends because their power dynamic is all-consuming. (We're hoping that the master is not being so callous as to ban friends and social contact. That's a red flag.) If you've agreed to restrictions which make it a lot less easy to just up and leave—especially around money, jobs, housing, or friends—you may find it a lot scarier to contemplate leaving. However, even starting from scratch is better than staying in a bad situation.

5) **Intimidation.** If the slave is someone with poor confidence or low self-esteem, an unscrupulous master can bully them into believing that it's wrong for them to leave.

6) **Habit.** If they've spent years trying their best to obey this master humbly and automatically, it may be very hard to be able to break out of that and disobey, especially if it's the ultimate disobedience—leaving, or threatening to do so if things do not change. Some may find themselves reverting to habitual deference and obedience, even if a part of themselves is screaming not to do it.

I could also write an even more frightening list of warnings about slaves who ended up in terrible, abusive relationships, including the tiny percentage who end up being murdered by their psychopath masters, but the truth is that most M/s breakups are less violent and dramatic and more simply dysfunctional, riddled with dishonesty, poor relationship skills, lack of communication, jealousy, arguments, insults, hiding emotions, weaponizing emotions, etc. You know, the same trouble that breaks up egalitarian relationships! Except when you're on the slave side, you're more vulnerable and you can get very hurt.

That's not to say that masters don't get wounded during breakups—they have feelings too, and they can also get hurt. But I'm talking to slaves here, and the best way to avoid all that is to pick the right person—and that means doing your due diligence and checking them out thoroughly.

Take as long as you need to find out what sort of person this would-be master is. Don't let them rush you, or demand more trust than you're comfortable with. (You can also remind them that they need to take time to get to know you and your own trustworthiness as well.) Here are some red flags that should at least get you to ask questions, and be wary.

1) They tell you that you must obey them immediately, before everything is negotiated and agreed. This also includes demanding that you call them by a title which hasn't yet been earned.
2) They demand things which haven't been negotiated yet, such as gifts, money, naked pictures, sex, BDSM play, or information about your workplace or family.
3) They are dishonest—you catch them in lies or serious evasions which turn out to be lies. Backpedaling and justifying when caught are more red flags.
4) They don't want to meet in person.
5) They refuse to discuss limits and limitations like reasonable adults.
6) They agree to your boundaries, and then try to cross them. They don't take no for an answer.
7) They change major rules without discussing it with you.
8) When you mention safety concerns, they blow you off or tell you that it's silly to worry.
9) They don't walk their talk. They say they will or won't do things, and then renege on that.
10) They tell you that "real slaves" don't have your limits, or any limits.
11) They can't control their temper.
12) They don't seem to be all that interested in you and your concerns, opinions, disabilities, or anything that gets in the way of seeing you like a cardboard slave cutout.

13) They are nasty to service personnel—waiters, cashiers, etc. This suggests that they don't respect people in service, which does not bode well for their slave.

14) They are unnecessarily mean to you and to others who are not their slave. Especially helpless animals or children.

15) They want you to cut off contact with family and/or friends and/or groups, even if you have good relationships with those.

16) They don't want to talk about past relationships, and they don't want you looking into those.

17) They body-shame you (unless that has been specifically negotiated), or attempt to shame other parts of your identity, or say things which seem aimed at undermining your confidence or self-esteem.

18) They push you to move in with them right away, or for you to let them move in with you right away.

19) They start telling you that they love you when they barely know you.

20) They ask for your bank account information or your passwords.

21) They make out like everything is your fault, and they refuse to take responsibility for their actions and emotions.

22) They want you to do things which jeopardize your safety, such as public nudity or public sexual acts.

One of the great things about having a community of people who share versions of the same lifestyle with you is that they can help you get a more objective read on a potential master or slave without judging you for wanting to be in that kind of relationship to begin with. If you're the kind of person whose "people picker" is broken—if you tend to pick exactly the wrong sort—it might be good to have two or three people whom you go to for second, third, and fourth opinions. Two or three is better than just one, because everyone has biases and it's good to have multiple views to compare.

However, after you've cleared all of these out of the way, there's a whole other list of red flags which will be *personal to you*. They don't mean that the master is a bad person; they just mean that this master isn't compatible with you. Smoking? Politics? Wanting or not wanting children? Monogamy vs. polyamory? Sexual ethics? Tattoos? Wanting you to stay home vs. working? Remember that you need a lot of compatibility, and don't settle. Every place where the two of you aren't compatible is either going to be a place where you will have to sacrifice what you want, or where the master isn't going to get what they want out of the dynamic. Neither are happy, and sometimes it's better to politely bow out than to commit yourself to a relationship with an otherwise good person where you will both continually have to make painful compromises.

Again, take as long as you need to get the answer to all these questions. Someone who isn't willing to be patient while you go through this process probably isn't right for you anyway. If you are really a slave at heart, choosing the right master is the most important decision you will ever make. Treat it like that.

Slave sherry is in devoted service to her Mistress, Lady Jean, and lives with her Mistress and her Mistress's other slave, bennett, next to the ocean. Slave sherry loves cats, dogs, walks on the beach, nipple clamps, and walks on the beach while wearing nipple clamps.

What Have You Got to Offer?

slaveboy shane

I meet a lot of submissives—especially but not limited to male submissives—who want to find a dominant who will order them around and give them lots of kinky sex. There's nothing wrong with that, but I also spend a fair amount of time talking them out of jumping into a full-time slavery situation just because it sounds hot. That's not to say that some of them couldn't become good slaves for the right person, but one of the biggest problems is that they don't have anything to offer a potential master or mistress, and that's going to hamper them in their search.

Many of them stare at me in complete surprise when I ask them, "So what have you got to offer a potential Mistress?" It's never occurred to them that they *ought* to have something more to offer than a willing limp body on which to perform despicable sexual deeds. Good masters, though, are in short supply, and there's a lot of competition. Sure, there are plenty of flashy jerks in leather vests or corsets, waving a whip or an ego and claiming to be Super Dom/me, but most of those aren't worth the cowhide they're wrapped in. (And many of them are just looking for free sex or free money or free housecleaning, or somewhere to vent their bad behavior and call it dominance.)

So how do you set yourself apart from the swarm of pathetic do-me queens who are vying for the attention of decent dominant people, and end up in a more permanent situation? When I was looking, I talked to a lot of other slaves who were already in good relationships. I learned not to ask, "How do I get me a Mistress?" thinking that it was all about what clothes to wear, or where to "shop" for one. I learned that it was more informative to ask the slave and their Master what qualities drew them to that person rather than another one.

I also learned that it wasn't all about looks. People like me who aren't the prettiest people in the world tend to blame the lack of a partner on lack of good looks, but many of the slaves I talked to weren't all that beautiful either, and yet their Masters and Mistresses valued them. Yes, there are shallow people out there who only want someone physically good-looking, but there are plenty who don't care.

On the other hand, I had to learn, also, to not be one of those people. A would-be slave who is too set on getting a Mistress or Master who is model-attractive so that they can have a focus for their sexual fantasies is just as shallow as the Mistress or Master who won't choose them because they're not good-looking enough. If that's more important to you than finding a partner who will treat you well and communicate honestly, then find an attractive professional and pay her to have scenes with you. (Or if you're looking for a male Master, it's a lot easier to find an attractive top to play with, and don't try to go beyond play.) But when it comes to making yourself someone worth getting involved with, I noticed that the "desirable qualities" mentioned by the couples I spoke with usually fell into these areas:

1) **Skills.** Even if you're not service-oriented, having a wide range of practical skills you can offer them will make a difference. I'm not talking about sexual skills, because you don't know what they're going to want sexually. I mean being able to get stains out of clothing, or change a tire or the oil in a car, or barber a beard, or keep accounts, or deal with people on the phone, or give a good (non-erotic) massage, or do internet research on anything. Yes, it's also true that you won't know what your future dominant is going to want for skills, either, but being generally useful in many ways is more like to interest a wide range of people than having certain specialized sexual or fetish knowledge. Besides, many dominant types might find it fun to train you in their favorite sexual or fetish skills, where getting you trained to do their taxes will be far less enjoyable for them. So, while you're waiting, start stacking up skills. (Keep in mind that even if your future dominant may not want those skills, they may like the idea of being able to offer them to others via you, their useful and talented slave. Being able to pull out a special skill for an honored house guest gives credit to the house.)

2) **Self-awareness.** Learn about the inside of your head, so that you can offer a relatively comprehensive "owner's manual" to your future Mistress or Master. Keep a journal. Share with

others who might have insight into similar qualities as you exhibit. Think about why you do things, and why you like things. Don't shy away from embarrassing or challenging realizations about yourself, and don't sit around planning ways to hide all that from your future dominant, because they're going to want to get inside you, and the right person will be able to see all the inner crud and not be freaked out or judgmental. Instead, plan ways to communicate about those difficult traits and behaviors.

3) **Label and patch any major leaks.** If you have serious mental health problems, deal with them now. Don't assume that getting a dominant will fix them—it's more likely that they will screw up the relationship. That doesn't mean that you can't have mental health struggles at all, but they should be clearly labeled and acknowledged, you should have a source of outside support and help for them, and you should have clear instructions for the most helpful response a partner can give when you are not doing well.

4) **Connect with real people.** Find other couples who are having the kind of relationship you want to have, and ideally have been together having that relationship for many years. Talk to them about what they do. Actually meet with them, if possible, so you can see that they're real and not just making something up online, which happens. Ask them for advice. Do this with more than one couple, to get different views. *(Editor's note: MAsT—Masters And slaves Together, at mast.net—is an international support group for power dynamic relationships, and a good place to meet others for advice.)*

5) **Read everything you can find with a critical eye.** I don't mean erotic stories, but books on how to manage M/s relationships. More and more of them come out all the time. Get all the information you can. It's especially good if you can figure out what more vague or general concepts look like to you specifically. ("What does 'abuse' look like to me? What does 'trust' look like to me? What does 'structure' look like to

me?") Be clear about what definitions you have decided to use, and be able to explain them.

6) **Have your financial situation relatively together.** You don't have to be rich, although having no debt is good, especially if you hope to turn your finances over to the right Master or Mistress. Put together some savings in a place where they can gather interest, and promise yourself you will not touch them while your future Master or Mistress lives. That will be your emergency fund, in the event that your Mistress or Master breaks up with you, or dies. Mature Masters and Mistresses will not demand that you hand that over, and will be fine with you having an emergency fund. In fact, a good one will veto you if you offer to turn it over to them in a fit of emotion.

7) **Have your responsibilities clear and handled.** If you have children from a former relationship whom you must support, for example, have amounts, timeline, method, and source of funding set and sure before you complicate your life by becoming a slave. Obviously unexpected chaos arises no matter how much we plan, but settling areas of expected chaos and likely chaos (if possible) is a favor to your future Master or Mistress. It's not fair to bring them into the middle of a disaster. Especially not if you are going to expect them to clean it up. ("Here, Ma'am, I'm laying this flaming, stinking mess at your feet as an offering. I'm sure you'll know how to fix everything!")

8) **Learn to state your feelings in clear, brief sentences.** You can practice this on your own time, talking to yourself—"I feel pretty angry right now, but I'm also hungry, so that could have something to do with it. I'll eat and report back." Or "I feel sad and forgotten because my friend blew me off."

9) **Learn to be courteous.** Courtesy doesn't have to mean formal protocols; it can just mean acting and speaking toward others in a way that is gracious, welcoming, nonjudgmental, and polite. If you're not sure what that looks like, watch films and videos of people who are courteous, and figure out what brand of courtesy will work with your life. I find that it's

advantageous to know how to make a respectful incline of the head, or a very slight bow, or look like I'm listening, or keep my tone even and pleasant when I'm not happy, or make gestures which invite but do not pressure. It's OK to practice that repeatedly on your own (perhaps in a mirror) or with other people, if you want to get better at it before unleashing it on a potential dominant person.

10) **Learn to listen.** Active listening skills are surprisingly valuable for a submissive or slave. There are many places online or in books where you can learn how to do that competently, and probably dozens or even hundreds of friends and acquaintances for you to practice on. If you want a potential Mistress or Master to feel safe and appropriate opening up to you emotionally, being a good listener is a place to start.

11) **Learn to touch like a slave.** We're assuming that touching the future dominant partner has not only their consent but their full enthusiasm—i.e., they straight-out asked you or ordered you to do it. Learn to touch someone in a mindful and devoted way, as if their body was an incredibly valuable thing which it was a wonder and a privilege to be able to touch—which is the truth. Practice on objects or pets or other willing people. (Touching without consent docks you so many points that you will be flushed back to "remedial" and shouldn't be let out to date until you are no longer at risk for that unacceptable behavior.)

There's probably more, but this is a good beginning. If you can manage to get through this list, you've got something above and beyond the usual mass of would-be slaves to offer to a high-quality dominant.

slave shane is the property of his beloved Mistress, Lady Kestrel, and lives with her in a big-city apartment where he is the house-husband and occasional online breadwinner, supporting her in her hard-driving career and laying in ecstasy at her feet.

A Few Foundational Skills for Would-Be S-Types
Joshua Tenpenny

We often hear a lot of would-be submissives and slaves asking what they can do to prepare themselves for their longed-for relationship situation. The problem is, of course, that every M is different and wants different things. When I put together the book *Real Service*, I listed a lot of practical skills that could make a servant more useful and attractive to the right dominant partner, but the list here is deliberately *not* about what you'd conventionally consider "skills".

If you asked me to make this list a year from now, I might make an entirely different list. I was mostly thinking here about what things tend to make M-types wary of taking someone on. It is like a car making a funny noise. Maybe it is nothing, but maybe it is a sign of a serious underlying issue. If it is something you can get sorted out on your own, do it. If it isn't, at least know what the problem is and have some concept of how to work around it. Anyway, the list:

❖ This is kind of remedial, but I've got to say it: **Have your own life reasonably well under control.** Emotionally stable, financially stable, etc. Don't be waiting for an M to save you from the dumpster fire that is your life. Not that you need to be perfect, but most good M-types really prefer someone who is capable of functioning as a responsible adult. Having solid basic life skills gives you a foundation for whatever path this takes you. If things are in crisis, put your focus into getting your life as well under control as you can, given the circumstances. Unfortunately, a large portion of M-types who want to "rescue" someone are well-meaning fools who completely lack the skills to do you any good, and predators are often looking for someone helpless or desperate to take advantage of.

❖ **Be at least moderately neat and organized.** Ideally a little above what you'd consider normal, but no need to go beyond that. (If you are already well-organized, there isn't a lot of benefit to an M from you getting even *more* organized. If you really want to work on it, instead try the adaptability exercise in the next essay, and use a different method of organizing than the one you are used to. Super-organized can often mean rigid and unwilling to adapt to the M's preferences. But that is extra credit.)

❖ **Be your best you.** Figure out what you are good at, and get better at it. Have at least one hobby or activity that is emotionally fulfilling and meaningful to you. Work on self-confidence if that is an issue for you. Dress and present yourself in a way you feel good about. Treat your body well, respect your health, make good choices.

❖ **Be happy!** Easier said than done, but do your best to enjoy life. Be a fun and pleasant person to spend time with. Learn to handle difficult situations with a good attitude. You don't have to fake a cheerful, bubbly persona, but if you are routinely cranky or whiny, a lot of M-types are going to feel bad about asking you to do stuff for them, and they may feel like you don't want to be in the relationship. You can learn to talk about your negative emotions without constantly acting them out.

❖ **Learn to wait.** Be able to quietly occupy yourself for at least an hour. This isn't meditation; it's just not being a pain in the ass or a distraction. This is a hundred times easier if you have something you can do while you sit and wait. For many people these days, this is a smartphone, and they can spend hours quietly staring at it. If that isn't for you, maybe reading or knitting. (Or picking locks. Whatever. Make it something you can reasonably and consistently carry around with you.) Just learn to be OK with waiting and don't get antsy. Being able to sit quietly *without* anything to entertain you is a nice bonus, and ideally I'd like someone to be able to sit patiently doing nothing for at least twenty minutes, but having something on hand to entertain you is sufficient for nearly all practical purposes.

❖ If you are looking to live your life in service to another person, you ideally want to **have a flexible career and living situation**, not something that seriously ties you down to one place or schedule. It's the same with family obligations. Think about what you would have to do if you found an amazing situation with the perfect M-type ... halfway across the country. Don't put your whole life on hold, waiting for The One, but unless you have a good reason, try to leave your options open. We hear from a lot of long-distance couples who really want to live together, but the s is tied down with something they can't or won't part with.

If you have massive obstacles to any of these, at least figure out what they are and have some concept of how you can work around them. Give some thought as to how this is likely to affect a relationship, and be able to talk it out with an M-type.

For extra credit: Learn how to dance. Especially if you are a heterosexual man. Ideally you should learn some type of social dancing, whatever sort that people normally do at parties or events in your world. (If you prefer partners significantly older than you, you might pick something more appropriate to their age range.) Something more performance oriented also works. The style is not super important. It is vastly easier to learn a new style of dance once you already have a solid sense of movement and rhythm. You don't have to get great at it, but at least get confident and comfortable in the movement. Aside from the direct benefits of just being able to dance, the main purpose of this is to develop some poise and grace in movement, as well as confidence in your body. If you get any kind of instruction, even informally, it also gets you comfortable with people looking at you, critiquing and correcting you. That can be too much for folks who are really struggling with body image, but just watching videos and practicing alone is a fine way to start.

And let me say this again: This is especially true for heterosexual men. Very few straight men are comfortable with being looked at, and all but the most gorgeous men generally assume women aren't going to find them physically attractive. This is bullshit, of the same order as "women just don't enjoy sex". Being well dressed, graceful, and confident does a whole lot, no matter what body you have.

Exercises for Learning Adaptability
Joshua Tenpenny

One of the big issues for new s-types is that they have a certain mental picture of the way that power exchange is going to be, and they get emotionally invested in that. Then they actually get a dominant partner, and that dominant partner wants things done differently. Maybe the s-type assumes they will be doing a lot of housewife stuff, and the M-type is a neat freak who likes to do that themselves, or is very casual about housework and wants the s-type to relax and have fun with them rather than constantly being busy cleaning.

As the s-type, you do have to decide what is a deal-breaker for you, what you can adapt to, and what kind of life you can be happy in. Some situations are just going to be a bad fit. But if you are looking to learn how to be better as an s-type, and you don't have an M-type yet, one of the things I advise is working on broadening your sense of who you are and what you do.

Some folks are already adaptable in this way. Some may be already quite emotionally solid, but just naturally adaptable. And some folks have so little sense of self (usually from growing up in a very bad situation) that they need to work in the opposite direction, figuring out who they are, rather than letting every situation redefine them. But most s-types coming into an M/s relationship are a just little rigid (or a lot rigid) about how they think this relationship should go, and most *people*, in general, could benefit from being a lot more adaptable. (In my opinion.)

Also, this is assuming you've already got the Basic Foundation-type stuff as solid as you reasonably can. That stuff is the low-hanging fruit. It is either relatively straight-forward, or it shows you a problem that is very likely to come up early in a power dynamic relationship.

This is deeper work, for less of an obvious payoff. It goes more into what I consider the spiritual growth of the path of surrender. It isn't something an M-type is likely to really notice early on, because most s-types can fake it when they are on their best behavior, but getting better at this skill subtly makes all sorts of things easier. Facing any hardship, our suffering is frequently compounded by our resistance to change. As an s-type, it is even more so, because the relationship itself so often means we are trying to accept a situation rather than change it to suit us. So here are some random exercises, all variations on the same theme.

- ❖ When presented with options like what to eat or wear, ignore your first choice, and go with your second. If you don't have a clear favorite, pick something entirely at random, or let someone else pick at random. Decide which choices are fair game beforehand, and then just go with the choice without debate or complaint. Or make an arbitrary rule, like picking the third option that is remotely suitable. Don't do this for big-deal decisions such as what state to move to, but do it for small things such as choosing different dish soap or a different type of cereal. Pick a specific type of decision to make this way, and work on it for a month. You don't have to pick anything you truly hate or can't use, but eventually try throwing some less desirable options in there.

- ❖ Change your public image in some way. Clothes, hairstyle, way of speaking, whatever. It doesn't have to be something dramatic, just something a little outside of your comfort zone. It makes the most sense to pick something that could be considered some kind of improvement (make your speech a little more formal or polite, dress a little fancier or sexier, etc.) but if you are a bit of a perfectionist, trying something a little more casual than normal can be educational. Maybe try something a little more masculine or feminine than you are used to, or just something very different—especially if it is likely to shift how people see you or treat you. Don't do anything stupid or reckless, but in any social situation there are usually a range of "acceptable" options. Just pick a different one.

- ❖ Pick a specific genre of music/movies/etc. that doesn't strongly appeal to you, and try to get into it. Try to get a sense of what people like about it. For a bigger challenge, try something that "people like you" (whatever that means) aren't generally interested in. Or pick one you really dislike, and try to tolerate it at least passively without grumbling.

❖ Pick a hobby that doesn't appeal to you, and interact with folks who enjoy that hobby. Do the hobby with them, to whatever extent you can.

❖ Go to a social event that is not your usual thing. Try to have fun. Meet people. Try to fit in. Don't be an outsider—actually participate.

❖ Spend time in a culture different from the one you were raised in. Not necessarily a different country, though that is sometimes easier than something closer to home. Anything that surrounds you with folks who you aren't "your kind of people". Try to feel comfortable in that culture, embracing customs that are unfamiliar to you, and being humble about your inevitable mistakes. Don't obnoxiously intrude where you aren't welcome, or assume they owe you anything. Relate to the people *as people*, people essentially just like you, not as exotic specimens, or objects of charity, etc. Get an understanding of the general worldview and values, as well as the details of culture (how people speak to each other, dress, etc.). See the variations within the culture—what is considered "normal" as well as the ways people push back against the norm.

❖ Establish a daily routine, especially if you have no daily routine beyond activities you can't really change. Just add one thing. Nothing hard at first; pick something you enjoy, or tend to do anyway, and set it as a strict routine. Have a certain type of meal on one day of the week, or eat lunch in a specific place, for example. You can make it something a little more challenging, something you see as an improvement, but if you fail repeatedly at that, try something easier. Take something that you already do and enjoy, and deliberately and consistently do it a certain way.

❖ Change something about your daily routine. Anything! Start waking up earlier or staying up later. Eat dinner-type food for breakfast, or the reverse. Do laundry on Wednesdays. Switch to a different style of coffee. Stick with it for a while, try to get used to it. If this is hard for you, do something tiny, and pick the area of life you are least emotionally invested in. If it is easy for you, do something harder that will make your life better.

❖ Pick some small virtuous habit or custom that doesn't hold much inherent appeal to you, and do it. Developing good habits that you are personally invested in is also a good exercise, but it is a very different experience to work on one that seems irrelevant to you. Make your bed neatly every morning, or carefully fold your socks and underpants, or take cold showers, or drink 8-10 glasses of water a day, or take your shoes off in the house. Don't pick something you have big issues with, at least not to start out. Just some habit or custom whose alleged virtues you don't find all that compelling.

❖ Look at different sorts of protocol other M/s relationships have, and pick one that you can reasonably do in your current circumstances. Do it, consistently. Then pick something else.

Basically, you're teaching yourself to practice and get better at doing things you wouldn't normally do, and adapting to situations you normally wouldn't choose to be in. This is not an easy skill to learn, but being adaptable is invaluable if you sign up with an M-type who wants you to live a certain way. Being able to shape yourself to be part of their life and their wishes—and not with resentment, but with grace—will make your life as the One Who Follows so much easier.

Figuring Out Wants and Needs
Alpha and boi nik

Part 1: Alpha

In knowing oneself and being authentic comes the understanding of wants verses needs, and understanding the difference between the two—what they mean for you, and having the meaning match that of the significant other in your world.

For me it is very simple. Wants are things I desire but can function without. Needs are things that I require to be healthy and happy. If my wants are neglected, sure, I might get a little annoyed, but it won't harm me or those within my world. If needs are neglected, it may cause irreparable physical or emotional damage to myself or others or my relationships.

To figure this out, I made a lot of lists. This came about because I sat in discussion with a dominant friend one afternoon a few years back, who told me it was not only OK to sit and make lists of these things, but he also told me it was important. As a dominant, he felt it was important for a prospective slave to know what they needed from him. He let me know that it was OK to ensure any prospective master was able to meet my needs, and that I did not have to settle for less than I needed. That afternoon was when I first started to break down everything I could think of. We started by talking about the first things that came to mind. What kind of person did I need a master to be?

❖ I need them to be respectful. *What does respect look like?*
❖ I need them to be honourable. *What does honourable look like?*
❖ I need them to be able to be vulnerable. *What does vulnerability look like?*

How do I need that person to treat me?

❖ I need them to treat me with kindness. *What does kindness look like?*
❖ I need them to remember I am a human being first. *What does being treated as a human being first look like?*

What are the deal-breakers?

❖ Abusing me. *What does abuse look like to me?*

And so on. From here we expanded and expanded, and picked apart every term that could have multiple or broad meanings until I was able to articulate exactly what each item meant to me with no room for error, misconception, or miscommunication.

Some people may laugh at having these lists, but for me, they were vital in learning how to set my boundaries and what I needed to negotiate for with a prospective D-type. They let me see what things I could let go of, where there was wiggle room and where there was not. My lists help me to truly see just how complex my power dynamic relationships are. They give me and my others points of reference if ever there comes a time of uncertainty around what has been agreed upon.

Having my personal understanding of wants verses needs also gives me perspective in times of heightened emotions, I am now able to take a step back and assess if this thing that I am upset about is a want or a need by asking myself the simple of question of "Will it do irreparable damage or not? Will I cease to function if I can't have that?"

The other thing I love about my lists is that as I grow as a person, so do they. As I change, so too do they. I can add, I can remove, I can rewrite sections or the entire thing. My lists have become an extremely helpful tool of self-awareness and introspection.

Part 2: boi nik

I feel as though I have learned this lesson the hardest way possible but, then again, perhaps not. The obvious answer to this question is one that my Sir gave to me before setting this essay topic for me to write, and that was: Needs are something that will break you (or the relationship) not to have.

I know that Sir doesn't want to break the relationship. I know that he doesn't want to break me either, so this was probably a very obvious and easy way for him to get this across to me. Still, however, I had to forge my own trail as that is how I best learn, and this essay reflects that process.

Wants

To articulate the difference between wants and needs, I feel like I must first define what each of these things are. I have read countless articles on this point in M/s dynamic relationships, but the best and most stand-out one that I always come back to is this one called *D/s Hierarchy*[*] which prioritized them in this way:

1) submissive needs
2) Dominant needs
3) Dominant wants
4) Dominant whims
5) submissive wants

The author also went into detail about why they chose this hierarchy, but at no point did this essay depict any wants or needs themselves, so I would like to do so now.

Wants: Desires, wishes, whimsies, passing thoughts that cross the mind.

I personally have no difficulty in airing these. I expect that these will not necessarily be met, and that is OK. This is information that I am passing on, and it is information that is absent of anything which could be construed as emotional manipulation. I hold a lot of concern regarding potential for manipulation by choosing to use the word "need". If I start with saying "need", I feel like I am then backing the

---

[*] From a blog post by @kneelingwaiting on Fetlife.com. www.fetlife.com/users/56295589/posts/4835468

other person into a corner. And so, I think to myself: *Better to use the word "want", then.*

Which, having thought about it, is really manipulating the response in a different way. One that doesn't see to my advantage. This is one of the reasons why I personally find value in first using the word "manipulation" to indicate any verbal interaction (good or bad or neutral), and then to specify that "coercion" is one specific kind of manipulation where the desired outcome seeks to either disadvantage or control the other person. But at no point here—when I am considering the ups and downs of "manipulation" vs. "coercion"—do I consider how the thing feels to me, whether what I'm feeling is a need or a want. I only think about how it will be viewed externally.

I feel as though this is the first thing that must change for any slave within an M/s dynamic. Easier to say than do, in my instance I suspect, especially knowing as I do how Sir has already existing manipulation/coercion issues of his own. It also explains to me why I have such difficulty with identifying my own wants from needs: it's not a distinction I am used to making from a place of honesty within myself.

A slave within an M/s dynamic, then, must consider honestly how the thing feels within themselves, not allowing consideration of external responses to interfere with that honesty with themselves and their Sir.

Needs

The definition of this one was so hard for me to figure out! It has, in fact, taken me a solid year, culminating in a breakdown on my own at home when the doors finally swung open. After quite some time, I came to realise that the difficulty I had in identifying needs as separate to wants was something that began in my childhood.

It was at this time when I equated needs and wants as very similar. Like my wants, these were not often met during my childhood. Instead of accepting that, however, I elevated one particular fear I had to the shelf of "needs". This then became a misinformed need that I lived my life by for decades: The "need" (read: fear) to not be abandoned like I have been in the past.

I didn't expect my need to be met, and in fact I learned that it wouldn't be early on. In fact, I believed I had to fight for this one elevated "need" to be met, and in doing so have likely pushed away more people than I care to remember. But fears are not needs any more than wants are needs.

Discovering that I no longer knew how to air my needs in the wake of this—*and* that I was not comfortable with doing so if pressed— has been a difficult road to walk. But it is one that has taught me from experience the importance of having my needs met.

> *Needs: Urgent, must haves, non-negotiable, important, and possibly inclusive of an imminent time frame.*

For good communication to happen, needs must be voiced. Honesty is the most important thing in any dynamic, any relationship. For Sir, lying is a deal-breaker anyway, but for any instance of good communication to occur, there must be honesty.

At the moment, I don't feel as though I'm communicating my needs very well. I identified in a recent writing that I'd noticed how Sir is far more comfortable with the use of the word "need" where I am concerned than I am, and this section of the essay is an extrapolation from that point.

My current working definition of the word "need" is flawed because, to me, a need presents itself as nothing more than a symptom to show me that something is wrong. Yet, if I was communicating my needs well—if I was in touch with my own needs all the time as opposed to just when something is not going well—then surely those needs could be something more sophisticated than a belated warning system that jumps to the forefront every so often. My needs could be so much more than reactionary, feelings that leave me (and probably others) feeling as though I haven't been paying much attention to myself up till the typical knee jerk response.

This observation that I've not been communicating well makes me think, though, about why I've habitually, consistently prioritised my own needs so low instead of owning them. And the reason for that is my Primary Need is always to make my loved ones happy. This first came out of a need to be liked, instead of from being a slave.

Like wants, needs will be information that is passed on from slave to Master. And, over time, I hope that I continue to grow into being more comfortable in airing and owning to this information. Not having my needs met in childhood was not OK.

The difference between wants and needs for a slave within an M/s dynamic relationship.

My childhood was not an M/s dynamic, but it has incidentally shown me both what the difference is between wants and needs. *The difference between needs and wants that are passed on as information to the Master is in how they are handled.* The very simple truth is that needs must be met within an M/s dynamic relationship, but wants don't always need to be met.

With regards to wants, the slave has decided to put their own pursuit of these aside in favour of the one they want to serve. More than that, the slave puts trust into the one they serve to meet as many or as few of these wants as the Master feels appropriate for reasons of growth, learning or other priorities.

Some slaves might find themselves compatible with a Master who is very restrictive about which wants are met. Some might work best with Dominants who are much more generous. In a long-term M/s dynamic relationship, it would be my assumption that things would ebb and flow between these two extremes over time due to circumstance, situation, and negotiation. In any case, the key to a slave's wants in an M/s dynamic is that they are given at the discretion of their owner.

Regarding needs: The slave's needs will come down to something that will harm them if they are not met. The only other need that a slave will possess at all times is to serve and please their Master.

The final difference I see between a slave's wants and needs in an M/s dynamic is in how urgently the slave would like the matter to be viewed by their Master.

In conclusion, one last thing of note that I would like to suggest on the subject of wants and needs is the following: It is important that a slave's voicing and wording of *both* wants and needs comes from the right:

- ❖ motivation
- ❖ station
- ❖ as much self-awareness as possible

Checking through these three things is the course most likely to ensure the following for the slave:

- ❖ good communication
- ❖ honesty
- ❖ appropriate self-esteem

Even so, I am aware that needs clashing is a main culprit behind incompatibilities. I have therefore spent a life attempting to subsume my needs—or meet them myself—so they rarely become another person's problem.

In doing so, not only have I not communicated well, but it's just another tool I've been using to keep others at an arm's length. This is something I am trying to change.

Alpha is a 39-year-old transman who identifies as an Alpha Slave, Daddy and Wolfdog. Alpha is the Owner, Alpha and Daddy of Boi Nik, a 37-year-old multigendered slave, little, and handler of Alpha's dog self, Shadow.

Qualities of a Good Servant

Joshua Tenpenny[*]

It seems that there aren't a lot of standards for what it means to be a good s-type; in fact, there is a distressing tendency for people to casually assume that "of course submissives can't be expected to act like a reliable, committed, self-disciplined adult – they're submissives, aren't they?" This kind of infantilizing of all s-types is counterproductive, as it hardly encourages them to excellence, and indeed it does the opposite. It may stem from a general discomfort with the state of submission on both sides of the slash, where that discomfort is translated into pretending that servants are a lesser class of human. Instead of this, it would be better to see this position as an honorable one – and that means having standards. So here are some suggestions of ideal characteristics for people in service. (Genders are arbitrarily alternated.)

- She is genuinely moved to service because of the emotional happiness it gives her, not because she feels that it is required for a particular fantasy role. She is aware of the difference between fantasy service and reality.
- He honestly enjoys working under the direction of someone else, and rarely suffers from reflexive resentment from being told what to do. He's not exceptionally attached to doing things his own way.
- She enjoys helping people and being useful, but doesn't take it personally if someone refuses her help or doesn't find her service beneficial.
- He takes pride in his work, and is motivated to do a good job without needing praise or recognition.
- While she is able to relax and take time for herself, in general she'd rather be working than sitting around doing nothing.
- He isn't a martyr. While he might be quicker than some people to inconvenience himself for the benefit of others, he doesn't go out

[*] Reprinted from *Real Service*, Alfred Press 2011.

of his way to inflict hardships on himself for little discernible benefit. He tries to avoid making other people feel guilty over service he has rendered them or hardships he has endured on their behalf.

∽ She does not need to be sexually aroused to render quality service, and sex is not her main motivation for doing it.

∽ He does not have trust issues so huge that even an extremely honorable master will be under constant paranoid scrutiny for the inevitable betrayal. He can realistically assess whether the judgment of a given master is worth trusting, and can relax into being carried by their will.

∽ She has a sense of honor and will strive to do the right thing even when it is unpleasant. She obeys not because she is afraid of consequences, but because she has made a commitment to do so. She takes pride in being able to remain obedient even when it is extremely difficult for her.

∽ He is reliable. If he says he will do something, you can trust that he will make every effort to do it. Keeping his commitments is very important to him.

∽ She has reasonably good self-control, and does not require continual external management of her volatile emotions. She is not actively impaired by serious mentally illness.

∽ He has no addictions, obsessions, or compulsions that seriously interfere with his ability to follow orders.

∽ She is capable of acting with discretion when allowed access to confidential or sensitive personal information. She is not inclined to gossip, and can keep secrets without drama.

∽ He can clearly and respectfully communicate any difficulties, concerns, or potential conflicts regarding his orders, in a manner appropriate to his role. He does not take it personally if the master rejects his suggestions.

∽ She is willing to admit when she does not understand something, or doesn't think she is capable of it. She is willing to fully apply herself to a task, even if she thinks it is beyond her capabilities.

- He is not looking for a service relationship in order to avoid real-world responsibility or accountability. He sees himself as a mature and responsible adult, capable of making good decisions.

- She realistically evaluates how the other responsibilities and commitments in her life effect how much service she is able to offer and under what circumstances, and clearly communicates this to the people she serves.

- He understands what he is hoping to get out of a service relationship. He can clearly communicate what he expects in return for his service, and what he would like but is willing to compromise on. If he is not getting these things, he discusses it with his master in a timely manner, rather than silently building up resentment.

- She accepts that her master is a real and imperfect human being. She does not hold unrealistic ideas about her master's perfection, but is not excessively critical of her master's flaws.

- He's comfortable working "behind the scenes" and isn't particularly concerned with whether his contributions are publicly acknowledged.

- She finds service to be an honorable and fulfilling way of life that makes good use of her skills. She does not feel it is a waste of her time, or that the work is "beneath her".

- He can appreciate that different people have different values and priorities, and can act according to his master's priorities, even when they differ substantially from his own.

- She is genuinely comfortable with her place in the household hierarchy. She does not look for ways to feel superior to other servants or to the people she serves. She does not attempt to look good at the expense of others.

- He has good observational skills, and can figure out his master's habits, preferences, and priorities over time.

- She can understand her master's view of life well enough to be able to extrapolate what her master would want her to do in any given situation, and follow those unwritten orders in a manner appropriate to her position.

- He has a good sense of his own worth as a person and as a servant, and will not serve a master who does not value him. He knows that he cannot honorably serve a dishonorable person.

- She can realistically assess her skill level, experience level, and how her physical and mental condition at any time will affect her job performance. She knows how to communicate this information clearly to her master in a way that is useful to them.

- He can understand his master's relationships with other people – such as other servants, submissives, slaves, egalitarian partners, family, and friends – and values them because they make his master happy in some way.

- She can verbally defend her chosen lifestyle to questioners, where appropriate, in terms that express how good the power dynamic is for her self-esteem and overall welfare.

When You Want to Be Destroyed
sheldon

It happens to some of us. We fantasize about all sorts of hideous things happening to us—pain, torture, imprisonment, horrible mindfucks, mutilation ... perhaps even the entire obliteration of your personality and maybe your life. Some of us may also dream about a slower sort of destruction—wanting to be brainwashed into being a mindless robot who lives only for the one who has brainwashed them, and who gives them purpose. By the way, I'm not going to go into juicy details, so if that's what you hope for, you can give up now. Those of you who have these fantasies also have probably already scoured the places where those stories are found, and you probably also have your own specific set of them. We're all different, and all our nasty perverted minds are different as well, so go collect your own porn. This isn't about what we want sexually. It's not even entirely about *why* we want it. It's about how much of it we can actually have and still stay sane.

When I was younger, I obsessed about being in a full-time 24/7 Master/slave relationship, because I thought that it meant full-time 24/7 of the above. I wanted to give up my life and live in the evilest erotica story possible. I told myself that I would be willing to give up my job, my money, my friends, my future for that—and I even toyed with being OK with the possibility that I would lose my life as well—but what a way to go! I did a lot of looking and a lot of talking to masters of both genders. I'm bisexual, so I was just as OK with being destroyed by a woman or a man. I also got into a long string of relationships—some only a couple of weeks, some many months. A few only lasted mere days.

As my search progressed, I became less and less naïve, and less willing to be taken advantage of by someone who wasn't going to give me what I wanted. When you hear that, you'll probably start thinking, "This guy is not a real slave, or a real submissive. He's a fetishist who just wants a scene, and he should stay the hell out of the deep end of the pool where the real M/s happens." Sometimes, during my search, I wondered about that myself.

At the same time, I did have some joy and satisfaction in service. This was the tiny thread I held onto in order to convince myself I was more than just a fetishist. It did make me happy to make a dominant happy. It did, sometimes, make me happy when I got a pat on the head and a "Good boy". It also sometimes made me obscurely angry. When I examined that urge, I found its ugly root: I wasn't a good boy, in my eyes. I was a horrible, worthless person, and them saying that I was good in any way simply proved that they weren't the wise dominant I hoped for. Instead, they were blind and possibly stupid, because a wise person would be able to see my internal hideousness, and validate it. Sometimes I would even follow up that compliment with bad behavior, hoping to be punished, because that made more sense.

I hadn't yet come to the part where you learn to trust and believe the dominant's view of you, even over your own. I didn't trust any of them that far. I was still using them as props in my ongoing fantasy of destruction, and if they refused to play the part I had rigidly assigned them, I ceased listening.

I believe that the urge to be destroyed comes from two separate sets of impulses. One could call them List A and List B. List A includes childhood trauma, low self-esteem, feelings of worthlessness, risking your body and mind because you don't value yourself, etc. If you feel like your life is a horrible place you're trapped in and you can't seem to find a way out, it's understandable that you would want a dominant superhero to come into your life and do something about it, whether it is to reinforce and validate your self-hate by doing horrible and well-deserved things to you, or turning you into a blank slate and rewriting you to be something entirely different from your own worthless self … someone who was at least halfway worthy, if only because they were the superhero's creation.

As my friend Dreidel once wrote:

1. *I hate myself.*
2. *I hate who I am.*
3. *I hate how I live.*
4. *I hate that I can't make myself change.*

5. *I hate that not being able to make myself change makes me worthless.*
6. *I hate this pain.*
7. *I hate that I can't stop this pain.*
8. *I hate that until I stop this pain I won't be able to change.*
9. *Repeat #1.*

The crazy thing about being saturated by List A, whatever it is for you, is that when you're trying to be a slave with those motivations—and this is usually unconscious—you convince yourself that you are the most self-sacrificing slave in existence, and the right dominant will see that and make use of it. In reality, you're probably one of the most selfish slaves in existence, and that's a hard truth to make yourself see. It's not really all about what the master wants—unless the master wants the activities which get you hard or wet, and/or which validate and reinforce your little story of self-disgust. Masters who don't want to play that game are scorned. You might even make up something in your head about how you aren't worthy of them, finding some way at last to cram well-meaning people nonconsensually into your playbook.

As an example: How many of you dream about being kept in a cage like an animal, preferably permanently or at least long-term? (I'm not talking about wanting to do it for a weekend as part of a scene. That's more honest.) How many of you have wondered what a future master might get out of a useless human being who must be fed, watered, monitored, and checked for health issues? That's a lot of work for very little return. Some dominants might be willing to go through that kind of work over a short period for kinky fun, but it's going to pall pretty quickly. Pretty soon they're going to be thinking how much more they would enjoy a slave who was actually walking around and could cook them a meal or get them a drink, instead of them having to "serve" the slave.

Ah, you say, *but the right master for me will be entirely fulfilled just by enacting my fantasies.* I hate to tell you, but that's them serving you, not the other way around, and most healthy dominants want someone who will make their lives easier, not more complicated. If you really want to be kept in a cage or some other (actionable and non-lethal) fantasy which will require a fair amount of work from the dominant for possible little return, then either find someone who would be into it as a regular scene (maybe a weekend every month) or, better yet, pay someone to do it for you on a regular basis. That way you are both clear what they're getting out of it, and you don't have to worry. Another possibility is that you buy yourself a cage, imagine your fantasy dominant, and jerk off, not bothering another human being with it.

If you are ruled by List A, the best thing you can do for yourself and for that future master is to get yourself into therapy. If the self-hate and self-disgust have latched onto your sexuality, it's possible that ironing out the psychological problems will not change that you find being that fucked up humiliatingly hot, but we'll get to what to do about that in a moment. It will—and I assure you that this is true—shift their importance so that you are not obsessing about them all the time, and also allow you to have a much more objective view.

But I went to therapy once, you whine, *and it didn't do any good.* That may be because you got the wrong therapist, or because you weren't willing to dig in and do the work. In fact, you were probably expecting the therapist to fix you while you sat passively, just like the Superhero Master would have done. This is work, and you have to commit to that, and keep at it even when it reveals things about you that are embarrassing and cringeworthy, and probably not in an eroticizable way. The more psychologically healthy you become, the more you can see where you are actually self-sacrificing and where you are actually selfish and disguising it as self-sacrifice. Then you can own the selfish parts, at least, and not try to pass them off as unselfish—and you'll have a much better idea of what your needs and desires truly are.

List B is different and far more nebulous. Hold tight, I'm going to get philosophical, and maybe even spiritual, here. The urges on List B may appear just as self-destructive as those on List A, but they have a different underlying urge. Sometimes they are mixed up with List A, and sometimes (more rarely) they appear without any of those. List B urges speak of a karmic direction for this lifetime. They tell you that it will be your job to walk into the fire of self-transformation and become something you are not. If you have List B urges bothering you, it's the Universe pushing you to learn the lesson that *who you think you are is not immutable.* Even core traits can be expressed in many different ways, some of them so different that they feel like they couldn't exist in the same person. (Except they can, if only at different points in our lives, and I won't even go into the whole time-is-not-linear thing, at least not in this essay.) The best way to prove to yourself that who you think you are is not immutable is to change, slowly but radically, into someone else.

Of course, we all change and grow as we age and go through life, but I'm talking about a speeded-up version of evolution. List B urges dare you to walk away from the anchors which make you the person you think of as *me*, and see how that changes you. Those urges ask you, perhaps subconsciously: What would I look like if I was someone who was not crippled by my flaws? Who would I have to become to get there, or even to take the first step? How can I transform into that person?

And now comes another whine: *But personal evolution isn't sexy! It doesn't get me hard or wet!* Besides the point that this is one good reason why one's pink bits shouldn't be making one's life decisions, it's not necessarily true, or doesn't have to be. If you do it right, you can get an erotic response to List B as well as List A ... and one may even be stronger once you begin.

The problem is that the two lists are often mixed up in one person. If you've got both lists going on, the List A voices may well try to convince you that they don't exist, that this is all perfectly spiritually healthy self-destruction. And you won't know if that's true or not until you've spent at least a couple of years working on yourself to dig out any vestiges of List A and work on it—and no, that's not work you should do alone. You, by definition, cannot be wholly objective about you. You need outside perspective to keep you honest while you do this work, and you need to be willing to sit with that perspective even when it makes you profoundly uncomfortable about yourself. Once you've done the work to sift out and deal with List A, then you can more cleanly approach List B.

So that urge for transformation! For erasing who you are and becoming something ... well, "empty" is one word that comes up in fantasy. Others might be "total devotion" or even "focused only on this one thing". This urge comes out in different ways with people who are not kinky s-types—following a guru or dedicating oneself to a spiritual path, implementing a serious meditation practice intended to "burn out" the unhealthy trappings of one's life, entering a monastery, etc. It's possible that the clean river running under the muck of your fantasy of self-immolation is List B urges. It's also possible that it's not, however, so do the cleanup first before you jump to conclusions.

On top of this, obsession with the tropes of self-destruction may or may not actually co-exist with having the appropriate personality for being led and directed by another human being. Some people find that while the fantasy is attractive, once they're actively under someone's authority, they really don't want to be told what to do, especially if they don't necessarily agree with the other person's ideas about where they should go and what they should do. That may or may not be because it's not the right master for them, and it's OK to try at least once more with someone different, but it's important to keep at the back of your mind the possibility that you're supposed to be doing this on your own, and that's part of the process. That idea may be disheartening, but sometimes the desire for an authority is a way of getting out of doing the work yourself.

If you do get into a realistic authority transfer with a master who neither judges you negatively for your self-immolation urges nor is willing to indulge those urges in any way which will be unhealthy for either of you—and that's a tough call right there—two positive things can happen. First, it's certainly possible to indulge those urges to a safer extent during BDSM play, if both parties find it fun and erotic, clear and realistic safety limits are in place, the Master is getting enough out of you in other ways that they don't feel like your fetish dispenser (very important!), and you are clear that this is an occasional treat, not the basis of the relationship. Reality, including jobs, home maintenance, health care, doctor visits, bill-paying, social events, and probably therapy for you all need to be valued in day-to-day life. It's not good if the self-destructive play becomes an addiction that you need more and more often, or obsess over all the time. If you find yourself doing that, be honest with your Master and back off for a while so that you can get that back under control.

Now let's take another look at that pesky personal-evolution thing. Some of the ways that I and others I know have had to evolve are:

- ❖ Becoming less attached to getting our own way.
- ❖ Becoming more resilient and flexible when faced with difficulty.
- ❖ Developing better distress tolerance.
- ❖ Developing tools for emotional stability.
- ❖ Becoming more dependable; keeping our commitments better.
- ❖ Addressing addictive behavior; not letting addictions overwhelm us.
- ❖ Becoming more compassionate.
- ❖ Becoming more loving.
- ❖ Becoming more tolerant of the flaws of others, and of the world.
- ❖ Working through our wounds and trauma.
- ❖ Developing patience.
- ❖ Developing self-discipline.
- ❖ Generally putting aside our egos.

The act of putting aside the ego is both one of the hardest things a human being ever does, and it is also the central basis of many, many religious and spiritual disciplines. It's also one of the best practices a slave can master (yes, that last phrase works). Whether we like it or not, most of our fetishized self-destructive fantasies are very egoistic. They are self-centered - how we think the situation should work and our opinions of ourselves take center stage, and there is often very little room for anyone else's views, including an actual human partner. It's especially tricky when the genitals are involved because genitals are one of the most self-centered bits of the body and brain.

Really letting go of the ego is being able to seriously contemplate living under the rule of someone whose views may be different—and learning to be flexible and adapt to their view when necessary. For those of us who are stuck in egoistic erotic fantasy, actually thinking deeply about what that would feel like ... may not feel good at all. It's possible that we have already spent parts of our lives—possibly even the early formative parts—under the authority of people whose ideas were not good for us at all.

This can make us less than skillful when it comes to discerning whether a particular Master or Mistress is going to bring us down a path that is the best possible one for us, especially when what we've been thinking we wanted isn't where we should go. Serious thought needs to go into it, and you need to enter cautiously with as much objectivity as you can muster. Don't go down either the route of mistaking discomfort with a difficult process for having chosen the wrong partner, nor the route of accepting everything that Master wants for you uncritically. The truth is somewhere in the middle. Above all, don't judge how productive things are by how much you're suffering—that can end up being masochistic mental masturbation.

Difficult as it is to believe, it's possible to transform the urges for self-evolution into something erotic, if you try. First, you must accept that you would be better off changing in these possibly banal-seeming ways, and that doesn't mean a grudging theoretical acceptance. It means really opening your heart to a realistic and non-romantic vision of yourself having changed in that way. Then, by yourself or with a Master's help, you walk down that road one step at a time. The Master's job is to hold you accountable for each step you take, and to help you eroticize the long, slow, struggle to the goal.

I'm not going to go into details of how to eroticize the acts of working to change yourself, because everyone's kinks are different, but it's largely about focusing on how you want to change, figuring out a simple and doable first step, making sure the Master is on the same page, and then while you're doing that step, you also focus on how the part of you which is the opposite trait is being destroyed in the name of the Master to whom you will be accountable. If you're trying to do this on your own, without a Master, it's harder. You don't get the chance to really put the ego aside. However, it can be good practice to begin with, even with a fantasy, because you need to learn to get used to making yourself do hard things. If you can't make yourself do the first step, maybe it's time to go back to therapy and talk that through. Don't sit around in a lump of misery waiting for a Master to come rescue your willpower. Make the first step smaller and try again.

It's been a long, hard journey for me, and I'm not anywhere near done. But when I look at myself now, instead of focusing on how much further I have to go, instead I dwell on how the me that I am now is so far different from the me that I used to be … that the old me would not have recognized me now. Much of who I was has been obliterated, and the me who is left is the sculpture which is emerging from the rough wood, once everything else has been slowly and painfully cut away. Actual self-realization has enough suffering for the most masochistic of souls, and can show you the real struggle underneath the fantasy.

Sheldon is the difficult, yearning, loyal, and sometimes obstreperous property of his Mistress and Dominatrix. His journey through self-transformation is still ongoing, and hopefully will continue until he breathes his last breath.

Pitfalls in the Path
Venerant

Introduction

Meeting the right person at the wrong time is such a common and familiar heartbreak. I found myself in a similar situation in 2017— right person, probably at the wrong time, definitely in the wrong relationship format. As I was finishing my undergraduate degree I had begun dating and practicing light D/s with a young man with whom I'd fallen intractably in love. We were young and trying to do a lot of things all at once: Practice functional polyamory for the first time, survive in a long-distance relationship, establish our autonomy as young adults in the world, heal from childhood and familial trauma, and develop a comfortable sense of power exchange.

I would go so far as to say that needing to work through any one of those things is enough to sink an unsteady ship. It is no wonder that we foundered trying to tackle them all. In 2019 our relationship ended (painfully, but with relief) and we spent the next two years not speaking at all. In 2021 he contacted me out of the blue, seeking emotional honesty and company.

Our previous relationship had begun as an egalitarian partnership with dreams of something closer to 24/7 power exchange. Neither of us knew how to get there in a healthy way, and we ended up practicing an occasional control-based form of D/s. It existed beyond the boundaries of sex but certainly didn't expand into our daily lives. I can see now that this desire to be egalitarian in some ways but unequal in others was confusing and impractical for the people we were.

As an egalitarian partner, I needed constant availability from him. I needed quick response times when I called, strong implicit expressions of love and affection, and a sense that I was integrated into all parts of his life. My feelings of worthiness in the relationship were founded on these principles: That my partner would respond when I asked, return my affection, and share his life with me freely as I wished. And most importantly, that a conversation about my needs would always end in my needs being met because I was entitled to that.

I found these needs directly in conflict with the things I wanted by giving up my authority: To be vulnerable to someone else's whims when it comes to giving me attention, to be a selfless conduit of my theoretical Owner's desire, to have only what I was given and trust that I'd be given what I truly need.

The conflict produced feelings I didn't know how to manage, and my partner at the time certainly fared no better. How could he effectively own something so demanding, so self-righteous of her own needs, so opinionated and unwilling to change? How could I feel secure as property when it felt like I was being starved of the things I needed to survive?

I'm lucky enough to get a second chance at this right person at a different time and in a different relationship format. The second chance has asked me hard questions: Why do you still want this person in your life? Do you want him enough to change fundamental things about yourself to make it possible?

I want him because I love him, and I think I never quite stopped loving him. Even in the relief of our breakup and time apart I still thought about him often, still hoped he was okay, still missed the intimacy we had shared. Like many complicated relationships, the good parts were *really* good and that's what made it so heartbreaking to have left. Given another chance at this, I knew I wanted it and it didn't feel like an unhealthy desire to fall into old habits. It felt like a desire for something new.

In the two years between our breakup and our reconnection I had spent untold hours thinking, processing, and journaling about the relationship. I thought about the things we each needed, the things we were able to offer, and how they were incompatible. I had moved past a childlike "What if things could have been different?" and into a pragmatic "If we had the emotional and mental capacity to fix these specific things, could we have been happy?" In late 2021 I was in the midst of unrelated personal growth that had caused me to reexamine other fundamental truths about myself. It was not unreasonable to think that maybe the needs that had previously gone unmet were not fundamental to my nature. I felt ready for change.

The story I want to tell here is about how I was able to change: How I confronted the challenge of my own needs and learned how to reshape them so that we were able to fit together in the pursuit of power exchange.

Structural Choices

Throughout this story I refer to this person as my [redacted] to reflect that I have not been invited to use a title for him even though I am hopeful that one exists in the future. He is not my partner, my Dominant, my Master, or my Owner. Nevertheless, there is some relationship here that feels like "mine" and I feel comfortable referring to him as my [redacted]. I also use the term "power exchange" to capture a sense that one of us is intended to have power over the other and that there are things we are each offering and receiving from our engagement.

The choices to adapt my needs for this dynamic didn't happen all at once, nor are they things one of us imposed on the other. They are decisions about the relationship we made together (or at least, agreed to uphold together). I believe they are integral to understanding how we interact, and how we interacted even before we rekindled our power exchange. Throughout my story, I show a very egalitarian slant to the choices we have made, and this is because we have not formalized a transfer of my power. For now, I am autonomous and heavily involved in the collaborative design of the relationship. I view this use of my introspection and creativity as an enormous service I can offer to my [redacted].

A Veil Between Worlds

Even before we began moving towards power exchange, we knew we would need strong, intentional boundaries. One of the first things that we agreed upon is that if we wanted to devote our energy to a new relationship we couldn't get distracted by old scars. It felt natural that we simply wouldn't talk about some things: His family, my schoolwork, our respective other intimate relationships, etc. After a while this habit of not peering past the Veil between our lives became enshrined as a cornerstone of the burgeoning relationship. There are things we simply do not discuss.

Once we explicitly committed to developing power exchange, we found that the Veil needed to become stronger and more opaque to protect the new feelings we were cultivating. We couldn't afford to channel any of our limited energy into creating a non-egalitarian version of our friendship as well.

For many people, pursuing a 24/7 dynamic, the vision is a pervasive sense of authority that reaches out and blankets an entire life including sex, emotional intimacy, friendship, and domestic partnership. I won't deny that this is something I dreamed of in our previous relationship (and in the early stages of this new one). Instead, we have chosen to simply not talk about anything aside from our power exchange and the related feelings.

A close friend has expressed fascination with this decision: "You *only* talk about your relationship?" and I don't blame them. One might think there is not much to discuss when we are limited in this way, but I think the scope encourages us to be thoughtful, intentional, and far more introspective than we otherwise would.

Some Beasts Are Tamed Alone

This decision also helped segregate another portion of our work. Some things (trauma, triggers, reactions) need to be handled alone before we have a foundation for working on them together. The work we put into fitting together now is independent by design, except for situations in which the other person's perspective is absolutely necessary to reach alignment.

An example of this is analyzing feelings from our previous relationship. Being able to share our perspectives on the past lets us reach alignment in a way we otherwise could not. No amount of independent processing will help me understand how he felt in a given moment. Being able to share these things and dissect them together brings enormous catharsis.

We must be thoughtful and sparing in how we determine whether the other person is needed. Often it is very tempting to say, "This would be easier if we talked about it," without having done the necessary introspection first. When we work independently, we make ourselves stronger so that our union becomes stronger as well.

I would not have this any other way—choosing to work on my own demons has been incredibly empowering and fulfilling for me. I have been able to witness myself face down fears I once thought I could tackle only with my partner beside me. I have found myself to be so much more capable, emotionally intelligent, and self-reliant than I expected.

Chalk, Not Ink

The honest truth is that there are plenty of small ways we aren't compatible by default, either fundamentally or because someone hasn't figured out how to change yet. Our final structural choice is that decisions need not be forever. There is no scripture prescribing that we will always have a Veil between our respective lives, that we will always process independently, that we will never integrate our power exchange into the rest of our lives.

A second honest truth is that I don't *know* if any of these structures will change. I can't see far enough in the future to know what that would look like or even if it is something I want. What I know for certain is that I was afraid at the beginning of this journey and now I am not. Our structures have served us well and given me great confidence in our ability to meet future challenges together.

Preparing Myself

Early in the relationship I worried that we would reenact the pain we had previously inflicted on one another and that we were doomed to repeat those same mistakes. I wasn't sure if we had done enough independent work on our triggers and past trauma to be capable of being the people we needed to be. We fumbled around a little bit trying our best to be "friends" (i.e., egalitarian, and platonic) and prove that we had grown up enough to be safe for one another. As we got more comfortable as friends, we started making some of our structural choices around the boundaries of our platonic relationship and a need to be emotionally independent.

Despite our platonic intentions we slipped quite naturally into flirtations about kink. We would drop innuendos or comments about power exchange, though never with the implication that we might reach for something like that again. With power exchange on my mind more often, I became open to the idea of exploring sexuality with him and he accepted my invitation to be sexually intimate again. We embarked on the journey of making further structural choices together.

I was only able to ask us to explore sex and power after meditating on my independent needs and desires. I had to devote a lot of thought to how we might be able to fit together in a way that didn't hurt in an unhealthy, unsustainable way. Thus began the process of sifting through my old journals and trying to decide which pieces of my conflicting or impossible needs could be released. While I am positive that he did his own emotional work to reconnect with me, that is not my story to tell, nor was I terribly involved in the process. I have gotten to reap the benefits without knowing all the gory details.

I lay out my process here with the caveat that this is written in hindsight. I did not embark on this process with five clear steps and deliverables—I'm looking back and finding that the process emerges like clear water once the dirt settles. It's very clear when I reflect on what I was doing even though it didn't happen precisely in this order or with this clarity. Aspects of our power exchange arose while I was processing and reshaping these needs—what looks tidy on paper was messier in reality.

Process Outline: Previous Need

First, I identify what I think of as a need in the clearest, plainest language possible. Then I consider what behaviour makes me feel as though the need is not being met. This was painful, and I felt very angry and defensive thinking about how sad and hurt I was in my previous relationship. Simple affirmations helped me work through the anger: *I can stop this work whenever I want. That I am continuing means I am committed to something new, and I think what's on the other side will be worth it.*

Deconstruction

I try to read between the lines of what I've identified as a need. Is it possible that this shallow "need" is just a thin veneer over a deeper need I haven't identified? This language is a little opaque so I will give an example: If the previously stated need is "lots of sex", maybe that is a specific, implementation-focused way of "feeling sexually desired by my partner" and there could be other ways to feel that way, thus meeting the core need. For the more technically inclined, one might call this previous need an "instrumental goal" and the core need a "terminal goal". The same sort of terminology seems to be used in both psychology and machine learning/artificial intelligence (funny how that happens, huh)?

So, as I investigate a 'need' I must ask myself questions that dig at the *why*:

- ❖ How do I feel when this need is met?
- ❖ How do I feel when it's not met?
- ❖ Were there times when the need was not met, and I still felt OK?
- ❖ If so, why?
- ❖ Are there relationships in which I do not have this need?
- ❖ If so, what parts of those relationships contribute to me feeling fulfilled and happy?
- ❖ If I imagine myself existing in this relationship in a situation where this need was truly impossible to meet (e.g., I'm in chastity, or we live on opposite sides of the world) are there pieces that still feel warm and satisfying?

Furthermore, I search for experiences and thoughts that resonate with me. I read books and memoirs about the topic, searching for clues as to how other people have lived a similar life. Since I am fortunate to have open and kinky friends, I also interview others about their feelings around this concept to see if any of their thoughts spark new ideas in me.

Reconstruction

If I want the core need met, then I am best served by being able to identify it and extrapolate a variety of ways to meet it. I need to give myself new mental pathways between the core need and things I might experience (i.e., my partner's behaviour) that might fill that need. I will use an example again: If the core need is "feeling sexually desired by my partner" then him having sex with me meets the need, but could I also feel desired when he asks for photos, tells me he's aroused thinking about me, gives me detailed plans for how he intends to fuck me later? All I need is a new mental framework for understanding how his behaviour fits with my needs.

Triggers

With the old need, the newly identified core need, and mental pathway in mind I can see how some interactions are more likely to reinforce dependency on the old need over the core need. For me, some things trigger the fear/anxiety/hurt that I am accustomed to feeling when the old need is not met. To give myself the space to develop, I need to avoid those triggers. To continue with my example: Maybe I feel my "lots of sex" need being rejected when I proposition my partner and he refuses, even though he's showing me I'm sexually desirable in a different way. Feeling rejected makes me unable to see other, subtler things he is showing me.

Self-support

Once I am aware of my triggers, I try to give myself the supportive structure I need to embed a new framework in my mind. It is much harder to change and grow when you are also in pain. Because I am doing this work on my own (as opposed to in collaboration with an existing partner) this is strictly self-support and is based on things that I can do or enforce (e.g., Boundaries with my [redacted], affirmations, committing to not interacting in certain ways until I'm more confident in my mental pathways). To close out the example: I could commit to not propositioning my partner for sex (and thus avoiding the triggering situation of being rejected). This would make me more able to experience feeling desirable in ways other than physically having sex whenever I ask for it. This sort of commitment should probably be communicated so that my partner understands why I have stopped asking for sex.

Case Study

The previous example of needing lots of sex transforming into needing to feel sexually desired by my partner is not a real experience of mine. The real needs I transformed were more painful, emotionally entangled, and complicated for me. I offer up a case study of the primary one that laid the foundation for our entire relationship to flourish.

Previous need

I had a collection of needs that, upon further reflection, could be deconstructed and recombined. I needed physical visits more than one weekend every two weeks, I needed immovable scheduled plans in my calendar, I needed to be able to access him whenever I wanted, have him be fully present in our messaging, and to know that he is thinking of me when we are apart. This group of needs felt unmet when our plans got rescheduled, when he didn't answer my messages, and when he answered and I could tell that he was distracted.

Deconstruction

In our previous relationship, the only time I felt like he was thinking of me was when he was with me in-person, and it felt impossible to recreate this any other way. When we messaged, I interpreted a lack of response or lack of engagement as a sign that I was not important (or rather, that other things were more important than me) and our cancelled plans made me feel like the lowest priority in his life. That hurt.

When we were able to be together in person, I felt intoxicatingly happy and loved. It made it especially hard to be physically apart because all of the attention and care I received in person seemingly evaporated as soon as he wasn't in front of me. When we weren't together, I felt like our relationship hardly existed because we were so unable to engage each other with full attention. All of this made me feel like I couldn't trust him to keep me in mind when I wasn't there to monitor him.

Very early on in our previous relationship there were times when we weren't together and weren't actively messaging ... but I still felt important and cared for. I reached back into my memory and recalled times he left me notes, wrote me letters, created tasks and activities for me when he couldn't be there. These things felt like proof to me: *You are still mine even when I don't see you. You can trust me to keep you in mind when we are apart.*

This need for physical visits really puzzled me because I have a wealth of fulfilling, happy long-distance relationships. My beloved game master in a long-running duet roleplaying game is someone I've met exactly once for just a weekend. I see my best friend once a year for an afternoon. Some of my closest emotional confidantes live on the other side of the continent from me. If I compare these relationships, I find a few things in common:

❖ There is never resentment on either side when someone is busy and must be absent for a while. It makes it easy to reconnect without feeling guilt or shame.

❖ We share emotional intimacy easily via messages and do not depend on phone calls or being in person just because they are supposedly richer forms of communication. We have honed our ability to communicate using the medium in which the relationship exists.

❖ There is consistency in how we engage one another. I know which friends I can expect to message me first after a long absence. I know which ones are prone to dropping off the face of the earth unless I prod them and can view this as a comfortable, natural way that we work together. I am reassured of my importance by their obvious delight at hearing from me.

The most painful part of this deconstruction was thinking about whether the previous group of needs might be impossible to meet. In this version of our relationship, we have explicitly chosen to segregate our external lives, independent emotional growth tasks, and any other egalitarian desires we have of one another. It simply isn't realistic or healthy for me to want such immediate intense access to him in this position, especially given how intentionally we are separating ourselves. The things I once needed are not available anymore, and that is a strong motivation for wanting to change what I need. Another affirmation arose: *I can't have this person unless something in me is willing to bend to support the relationship.*

For me, unfortunately, reading books and other accounts of long-distance relationships did not help. Most advice seems to be geared towards feeling connected with regular phone calls, planning ahead for when you'll be together, keeping each other aware of events in your respective lives. This is directly in contradiction with what we had already decided: Our relationship is limited to our power exchange and our separation of D/s and daily life lets us focus on that.

Instead, I found solace in a strange place: Posts from couples that had recently opened to polyamory. A common pattern is that a husband suddenly finds that his wife is far more popular than him and he is left alone while she goes out on dates. He wants to be happy for her but all he feels is loneliness, self-pity, and a bit of resentment. The resounding advice for such gentlemen is: Find something to keep yourself busy.

If I could fashion a rich, fulfilling life that is not directly connected to my [redacted] then I would lessen my dependency on him for things like emotional support, entertainment, intimacy, and partnership. We would be left with the core of power exchange and whatever else he chose to offer would be a gift, not something I demanded. If we choose to integrate our lives further, maybe this will be something I revisit. For now, it serves us well.

Through this process I deconstructed my collection of related physical access and communication needs into something a little more abstract: I needed to feel like I was important, that he thought of me often, and was willing to prioritize me.

Reconstruction

At the outset of our new relationship, I was lucky that my need for physical visits had simply changed without my active involvement. I have a rich enough life nowadays that I can't offer anyone a full weekend every two weeks! When it comes to messaging, I have become more sympathetic to the reality that we lead separate lives and that sometimes he is unable to respond. After all, there are certainly times in my life when duty calls in other areas (family, work, time for self-care). Modelling my expectations for my [redacted] after how I treat my treasured online friends worked wonders for reshaping this need. It also gave me an active way to make it easier for him to engage me: It feels a lot better to message someone who isn't bitter and resentful when they hear from you.

It naturally follows that if I would rather have proper engagement than small talk then I need to create an environment where this is possible. I need to show that it's okay to choose to not message me (or to say goodbye) instead of placating me with small talk. Just reframing this experience in my head using a brief affirmation helped: *If he is not messaging me, it is because he is not free to give me the engagement I deserve. I would not want him to message me if he were not able to engage.*

The result of this reconstruction is that I think my need is to feel that he is willing to give me his full focus and attention. This is something I can still feel when he chooses not to engage because he doesn't have attention to offer. This in itself is a sign that he is thinking of me when I am not present and considering what I need and deserve.

Triggers

When I get "left on read," I feel forgotten. When I don't hear from my [redacted] as often as I'd like, I feel like I am not important enough to make time for. When we are having "small talk" or discussing things where it's clear neither of us really cares, it makes me feel like we are just numbly going through the motions instead of engaging one another fully. I had thought that these were all independent triggers, but I realize now that they are all just rejections of a bid for attention. Being rejected in this way feels so bad that it makes me spiral into thoughts of unworthiness and lack of care. The same spiral occurs when our plans are rescheduled or shifted, since this is a commitment to future attention that is taken away.

Self-support

Avoiding these triggers is hard; they are all rooted in how we communicate and how we see one another. The best thing I can do for myself is impose a clear, inarguable boundary on how I communicate so that I experience consistency and am not left to mentally spiral about being ignored or forgotten. So, to address the trigger of "my bid for attention being rejected", I told my [redacted] that I wouldn't be initiating conversations. I asked him to message me at his leisure and only when he had the focus and attention that the relationship deserved. With this system, I knew whenever we were talking that I had his full attention, and he was actively interested in giving it to me. Similarly, I asked him to be entirely responsible for our scheduling so that I didn't experience begging him for time and being rejected like I did in our previous relationship. He is a kind and thoughtful person and so he accepted my request for him to be our initiator even though it might have chafed at his own feelings of being desirable. I'm grateful that he was willing to try this for me and our relationship; it built a lot of trust between us.

Reflection

This structural choice to never start conversations has worked wonders for me. It has allowed me the consistency and space to reshape my expectations into something that works for our relationship. It is also the structural thing that the wider kink community finds the most uncomfortable about our relationship. I constantly find myself defending it to others as something I requested for myself to help me feel safe, not an abusive withholding tactic on his part. Yes, it's possible that I simply won't hear from him for a week, and I have no way of reaching out; yes, it's possible that he'll just stop scheduling physical visits with me; yes, that is exactly what I want, and it enables me to welcome him properly into my life when he is ready to be here. It lets me see his attention as a gift instead of something to which I am constantly entitled. It has also opened my eyes to other proof that he thinks of me when we are not together—things like coming into our conversations with new ideas and energy, telling me about his fantasies and daydreams about me, showing me context-light things he sees in the outside world that remind him of our power exchange. The pain of bids for attention being rejected made it impossible for me to see these other aspects of his behaviour.

Continuing to Walk the Path

We are one year into our new relationship, and I have changed. When I dig at my needs, they are surprisingly sparse. I won't fool myself or the reader into thinking that this is because I've wiped out huge portions of myself in order to fit someone else (as hot as that may sound). The reality is that none of this is possible without a high degree of compatibility, and the things I've had to change turned out to be not so integral to me after all.

In the early stages of this new relationship, I was afraid that I would be unsafe and unfulfilled if we chose to walk the path of ownership. Now I see that regardless of which path we take, some things about him are unchanging and these things are compatible with me. They are things I can take for granted: He will be honest and forthright with me, he will communicate with me, he is committed to his own self-examination and growth. These immutable facets of his character line up with immutable needs I have such that I don't have to look too closely at them. If he weren't committed to his growth, I wouldn't be able to follow him and I don't think I would be able to change myself into someone who would.

The core needs I've wound up with are:

❖ I need to feel special to my [redacted]. I want to know that the quality of our relationship is unique and there is some aspect of what we do that he doesn't get anywhere else. I'm not entirely confident that this is different from "I need to be his only piece of human property" because, truthfully, we haven't gone far enough down the path for me to investigate that feeling properly.

❖ I need to feel that my presence is helpful to my [redacted]. Sometimes I'm able to create this feeling for myself—I can tell when he is benefiting from my existence, and I can make myself more helpful so that I get more of this feeling. If I am lacking in it, I can ask if he is finding me pleasing and useful. More and more he is affectionately willing to tell me when I am being pleasing (be still my heart)!

❖ I need to feel that he is willing to give me his full focus and attention. I don't need the attention to be actively on me (e.g., Talking to me, interacting with me) but I need to trust or have evidence that he is thinking of me. This feeling is given to me by his focus and engagement when we are speaking, at the lack of going-through-the-motions interactions, and when he clearly has had thoughts or ideas of me when we are not in contact

❖ I need to feel that he is aware of how I reshape myself for him. I don't need to be thanked or directed but I need him to notice and for that awareness to be communicated in some way. Sometimes this could be a neutral observation ("You've been more assertive lately,") or sometimes eyes lingering on a change I have made to my apartment to better host him. It could also be him taking it as fact that I will do a certain thing despite never having explicitly discussed it.

❖ When (if?) we formalize our ownership dynamic, I think I will need to feel that he views me as something he has sovereignty over and not just an autonomous person he can be especially commanding or influential over. I think this is attached to some of the aforementioned needs—feeling special to him and having awareness of how fluid I make myself for his benefit.

When I compare these needs to what I thought I needed in our egalitarian relationship I find myself pleasantly surprised and a little sheepish. These are flexible, open-ended, and leave room for us to work together to encourage my feeling of fulfillment. Considering my needs in this open-ended way means I am more resilient against the fear that they won't be met. If there are many ways to fill my cup, then it is not the end of the world if one or two run dry. As an additional note, they are not demands, and this makes my submissive heart sing.

Having undertaken this process of investigating my needs and reshaping them gives me much more confidence that I will be able to do the same thing in the future. My perception of my needs has shifted from being pieces of my identity to expressions of how I participate in a relationship. As such they have become collaborative things we will work together to meet.

I find it deeply reflective of our intended dynamic to have such paired responsibilities: I can shift my needs; he will find ways to give me what I deserve.

Venerant is a property-oriented s-type who has been practicing consensual nonconsent, emotional sadomasochism, and power exchange in her intimate relationships for ten years. She and her [redacted] are presently cultivating an ownership-oriented relationship based on shared vulnerability, a sense of worthiness, and an endless, starry-eyed fascination with one another.

Part 2
Walking the Road

Negotiating With Reality
Kimber

My biggest struggle in the beginning, when I was still looking for a partner, was coping with the limitations of vanilla life. I spent eleven years as a live-in caregiver for an aging parent while working full-time, all without a vehicle. I did both online interactions and real-time interactions outside of where I lived. I live within range of a BDSM club, so I was able to get away quite a few weekends. I created a social life outside of my home environment, and that support system was invaluable to me. I also had private meetings with the dominants I was serving at the time. When I was given tasks to do that could not be done in the house, I would arrange for some private time to do that.

Proper negotiation made a huge difference. After several mistakes and lessons, I learned what my boundaries were, as well as becoming more adept at negotiating. I learned to make sure that they understood reality, and that I was not able to drop everything on a moment's notice. That became a very good benchmark to determine whether someone really understood what these lifestyles are all about, because I ended up having some wonderful relationships with those dominants who respected my boundaries and my reality. But if they couldn't do that, I learned that they were not worthy of my time and my service. That is an important fact to internalize.

The problem wasn't even that the unsuitable dominants were looking for a full-time live-in relationship, which I couldn't give. They were looking for things like me being naked or in lingerie all the time, or they would want me to present myself in an inappropriate outfit in front of the aging parent for whom I was caring. (That's why I'm using the term "not worthy".) They assumed that I would be willing to be dressed up like a sexy schoolgirl 24/7, regardless of whether there was an elderly ill parent in the same space.

I am also polyamorous, and I do have a primary partner who is not my dominant but will get toppy with me during play; our relationship is open, and we discuss how much time we will be spending with others. So, between my primary partner, my job, and my former caregiving situation (my elderly parent passed away in 2018), there was a lot of my life that I had to hold onto, that I couldn't give away to a dominant partner. Many of the dominants I talked to decided that this wasn't for them, which was OK, but I think a lot of s-types may be in the same boat, having prior obligations which cannot be given away.

Whether it's your chosen family or your birth family, there comes a time in the stages of our lives where we must do what is right by them, even if in some cases that means we don't always get to do what we want to do. I think it's important for s-types to recognize that you can get at least some of what you want and need out of the right D/s dynamic, but until you're in a place where your regular life is not stable—if you're taking care of others or your income is such that you can barely take care of yourself—I found that for me, anyway, I couldn't give everything in my life if I couldn't meet my own needs. It's Maslow's Hierarchy of Needs, but for the kink world. If most of your attention is on survival or other responsibilities, you aren't going to have that much to give a dynamic.

I know that some s-types say that the right dominant would just "rescue" them from all their responsibilities, but what I would say to them is that if you are not a functioning human being, how do you expect to attract someone who is going to be healthy, and be able to take care of you from a solid place? You are more likely to attract people into your life who are also unhealthy, and who may use you or treat you badly. Do you really want that tradeoff? If someone wants a D/s dynamic because they don't want to be responsible for themselves, that opens the door for predatory people, in my humble opinion.

While I have not been a full-time live-in slave due to my circumstances, I have had many rules with my various dominant partners—clothing rules, orgasm control rules, requirements for health goals, bedtime rules, etc. I've had as many real-life "spillovers" from dynamics that started as sexual play as I could, given how caregiving took up so much of my time. I think I've come as close as I possibly could to having a real-life dynamic without actually living together. I've had a lot of experience with dominants who wanted me to do online dynamics, but I'm an in-person kind of girl. Online stuff can be entertaining, but I get bored very easily with it. If there were promises made and not kept about getting together, I would find that I couldn't muster enthusiasm for any rules, even if they were made to help me. Those rules meant to me that they had respect and caring for me, but I needed to build a good connection in person with the dominant partner to feel that.

I finally met the right dominant and was with him for four years, but he passed away in February of this year. I'm still in the later stages of grief right now, and still reconciling how the next chapter of my life will work. He was a wonderful man who saw me through the last years of being a caregiver, and was always supportive. While he was very dominant, we did have more of a Daddy/little relationship—it was a combination of more traditional Dominant and submissive/slave, but sometimes we would just get silly and slip into the Daddy/little dynamic. He was an M.D., and he used to teach medical play at kink conferences. He was a sadist, to be sure, but there was a strong spiritual component to our play because he was a bit of a shapeshifter. His spirit animal was a wolf, and he had even worked with wolves in real life as a younger man. Sometimes things would get very primal, and sometimes they were more like "standard" D/s—not that there is a real standard definition of D/s. Our time together would flow within minutes through many different permutations of D/s, and that completely worked for us. He once actually came out and helped with my caregiving, which is one of the memories I will always treasure about him. My parent needed some medical attention, so he came over and helped with that. I hadn't wanted to mix those two worlds, but he was willing.

One of the surprising things I learned from that relationship is that humiliation can be done without demeaning or disrespect. That was important because although we did a lot of humiliation play in various ways, I never felt devalued or disrespected as a human being. After every experience involving humiliation, he would hold me and reassure me that I had pleased him, and remind me that I was strong and beautiful. In the depths of subspace, his positive words would make me feel proud that I was able to give this to him, because humiliation isn't easy for me. Whenever I would do something which was a push for me, he would do that—hold me and reassure me that I had done well by him. I did a lot of hard things for him that I would never have done for anyone else, because I knew that I was safe with him.

Another piece of advice that I would give to new s-types who are getting into these relationships is to laugh! We were always joking and using humor with each other. Enjoy each other as people, and let the mood and the energy flow organically. Just because you might have started with a plan for this interaction doesn't mean that you necessarily have to force it. If the mood and the energy is different, enjoy what is happening rather than feeling bad that it's not going according to plan.

I should put in a disclaimer at this point that I am in training to become a mental health professional, ideally for the kink community. As a therapist in training, I know that when I first got into this and recognized it in myself, I was not mentally or emotionally equipped to process these feelings, and know exactly what I needed. It took a lot of work to get to where I am now, and it is critical for s-types to learn how to be comfortable with themselves and to be functional. I've seen some terrible situations where people were in long-term dynamics and their dominant partner took care of everything—and then the dominant passes away or gets very sick, and the s-type does not know how to function on their own as a human being. I think it's especially important for those of us who are getting into our forties and fifties and beyond. As you progress in your life experience and get to different stages of development, you need to look at your life realistically. If you are going to knowingly be involved with an older person, especially, there are some real-world factors you need to know how to take care of. My dominant was 75 when he died, and I was 52. No one talks much about what happens when you are with a power exchange partner all the way to the end.

Regardless of whether you were married, unmarried, living together or not, make sure that you have a support network beyond them—someone you can talk with about it, whether it's personal or professional support. Even if people you are close to may not know the exact nature of that relationship, they can still be helpful if they understand that the person you love has died. Give yourself whatever time it takes to grieve, and to honor the memory of that relationship. Not only have I just gone through it myself, I also know a lot of people in my local community who are going through this. Grieving has no timetable. and it's a disservice to you and to the one you loved to try to force yourself to be OK before you're ready.

When we're in the early stages of our life, we all think that we're ten feet tall and bulletproof. This can continue on, particularly if one has a masochistic bent! For two or three years, I went through a very large masochistic "I am the ultimate pain slut!" phase. If I didn't have large bruises on various parts of my body, then my trip to the club was not successful. Later in life, as things have changed and I've gained experience, I still enjoy that kind of thing from time to time, but I want to remind people that as you get older, your tastes are going to change. Your body and your tolerance is going to change. The reality is that even if you're with the same person for thirty or forty years, the things you're going to be able to do together are going to be different as you both progress through life. Allowing for that without judgment, and without demeaning each other, is an important part of a long-term dynamic.

And as a final piece of advice to a very bratty sub friend of mine: Make sure that you put nose-licking and wet willies on your hard limits list, because if you don't, that could come back to get you in trouble!

Kimber is a 52-year-old s-type who started her BDSM journey in real-time at 17 while attending college in New Orleans. Over the years, the journey had many adventures in topping, switching and both public and private experience. In everyday life, she is working on a master's degree in Marriage and Family Therapy, with a hope to assist the poly/kink community with mental health and relationships.

The Thrill Is Gone?

Renee

This is something I wrote for a thread where a slave was feeling lost because his mistress wasn't as high protocol and demanding as she had been in the beginning. It seems to be a rather common problem by the number of posts we see about the subject.

I went through something similar years ago. When our relationship was new, my Master had all kinds of high protocol and ritual I had to learn, and I did. I internalized all of it. To me, it *was* part of the whole slavery thing, and while it wasn't easy to learn and find the "headspace" to do things that made me feel silly or embarrassed, I wanted to *be* a good slave, so I did them all.

Eventually, after these things became a part of me, he started easing up on the micro-management, protocol, and ritual. At first that seemed OK because it had been rather overwhelming at times, but as he eased up more, I began to panic.

I wondered if perhaps he was bored with me. I worried that perhaps I wasn't pleasing him or doing "it" right. I couldn't figure out why he would no longer have an interest in me being "the slave". I thought that because to me those things were part of being a slave.

So, with tears in my eyes, I sat down in front of him between his knees on the floor and asked him why he didn't want *me* to act like his slave anymore. He just smiled at me and said it was because I didn't need to *act* like his slave anymore. He told me I *was* his slave.

He went on to explain that the micromanagement, protocol and ritual were part of teaching me to serve him, to get me used to having my actions revolve around him and his desires even when I didn't feel like it or wasn't in the mood. He went on to explain that he had no intention of becoming a slave to the dynamic and his desire is to be obeyed and served, not to have to be *on* all the time to role-play. He wanted my obedience to become a part of me, for serving to be just what I do and how I think, and once he accomplished that, that part of training could be wound down—and that's what he did. He didn't need me to act like a slave because I was a slave. There was no more acting required.

After that I felt better. I was his slave (and still am). I don't have to get in any mindset or mode. I don't need ritual or protocol or micromanagement to be who and what I am. He taught me that serving him and pleasing him, obeying him *is* what he desires. *That is* being a slave.

You can find that feeling of serving, of being a slave, by thinking of what your mistress does want as an act of slavery, if you thrive on that feeling. To me, bringing him a glass of tea when he's thirsty is as much an act of slavery, and makes me feel as good, as any protocol or ritual would. Why? Because I've done what he desires. I've pleased him. More importantly, I've pleased him without making him jump through hoops putting me in some "mindset" to get that tea.

Instead of thinking about slavery as whips and chains and protocol and all the other bullshit you read about in some BDSM fantasy, think of it more realistically. What is it you really want out of slavery *for yourself*? Then ask her what she wants in a slave? You might find that feeling you're looking for by serving in a way that pleases her instead of having an unrealistic expectation that enslaves you both to the dynamic and pleases no one.

Renee is an attorney and the devoted monogamous slave of a polyamorous master. She shares him with his other slave-wife, and often dispenses advice to new s-types.

D/s When You're Not Submissive
MalikaSG

You Are Not Alone
First, let me just say that I don't identify as a submissive. I have never desired to submit to anyone except for him. But I have learned a lot on this journey by going to various types of online gatherings, Zoom classes, and by talking to those who identify on the little-letter side of the slash. So, the first piece of advice I would give to s-types is: Don't think that just because you don't fit into a certain "type", or category of submissive, that you can't learn something from those who do. Don't think that just because you're not a slave that you couldn't learn something from slaves. You're not an island. I used to think, "Well, I'm just submitting because it's him. I'm not like all the other s-types. I don't even know what 'slave heart' is! That's not me!" But you do yourself a disservice that way because there's always something to be learned from everyone.

I'm not a label person. I don't think about it. I do know that I have more of a dominant personality, a dominant side. I desire to be dominant more than I desire to be submissive, but that still doesn't get in the way of how I feel about, how I interact with, and how I view Sir. It's separate, but it's equal, and it doesn't hinder our dynamic.

I'm lucky because Sir encourages me to explore all the different sides of myself and to be who I am. I'm allowed to vocalize what I want and how I feel, without feeling as if I'm disrespecting him or our dynamic. I am fortunate to have that.

Am I Good Enough?
Another thing I would advise is to try not to get in your own way. I did that a lot, and I still struggle with it, because I am in a dynamic like this for the first time. Sir has had many years of experience, and more than one s-type in his charge, so I would always compare myself to the previous submissive. I thought, "Well, I can't do all the things that she did, so am I good enough?" But when I did that, it put a strain on our day-to-day interaction.

He can always tell when something's going on with me, and I am the kind of person who likes to suffer in silence, so I wasn't going to tell him. That won't do! You go from having effective communication to having a communication breakdown, and that is not a good thing for any dynamic.

I had to learn to trust him. By that I don't mean trust in the fidelity sense, but to trust him when he tells me that he loves me, wants the best for me, and that I don't have to measure up to anyone. To do that, I had to learn to trust myself, first. I had to trust that I was good enough to be with him and to be in this dynamic. I had to trust that I am worthy of his sacrifice, and worthy of his love.

I don't think that any dynamic can work if those involved don't have a strong sense of who they are. You have to know where you're going, to figure out what you need to help you get there. I know that at eighteen I didn't have a clue. (Even at forty-seven I sometimes think, "I don't really know for sure...") I'm much better at that now; when I start to have those thoughts, I just take a beat and think of all the things Sir has said to reassure me. I think about who he is as a person. I know him, so I know that the things I'm doubting, well, I don't really have a reason to doubt them. I just had to stop overthinking, which is something I do a lot. Getting in your own way is going to happen every now and then, so you have to give yourself a break. I'm notorious for being way too hard on myself. Sir's never fails to tell me, "You're capable! You can do this! You just have to believe in yourself!"

So don't get too caught up on labels, or what you should or shouldn't be doing in your M/s, because it's different for everyone. Each dynamic is unique to the people who are in it. You will hear people talk about "Old Guard this..." and "Leather that..." and "Master/slave is supposed to look like this..." It's not going to look like that for everyone, because not everyone is geared to do those particular things. I am a full-bodied woman with really bad knees, so I'm not going get on the floor and crawl to anyone. If I feel bad about that and get too caught up over what I *don't* have to offer because I think it means I'm not submissive enough, I won't be able to focus on giving Sir what I *do* have to offer.

Which leads to one of the most important components, self-esteem! When I found out that we were going to the Master/slave Conference, I started freaking out. I've never been to a conference before, and MsC is a big one. I had so much anxiety over what to wear, thinking that I don't have the kind of clothes that are appropriate for a conference like that. I convinced myself that I was not going to fit in. But it all comes down to whether I like what I see in the mirror or not. If I'm OK with that, it won't matter what I wear. This kind of self-doubt could negatively affect your dynamic, either directly or indirectly.

Peer Education

If you have questions, don't be afraid to ask—everyone had to learn, at some point. Sir is a uniform enthusiast. He has many and several pairs of boots. I was very concerned because I had no knowledge about maintaining and caring for them when we entered our dynamic. So, I went to classes and asked questions. Doing that allowed me to gather resources to help me. I also, now have friends who are titleholders in boot blacking! Which is fantastic—I'm going to learn from the best of the best. Being as educated as possible will allow you to cultivate the skills that you need in your dynamic. But if you don't know how to do something, don't be too hard on yourself!

If someone offers you a book, read it! Even if it's not something you want to read—whether it's wordy, or you're thinking, "This isn't part of our dynamic?"—just read it anyway.

Even if the only thing you get out of it is, "This is bullshit," read it because chances are you will learn *something*. It may not manifest right away, but one day you might hear something and remember, "Hey, I read this somewhere!" I have a stack of books about various aspects of kink and M/s. They were all gifted to me, and I have found them useful.

Negotiation

I was lucky because I already knew who Sir was, as we had been friends for twelve years before we started our dynamic. I did have to get used to the idea that Sir is different now than he was ten years ago, twenty years ago. I feel like I've gotten Sir Guy 2.0! He's done a lot and learned a lot. He has been to many places, and now I have the older, more mature, experienced version of him. Many things I want to learn and experience, and he's already done. For a while, I would say, "How come you're not excited about this?" And he'd say, "I've already done it." That used to upset me, but then Sir reminded me that he has never done those things with me, so it's still going to be a new experience for both of us.

Don't dwell on the things your D-type has done in the past with other s-types. As long as you are secure in your dynamic and relationship, there's no need to worry. Instead, look forward to the experiences you're going to have together. Try to live in the moment of that.

And by the same token, leave your own past stuff in the past! If you've had a bad experience and you learned from it, take the lesson, and leave the junk. Not doing so can also cause a rift in your dynamic. Even if you think you're hiding it well ... you're not. I had to learn this lesson. I had a really bad experience as part of a polycule. It was my first time in a polyamorous dynamic, and I thought I was safe because I had known the people for twenty-five years. It ended badly, causing a lot of emotional damage, and I had to make sure that I was OK before I got into another relationship. The first thing I asked Sir was, "Is this going to be a poly dynamic? Because if it is ... I can't."

So, we talked about it—and this is really important. Talk about everything openly—as equals—first. Don't think that just because you identify as an s-type that you must negotiate as such during the first conversation. Until you've worked out the details, crafted and signed the contract (if that the procedure used), you are on equal footing.

You have to be honest about how you feel, what you want, and what you can't tolerate—or otherwise you're going to get all the things that you don't want, and you're dead in the water. I was lucky that we were able to have an open conversation about wants, needs, and expectations. It took me a while to be confident enough to say the things that I needed to say without being afraid that Sir would disappear when I said them. Once I did, it made the negotiation process easier.

Warning

Be careful of gaslighting. I met a woman recently who had run her own business successfully for years, who had raised children on her own, and who was incredibly capable, smart, and beautiful. She was naturally inquisitive and was not afraid to ask questions. Then she met a dominant, and all of that changed. She began to question her intelligence and her business savvy. When she asked him a question, he would reply, "I want you to do what I tell you. If you have questions, then that means you don't trust me, and you're not serious about our relationship." Be careful of those red flags. Don't ever let anyone make you doubt yourself by dangling dominance and submission in your face.

If you see the warning signs, don't be afraid to walk away. Don't think that if you walk away, you're never going to find what you're looking for—because you will. It may not happen right away. In fact, it may take a long time, but you can use that time to grow, become stronger, and learn more about yourself; so when it does come, you'll be ready.

Long Distance

This single most difficult thing for me right now is that our relationship is currently long distance. Trust is huge in making that work—it's paramount. If you're always wondering what your partner(s) is doing, it's going to drive you crazy. Sir and I set a goal to be living together as a unit in the same space, in less than five years. Permanent long distance is not something either of us want, and we made that clear from the beginning. To maintain our dynamic, we have certain rituals. I send him a video message every morning; we talk every day at my lunchtime; and on weekends we talk every day at 1 pm. We also have a nightly phone call; no matter what happens, one of us is calling the other. Saturday nights are our date nights, and on those nights, nobody interrupts us, and we turn off our phones. (Well, OK, sometimes we're on our phones sending pictures and saying, "Hey, did you see this thing today?")

We have to keep the lines of communication open and share our lives. We share our music, we watch movies together, and we try to spend as much quality time together as possible. Not quantity, because sometimes we barely get five minutes during the day to talk, but quality. We make those five minutes count.

Be honest when you're feeling like you miss each other; don't let those feelings turn into resentment. I did that; I would be so tired of being a thousand miles away from him, and instead of talking about it, I kept it to myself. And the longer I did that, the more resentful I got.

Sir could tell that something wasn't right. We finally had to seriously talk about it—and talking about things even when they're hard is also really important. That was a very hard emotional conversation.

We send each other things. When I least expect it, something will show up in my mail—anything from books to cute coffee mugs, most recently a beautiful ring. He wears a particular scented oil, and he sent me some so that I could have his scent with me all the time. The little things count more than anything else.

I am required to check my mail every other day. I live in an apartment complex, and my mailbox quite a distance from my building. I'd go every couple of weeks. When Sir heard this, he laid down the law. "You're going to go get your mail every other day. Let me know when you leave, and when you're back in your apartment." This is required whenever I leave, for any reason. This was kind of difficult, at first. However, I did get used to it over time.

Honorifics are not required. Sir said, "You call me what you feel comfortable calling me—whatever speaks to you. And if that changes from day to day, I'm fine with that, as long as you respect the dynamic and our roles in it." Since we're not very high protocol, it's really relaxed. He said to me, "I value your opinion, I won't keep you from speaking your mind. I like the fact that you're strong, but remember that when everything is said and done, I'm the one who makes the decision." He understands that I've never been in this type of dynamic before, and I never wanted to be, but I'm willing to relinquish my control because he is who he is. He has let me know, on several occasions, how much that means to him.

Why This Side of the Slash?

I was afraid of losing myself at first. I didn't know very much about this life— I didn't want to become someone's *thing*. I still wanted to be me, and I feared an authority-based dynamic would rob me of my individuality. I was also trying to wrap my head around the dominant side of me, at the same time. It's pretty strong, but I've never explored it before, because it kind of scares me, to be honest.

I've told Sir that I would like to explore my dominance at some point; I've been very clear about what it is that I want. When I told Sir that I wanted to explore this side of me, I added that I would very much like him to be a part of it, because there are going to be things I don't know. I'm going to have questions, and I trust his judgment. When vetting, a second pair of eyes, so to speak, is better because they may see something that you don't.

I met Sir on Fetlife when it first started, and we became online friends. I was fascinated by him—he was smart, handsome, and had a very sexy deep voice. Most importantly, he paid attention to me in a way that didn't make me feel like a fetish, or some kind of new shiny toy. He saw me as a person. We would talk on the phone and he would read his stories to me. But he was in New York, and I was in Arkansas, so I knew this was impossible. Still, I enjoyed spending time with him, and as the years went by, I never forgot about him.

I had told my mother when I was nineteen years old that I was never going to get married. She asked me why, and I said, "Because there's not a man out there strong enough to handle me. I need someone stronger than I am, and there's no one out there like that." And along came Sir Guy. I immediately felt a need to step back and let him take the lead, but I never told him. We didn't speak much, for years, but every now and then I would call him. I didn't want him to forget me. In April of 2020, we began talking every day. I lost my mom to dementia the year before; Sir was now his mother's caregiver, and we offered each other comfort and support. All the fascination I used to feel for him just came flooding back, and one day I said, "I would really like to try and be in a relationship with you. I would like to be yours."

Those were my exact words, and from that point on, we started talking about what that would look like. He asked me why, and I said, "Because you're you. I can't see myself submitting to anyone else in the world but you."

It was really weird at first, though. Why was it that I liked when he called me his girl? Why did I get butterflies when he scolded me? It was so new. In my previous relationships, whenever someone tried to control me, it was "No way, man. I'm outta here."

But my dad was career military; he was a tough dude, and I gave him trouble all the time. He was my favorite person growing up. My Sir and I don't have a "daddy/girl" type of dynamic, but he and my father do have certain similarities as people, similarities I didn't even notice until we were already in our relationship. I appreciate those similarities, and to be fair, a lot of my interest does stem from the sort of person that my dad was. My dad always wore suits, and I love suits. I love the look of them and the feel of them. I like to wear them. I do like strong, disciplined people, but I think some of that is because I am a free-spirited Aquarius. I hate routines and rules! So, when I'm with someone who has those qualities, I can learn from them, I can harness that. He can keep me focused and keep me in line. I need that, and I didn't realize I needed that before, but no one else has been able to offer that to me.

I can't imagine my life without him now. It feels crazy sometimes, but I've learned so much since I've been with Sir. He asked me, "What have you learned about yourself since we've been together?" And I asked that of him too. I think asking this question is important, because that's one way to know whether or not your dynamic is working. Each stage of personal growth help can help to make one's dynamic that much stronger.

MalikaSG (She/Her) lived the kink life both privately and publicly for nearly 15 years, and began her Leather journey in late 2020. She is the Queen of The House of the Black Panther where she is the partner of and serves the Head of Household, Sir Guy.

Malika is the Founder of POC Arkansas (est. 2021). She member of a various BDSM, kink, and Leather organizations. Malika has organized and facilitated discussion panels on the POC kink perspective and bigger bodies in the kink community, in collaboration with various lifestyle groups.

With her loving Sir, MalikaSG delivered the Keynote address for the Inaugural Service Oriented Conference, 2021 and the Endnote address at the Latinos In Leather 2nd Anniversary celebration, 2022.

Following My Captain
passerby

I met my current dominant in high school when we were in the same ROTC-style program. We all had the experience of following a chain of command, of having superior officers, from high school on. We learned about respecting rank and office if not necessarily the person, and the difference between lawful orders and unlawful orders. It was a really good experience for a young person. I know that on Fetlife we like to pretend that we didn't start our journeys until the age of eighteen, and if we did anything earlier, we don't talk about it.

He was the unit leader, and I was his assistant and his executive officer while we were students. He went off to join the Navy, and I went off to experiment sexually. My first foray with BDSM was getting involved with a man who was much older than me, who was a predator-type. I had two children with him, and a third child I hid while I was trying to get my divorce to go through. After that, I became a very independent person. I engaged in some professional-dominatrix work to support my family, and it was a way of taking back the control I had ceded during that relationship. I decided that I was never going to submit again; I was never going to put myself in a position of being harmed again, which was a wild swing for me.

I am Mechica—the American version of that is Mexican—and Apache. My grandfather used to say that these terms were created by governments putting up a border—some of us were on this side, some were on that side. Colonization brought a very patriarchal style of household, surrounded by the Catholic Church. Growing up, I had to let go of Catholicism and this ideal where the women were always submissive. I was always asking the nuns why women were judged certain ways. So while we were growing up, we were taught that men lead and the women follow, but in our homes I could see that was different—nobody ever crossed Mama! To this day, I look to my grandmother who has been dead for over fifteen years, and she is still the leader of that extended family. Nobody was ever able to fully replace the matriarchy. Even though my grandfather was very strong and respected at his work, there was no question that the house was Grandmother's castle. You approached her and her home with respect, you didn't fight with your cousins there, because this woman was the leader and she was who you looked to for advice, and you didn't disgrace her by bringing conflict into her space. We were really taught that the women in our culture were spiritual, the connection between life and death—because we bring life in the world.

But when my parents were growing up, the whole point was to assimilate—to speak English well, to leave certain parts of your culture out so they couldn't be seen, to be white-presenting people in society. At the same time, we were taught that the women were the leaders in the home, but that you had to put out a certain image that the man was the leader outside the home. I grew up seeing both men and women in very strong positions. So even though the machismo of Chicano and Native American culture was magnified when I grew up, they are matriarchal cultures underneath, so it wasn't unusual to have a female-led household. My kids have always known "Mom's in charge!" This was my fallback after my first failed experience with power exchange.

I was determined that I was never going to submit to anybody, and I certainly wasn't going to call anyone Master. In fact, when I hooked up with the Captain, who is now my partner, I told him that I don't do slavery. That would never be a thing for me. I couldn't cede that control, because I couldn't trust that anyone was going to do for me and my family what I would do. I thought of it as putting myself in a position of weakness, which with the wrong person, it very much is.

I see that a lot with new s-types who say, "Well, I just don't know what happened—I gave them permission to do these things to me, and then they hurt me!" I don't want to victim-blame, but in this lifestyle there has to be a facet of personal responsibility. You must decide what your boundaries are and stick with them, and not let them be chipped away because somebody says all the right words.

I moved to Montana because neither my family nor my first husband's family were there. I'd gotten involved again with that same

ROTC program, and was working for them. I entered a somewhat traditional marriage with a man who seemed more submissive than me; when we'd started dating, I told him that I am bisexual and polyamorous—monogamy was never going to be in the cards for me because I wanted to be with women as well. He was fine with that for the first couple of years. We had a child together, and then I decided I wanted a play partner to top me.

At the same time, the ROTC program was having their reunion gathering, and I wrote to the Captain and said that many of our old classmates would be there, that we all missed him, and would he come out to see this? He came out and we ended up wandering around together trying to get all the new students into their chow lines, and he just stepped right back in and started being the leader again. It had been over ten years since we had graduated, but it was like no time had passed. We all just fell in together with the same routine we'd had in high school.

After the event, I got together with the Captain over a meal and we discussed what I was interested in, and what he might want. I'd talked about it to my husband, and he didn't have a problem with it at that time, but about a year later when I'd been seeing the Captain for some time, he decided to veto the relationship. That's not the way I do poly, because that trounces on someone else's rights. I we ended up getting divorced, and I moved on with my life and took custody of the kids.

My Master and I are both working for the National Guard ROTC program now, and I'm having a relationship with someone who outranks me at work, so we must be very careful to behave in our professional life so that most people have no idea we're involved. We have different last names; we continue to live in separate households. At first, I didn't want to be one of those women who brings a new man into her children's lives and then it doesn't work out. (Also, he likes it quiet and peaceful in order to work, and I have a houseful of kids.) He has his home and I have mine, and we run them separately ... but my Master is entirely in charge of both.

The turning point was when I was working in an unpleasant, stressful side job, and I'd been talking to my Master about just how bad my boss had gotten just before I had to leave on a work trip. He messaged me while I was in Washington and told me, "Your son has the new house keys."

"What new house keys?" I said.

"You're done working at that job," he told me. "And since that was how you were providing a home for your children, I have come up with a solution. I've rented you a house, and now you have an option. You don't have to stay and be abused at this job; you have other choices." He'd observed how things were, he'd implemented a solution, and then informed me about it. Ten years ago, that's not something I ever would have wanted someone to do—telling me that I was going to move and quit my job. It would have been the end of the relationship. But when he did that, I realized how much trust I had developed with him. When we'd started out, it was just topping and play. It was his own behaviors over the years—not pushing limits, not ever acting like what I could give wasn't enough—which solidified the foundation we'd started when we were teenagers. I'd seen him lead other people and make good decisions for them, and it felt natural to step back and let this man lead, where I didn't trust any others to do so.

He did a lot of work to build up trust, and he did it silently. He never pointed out everything he was doing to make me trust him—he just *was* trust. No one I knew was stronger about their own moral and ethical behaviors than he was. That was not something I could control with a contract, or say, "This was our relationship agreement, and we have to stick to it." I didn't have to worry about those things—he just wasn't going to cross boundaries. If he didn't know something, he would go learn about it, until he could say that he had the knowledge. He didn't make decisions until he had heard people's input. He taught me the difference between abusive men who use this lifestyle to get what they want, and a man who was worth following.

He makes all the final decisions for my life, but he values my counsel. He wants to know what things I've seen that he hasn't. I do now describe our relationship as "I am slave, he is Master,", I feel like I have more freedom and understanding and safety now than when I was adamantly in charge. In my weakest moments, I can trust him to keep me safe. Getting to a place where I was willing to re-examine submission was a hard journey, but he made it easier by his own strength of character.

Since then, the biggest struggle has been letting people see that I was OK asking someone for permission before I agreed to anything. I'd always been the kind of person who would respond immediately when friends asked me if I would like to do something, and having to stop that reaction and step back, saying, "I'll get back to you on that; I have to discuss it with my partner and I'll let you know," made people react as if I'd committed a heinous sin. I would get, "I don't know who you've become!" But with his word behind me, I had the strength to stand up to people who wanted to control my behavior, and I didn't feel like I had to defend anything. I had not experienced, as a child, having No mean No, but when I was speaking for his No, I could stand up for it. (I teach my kids that they can say No to me if it's really important to them, and I'm going to listen to that with a respect that I didn't have growing up.)

We have a total power exchange relationship, and that can really scare a lot of people. "What if he decides to lop off your arm? Surely you have some limits!" It's interesting to try to explain to people that while all human beings have limits, I've consented to give over those limits to him—because his interest in my well-being supersedes that of my own.

It's such a pet peeve of mine when I hear s-types say, "I want someone to break me. I want someone to force me to do this," because I believe that good power exchange relationships don't come out of breaking somebody down. They come out of helping somebody to heal. It wasn't his responsibility to break me of my bad habits and my fears. Instead, he took responsibility for making me a firm foundation so that I could go heal myself. I get frustrated when new s-types go on about how they can't take care of themselves, and they need a master to help them maintain their lives! Having been a broken person, I know that you don't put that on your partner, no matter how domly they are. They are not your mental health professional.

It's important for s-types with problems to find some sort of healing outside of the relationship, so that they're not bringing that heavy luggage in and dropping it on the dominant's shoulders. He gave me a strong, steady foundation that wasn't going to be yanked out from under me, but he wasn't going to do the work for me. He wants a strong partner who, in an emergency, can step up to the plate. Because I have autism, I'm not the most tactful person, so I'll tell a new s-type straight out, "What are you bringing to this relationship? What happens if your D-type dies tomorrow? Are you just going to run out and find another one because you can't survive on your own? Or are you going to honor that relationship, hold it close, survive on your own, and respect what good happened in your life before you run out and start taking job applications for the next person to fix you?"

I'm also frustrated by the s-types who say, "I will be anything you want me to be! I will do anything!" From a dominant point of view, they might wonder, "Well, if you'll do anything for anyone, what will I have that is special for me? This doesn't make me feel special. What will be mine and mine alone?" What do you bring to the table besides being willing to let someone debase and humiliate you? That can be fun, but what real value do you bring to the relationship? As I get older, I have no patience for s-types who just want someone to take care of them 24/7. Yeah, good luck with that. You'd be better off hiring a home health care nurse. That's not what this lifestyle is all about.

Value the qualities that make you *you*, and I guarantee that when you find the right partner, they will value those things about you as well. We have plenty of sadists out there who like to hurt people, but at the end of the day, will you be valued for your submission? And will you just turn around and give it to the next person? I don't want to slut-shame anyone because I believe that people should be able to follow whatever sexual interests they have, but if you can't value yourself and the gifts that you're going to give to somebody, then they aren't really gifts at all.

Actually, I didn't gift my submission—he earned it through trial and error and competence and compassion and education, and the code he continues to live by in order to receive that. I bring a lot of skills and knowledge to the table, and he values that. Yes, he makes the final decisions, and yes, it's not always the decision I want, but because I know he listens and I know I have been heard, I know that he's made that decision carefully. Sometimes it's a wrong decision, and then we have what's called in the military "after action reports" where we dissect that. "Well, that didn't go the way we thought it would. What can we do differently?" He is fallible, and I have to understand that he might not make the perfect decision all the time. If you hold your partner to a godlike standard and expect them to have no faults, you're setting everybody up for failure. No matter how gifted and talented we are, humans make mistakes.

But I've seen him in command, and I know that the welfare of the men in his unit is of paramount importance to him. I know that I could trust him with my life. He was able to take total control of my life because he could see that I had that trust in him, and that the occasional mistake wasn't going to end anything, that it would all come crashing down because he was fallible. My trust, my patience, and my willingness to communicate, gave him as much as he gives to me. He makes decisions for me, not because he's an adult caretaker and I can't make them for myself—I certainly can—but because I am trusting him to make them, to have that authority and use it well.

passerby is a switchy, owned Two Spirit indigenous person of Irish, Mexica and Apache descent who has spent many years dividing their time between activism, raising awareness of indigenous issues, and advocating for criminal justice reform for POCs. As an activist, they are a member of The Brown Berets, a Chicano organization that fights to protect people of color and raise awareness of issues surrounding colonialism and the assimilation of indigenous nations. They also contribute their time in the fight against oil pipelines on native land and work to educate others on the connections oil pipelines have to the epidemic of missing and murdered Indigenous women, girls, and Two Spirits relatives. They have spent many years as a cannabis reform educator, striving to educate others about plant sovereignty and non-violent drug offenders serving life without parole. Occasionally they wear a uniform, offer survival and marksmanship training, and get their hands dirty in the field while accompanied by their two HellHounds who have decided to go by the aliases "Sirius Black" and "Polar Bear" for this purpose.

Communication Journey

Harley Quinzel

Our story began when we were both just coming out of toxic relationships; I was separated from my ex-husband and working on a divorce. A long-term online friend was in the process of purchasing a new home and offered a room for me to stay, so I packed up everything I owned and moved to a new state to live with her. He had recently ended a ten-year-long toxic relationship and was attempting to be generous to his ex-girlfriend by allowing her to stay in the spare bedroom of his home as a roommate until she could find a place of her own to live. The day we met, we were helping to move our mutual friend to her new home, where I would be renting a room. Our mutual friend was having a rough, overly stressful day with the move and when he walked up and offered a hug to our friend, I found myself instantly wanting a hug as well. This was a very strange urge for me, because I am not a "touchy-feely" person by nature. I am often guarded and the thought of offering a hug to a stranger was outside of my "normal". The instant energetic connection was powerful, more power than anything I have ever felt before. It honestly took me by complete surprise to feel such a pull to someone I had just met.

Over the next few weeks, I was determined to keep to myself, and I succeeded for a short time. If I knew my roommate was going to have him over, I would stay in my room to keep myself from making a connection with him, going out of my way to avoid interacting with him. Traylen and my roommate played Dungeons & Dragons together with a small group every other week at our house, and on those days I made sure to stay in my sanctuary to protect my peace and independence. I had walls I thought I needed to hide behind. Because I was putting my life back together, I was focused on me, being independent and refusing any help when offered. But if I am being honest, the spark from the day I met Traylen was a bit terrifying, but in a good way.

I had often thought about that first meeting, the connection I felt, and wondered what it would be like to explore where that energy could lead. I just was not ready; I could not put my heart back out there for someone else yet. Even though I was no longer in love with my ex-husband, our relationship had left me with deep emotional scars by the time it came to an end. However, the day came when I walked into my kitchen to find Traylen and my roommate talking at her kitchen table. He looked over at me, a little surprised, and said, "You need to come sit down and talk to me." I looked at him and said, "No, I'm good, thank you." My plan was to return to my room as fast as I could. I will never forget the way he looked at me in that moment and the sound of his voice when he casually said, "That wasn't a request." If I am honest, normally I would have declined his "non-request" in a not-so-submissive manner, because he was not my Dominant. But there was that spark again, the one that pulled at something deep inside my core, the part of my life I just could not ignore.

So, I smiled sheepishly and went to sit at the table to have a conversation with this man, one that would change the direction of my life more than he would ever know. We talked about everything from our childhoods to previous relationships, to wants and needs for future relationships, and everything in between. By the end of the evening, we had talked for hours without realizing the time, concluding that our views and goals for our futures aligned almost perfectly. Most surprising was the fact that our views on D/s also aligned so closely; I was sure he had read what was in my mind and heart. That conversation ended with him stating that we needed to put our exes in contact with each other and the two if us needed to have dinner together—and just like that, something started to grow, something so refreshing and pure, I often wondered if it was fantasy instead of reality.

That conversation was the start of a relationship which was almost overwhelming. Over the next several days, we texted as much as possible. Over the weeks, the texts turned to phone calls. Within months, the steady phone calls turned to us staying together at my house as often as our schedules allowed, although staying at my place with my roommate was preferable to staying at his place with his ex-girlfriend staying in the spare room. If we were awake and not working, we were having the best discussions. Some were about our pasts, but many were about our futures and what we each wanted. It was a constant source of surprise how well our visions and perspectives aligned. After several months passed, we were into the deep negotiations for our dynamic and we both wanted a future together.

It was during those times when his ex-girlfriend was trying her best to keep us apart and caused a lot of drama for us within our local BDSM community. To avoid giving her a reason to be more dramatic, we had to alter how we acted around her, which was extremely hard for me. If we were not around her, we could hold hands and be us. If she were anywhere in our vicinity, we could not. It did not take long for the back-and-forth to take a toll on my heart, and I found myself doubting and wondering why we had to alter our behavior. His answer was simply that he did not want to give her a reason to cause drama in our community, knowing she would still be part of it.

One day, I finally hit my wall. While I knew in my heart that he was not putting her before me, it did not change the way I felt. I tried to explain my feelings to Traylen, and while he said he heard me, I did not feel that he had. At that point I made a near-fatal move, almost sabotaging our relationship. I decided I had had enough, and he was going to hear me. After years in a toxic relationship where the only way I could be heard was to scream and yell, I made the decision to do just that. On the very next phone call, I once again tried to explain my point. When I did not feel heard, I unleashed every bit of anger and resentment I had in the most un-submissive manner possible. I am not sure how long the rant went on, but I know I did not breathe through the entire thing. I also did not give him much time to try to respond. That call ended right after my rant.

Days went by with little to no communication from either of us; I was unsure if reaching out was appropriate, and he had not reached out to me. I convinced myself that our budding relationship was over; that he was done with everything to do with me, but after several days, he called and said, "We need to talk." At that point I was even more certain that my snap decision, fueled by emotion instead of by logic, had ruined what promised to be one of the greatest things in my life.

Instead, he said he had thought a lot about what I had said while screaming at him. He understood my point of view, and why I was so upset (He also said that the fact that he did understand my point is likely the only reason he was willing to have a conversation about it.)

We discussed how I felt about having to hide our growing feelings when his ex-girlfriend was anywhere nearby, and we discussed options on how to handle his ex while moving forward. We talked about it being time to have his ex-girlfriend move from his home for good, giving us the opportunity to move forward with our dynamic and relationship. He agreed with my perspective that trying to be the nice guy to the ex was hurting our chances ... and then he said something which would change the face of our relationship.

Traylen said there was only one way we would be moving forward with our dynamic and relationship. If we were going to build anything productive and lasting, we would never treat each other as we had treated, or been treated by, our exes. He would not tolerate being yelled at ever again. Years of conditioning had put me in that mindset, but I agreed that I did not want to have to communicate that way either. Part of that conditioning was a fear of never being heard, so I asked Traylen how that would be handled in the future. He assured me that if I felt unheard, I could simply point it out, and as the Dominant in our dynamic, he assured me that he would let me know he had heard me. He said that he might not always agree with me, but he would always take my perspective into consideration when making decisions.

From that day forward, if something happens, we simply do not argue. He's assured me that he will listen when I bring a concern to him, and I accepted that I would trust him to make the best decisions for me and us. It was in that moment we decided that we did not want to continue the cycle of toxic traits from our past.

To this day, now four years later, we have not had another "argument", and not raised our voices at each other. Have we disagreed? Of course we have. However, I know that he does hear me when I speak; my voice has value. Once he has all the information, he makes the best decision for us and I happily accept that, even when it is not the decision I may have wanted.

Our dynamic and relationship has been on solid ground since we made the decision to do better, to be better. We have gone on to plan and have our formal collaring ceremony and handfasting as well as our wedding. We were part of a local lifestyle house for years before starting our own house, and we are currently serving on the board of directors for the local education-based nonprofit, providing our community a safe place to play and learn.

After making the conscious decision to not perpetuate the toxic behaviors of our past relationships, we have not raised our voices in anger once. Arguing is a choice we make daily, to use our words in a respectful manner instead of in a confrontational way which will serve no purpose other than to cause future damage. I am thankful daily that Traylen saw beyond the anger of that one terrible choice and decided to give me the option to agree that clear, concise communication was the best option for us. I have applied that to other aspects of my life, choosing to not argue with anyone, not just him. That one choice—and the emotional rollercoaster of waiting to hear what happened after my outburst—has still been an amazing reminder that word choice matters. The words I choose directly impact the message he hears. I am careful to remember so that I am expressing the message that I want to express, not one that is led by uncontrolled emotions.

My pseudonym is **Harley Quinzel**; *my Fetlife name is* _HarleyQ_. *I have been in the lifestyle since 1992. My personal philosophy in life is that we should learn something new every day. My hobby is reading, which has caused me to have a personal library of books dedicated to the lifestyle. Because of that passion, I host a local book club which reviews traditional D/s books. Along with that, I am the co-leader of our house, an educator, board member, mentor, and presenter.*

Speaking the Same Language

sweet wisteria

When Master and I met and were forming our relationship, it did not take long for us to realize that our communication was a bit off. The biggest indicator of this was that he would say something and I, for reasons that were completely unclear to him, would end up upset, angry, or in tears. He had made what he thought was a simple statement and was taken quite aback by the reaction that followed, a reaction that to him made absolutely no sense.

The frequency of these outbursts decreased when we realized that Master is a logical thinker, and I am an emotional thinker. For me, words carry emotion. Words can be either "good" or "bad". These are foreign concepts to the logical thinker where words are just words, emotionless and neither good nor bad.

The first word where we truly noticed this situation occurred was *manipulate*. In my teenage years, I found my mother to be a very manipulative person who used guilt trips and other methods that ultimately were very harmful to me. Through those experiences and my eventual reflections upon them is how, to me, the word *manipulative* no longer was just a word, but it became a "bad" word that carried all those years of negative manipulative history with it.

When the emotional outburst that followed concluded, Master paused and calmly asked, "What did you hear me say?" I jumped on the word manipulative, told him the stories from my childhood, and ended by saying that because he was intending to be manipulative, that meant he was going to do bad things to me that would surely cause harm.

What followed was a very long discussion about the definition of the word *manipulate* and how the act of manipulating another is not inherently a bad thing, and also how it intersects with a Master-slave dynamic. He wants to plant seeds in my mind with hopes that they will grow and flourish, and ultimately that I will want to do what he wants me to do. It is one tool that he has available that can help to bring us closer in alignment.

With this technique of me working on remembering that words are just words and there is no need to associate emotion to them, and Master asking the phrase, "What did you hear me say?" when I unexpectedly reacted to something, the outbursts continued to decline. Many years later, they are very rare, and we find it much easier to talk to each other because we understand how the other speaks and thinks a bit better. Having this established process for when the unexpected happens makes it easier to deal with heightened, unforeseen emotions when they arise, and we are able to return to our conversation and our relationship quickly.

sweet wisteria is the devoted slave of her master Stephen. If she's caused someone else's happiness or pleasure, usually it becomes her own. She likes knowing that she is the reason for that smile or sound. Those cues tell her that she has fulfilled her momentary purpose, and that sense of fulfillment makes her want to be the reason for that smile or sound again. On a somewhat similar note, she follow instructions well because she likes following instructions—it's amazing how that works, isn't it?

Goodbye Fear, Hello Communication!
Joy

My Master and I have been in our M/s relationship for almost six years. I am His property and we have a total power exchange (TPE). While I am a cisgender heterosexual woman and my Master is a cis/het man, I believe that most or all of the ideas discussed below are applicable to any M/s relationship regardless of gender structure or sexual orientation.

Master and I started out as friends and dance partners, and as we became "more than friends", we also introduced a D/s dynamic into our relationship. Soon after, we learned about M/s and decided to experiment with it as a "scene". Trying it out as a "scene" gave us an easy safety valve if either of us felt it was too much. However, the M/s dynamic fit us so well and felt so right that we ended the "scene" and made the dynamic permanent!

To begin, I would like to state that all the ideas and suggestions discussed below require a good, functional D/s or M/s relationship. This is important because dysfunctional D/s (and especially M/s) relationships can be downright dangerous.

What makes an M/s relationship good and functional? During a talk that Master and I attended a couple of years ago, Raven Kaldera mentioned that the most important quality for a master to have was honorable intentions—and I believe that this means both having good intentions and being purposefully intentional in governing the relationship. My Master does both of those things, and I truly and completely trust Him. If I couldn't absolutely trust Him, then I couldn't submit to Him. Likewise, I know He trusts that I am all in, meaning that I take our relationship seriously and am fully committed to it. Having that mutual trust has helped us to build a solid foundation for our relationship. It has made communication much easier as well; I wouldn't feel comfortable communicating fully and openly with Him if I didn't trust Him.

Presuming that those reading also have a solid foundation of trust, here are some things that have helped me to deepen my submission and better communicate with my Master:

❖ Trust that the Master or Dominant has positive intentions.

❖ Remember that an unequal relationship is still a partnership. Even though the M-type directs the relationship, there are a lot of things that the s-type can do to communicate with their M-type to support the relationship.

❖ Tell the Master or Dominant all the information. If the M-type doesn't have all of the information, they can't make the best decisions to guide either of you individually or your relationship as a whole.

Communicating sounds easy, but it can be very difficult for someone who has had neither good experiences nor good role models. In addition, if a person hasn't had good role models, they won't fully understand the value or importance of good communication. In my prior relationships going all the way back to my early childhood, I did not feel safe truly expressing myself. When I did try, I was often criticized, shamed, dismissed, ignored, or given the silent treatment. My father was verbally abusive and would completely reject me (and certain other immediate family members) for months or years at a time. Other members of my family have refused to engage in uncomfortable or difficult conversations. When things that were important to me weren't heard or acknowledged, it felt quite belittling and frustrating, and made me feel small and worthless. Over time, I learned to just cope with things rather than try to talk about them.

In addition, we are often conditioned by society to hide parts of ourselves physically and/or emotionally when we are uncomfortable or ashamed, because it feels safer and we falsely believe we are protecting ourselves. However, when we hide, we aren't being our true selves—and if we don't share our true selves, we can never truly be accepted. Feeling unaccepted can lead to a person feeling unacceptable, which is what really creates the shame.

I carried these feelings of avoidance and shame into my relationship with Master. At the beginning of our relationship, whenever I was worried, upset, or confused about something, I felt afraid to talk and wanted to retreat to a space where I could be alone and hide. This was especially true when we had heartfelt conversations about things that were hard to talk about; my fears and shame would cause me to shell up or shut down. Of course it didn't have to be this way, but I didn't realize how important open communication was and how many problems the lack of it had caused me in the past.

Fortunately, over time, Master helped me to open up and learn to communicate more freely, even about difficult topics and feelings. Master *made* me talk. He made it clear right from the get-go that communicating with Him was absolutely required. He said that He wanted and needed to know what I was thinking and feeling because it helped Him understand me better, helped Him guide our relationship, and helped Him protect me—His property. He also told me that since He owned me, my thoughts belonged to Him. Just hearing that made me feel owned and put me in an obedient and submissive frame of mind, which made it easier for me to communicate more readily. The more comfortable I have become with such open discourse, the closer and stronger our relationship has grown. Having first-hand experience that communication is valuable, productive, and safe has helped me to overcome some of the obstacles that had previously prevented me from opening up. This is especially true for those difficult conversations!

In the early part of our relationship, Master told me that in order for Him to make the best decisions for us, He needed all the information and I was not allowed to hold anything back. He also said there would be no shame in what I expressed and that no matter what I told him, He would continue to accept me. That made me feel grateful and relieved because I truly wanted to share all of myself with Him. However, I had never been so completely vulnerable with anyone before, and I wasn't sure I could be. It would have been so much easier if I could have just given Him a flash drive to let Him know all of my past and how my brain works! Yet doing the work of actually being open and trusting was the most important thing I could have done. Sometimes you have to be trusting and vulnerable to develop more trust! But that vulnerability has been extremely freeing, because it has given me first-hand experience that I can truly be myself and still be accepted. To me, this is one of the most important benefits of being owned, and confirms our relationship is safe and protective.

Both sides of the slash do work to support the dynamic. While the M-type is responsible for directing the relationship, the s-type can also contribute by communicating what they know about themselves, such as what they value, like, and need. These kinds of contributions are a useful act of service for your M-type, and may also help give them more confidence in guiding the relationship. For example, when an M-type knows what makes their s-type feel loved and safe, they are able to provide the kind of nurturing environment that will best help their s-type feel supported when they talk about difficult things. In our dynamic, when I notice something that seems to help me, I let Master know about it. This gives Him more tools to use and is a way that I can help set Him up for success—so that He can help set me up for success! This kind of communication serves us both! (A good starting point to help a person discover or confirm some of the ways that make them feel most loved is the *The Love Language*™ *Quiz.*[*])

In our dynamic, I am required to tell Master my thoughts and feelings as soon as I am aware of them. He has also directed me to tell Him things even when I am unsure if they are important enough to bring to His attention—we err on the side of more communication, not less. Of course, not every dynamic or master works this way. This is just how my Master designed our relationship. Since every dynamic is different, ask your M-type how they want you to communicate with them, and if or how they would like you to address issues or concerns. (In fact, the simple act of asking them how they want you to communicate is a great first step in communication!)

To facilitate communication when I am struggling, Master uses a number of tools and methods that have proven helpful over time and through experience. I also help by paying attention to what helps me calm down and gather my thoughts—even things like physical surroundings and body positions—and then I relay that information to Master. This is another valuable act of service I do for Master, because it provides Him with more ideas and tools that help me open up. For example, I know that physical touch is one of my most important love languages and makes me feel close, connected, safe, and loved. When we snuggle, it is much easier for me to talk, especially about difficult

---

[*] https://5lovelanguages.com/quizzes/love-language

things, as I feel held and protected while I get out what I need to say. Therefore, sometimes I will ask, "Master, is it all right if we snuggle while we talk? I think it would help." Another example is a little sacred-to-me carpeted space next to Master's bed that I like to call "my nook". I feel safe and peaceful when I'm kneeling in my nook, and Master knows how much I treasure it! I use it for resting, thinking, writing, and praying. In fact, when strong emotions make it hard for me to express something, I will sometimes ask if I can "go in my nook", which also signals to Master that I have something important to say, but am having a hard time saying it. Once in my nook, I find it easier to be introspective and figure out what's going on inside of me. Being in my nook also makes it easier for me to remind myself of all the reassuring thoughts that help me open up and tell Master what's going on. For me, it's a magical, sacred space.

Because being open and honest is such an integral part of M/s dynamics, it is greatly valuable to build time into your week for thinking, processing, and developing self-awareness. Time to reflect can help you better understand yourself, so you can more accurately and clearly share that information with your M-type. Try different things and see what helps you reflect and feel centered: journaling, meditating, praying, yoga, showering, driving, being out in nature, etc.

In addition, the right kind of environment can help a person feel open and attuned to their inner thoughts. My personal preference is an absolutely quiet, indoor, private space (like my nook), or outside in the sun surrounded only by the sounds of nature. I have found that when I kneel by myself in the backyard and put my palms on the earth, I notice the blades of grass and feel strong, grounded, and centered. This almost always inspires me to say a prayer for all the things I'm grateful for. This brings me a sense of joy, hope, and contentment with my life and whatever is going on with me and those I love. It's a feeling that "all's right with the world!" In addition, it is always helpful for me to be rested and warm enough, and have adequate nourishment so my emotions are stable and don't spiral out of control—I want to do all I can to promote healthy mindfulness and self-introspection. Below are some ideas that may help you find your own treasured spaces that provoke thoughtfulness and help you go deeper into a submissive headspace.

- ❖ Outside in nature: a backyard, beach, park, woods, mountaintop, patch of sunlight, garden, waterfall, pond, river, ocean, or any place pleasing to your eyes and senses that feels nurturing and restorative.
- ❖ Inside and cozy: snuggled in bed, relaxed on a couch or comfy chair with warm blankets or a beloved pet, in a patch of sunlight coming through the window, at a familiar desk where you're used to writing, or any interior space where you feel safe and comfortable.
- ❖ Sounds: music, pitter-patter of raindrops, voices of children playing at a nearby park, ocean waves crashing on the shore, gurgling river, pounding waterfall, birds chirping, silence, etc.
- ❖ Body Position: reclining on a beach chair, kneeling in a sacred space or before your M-type, resting on a towel at the beach, sitting on a giant rock that you hiked to at the top of a mountain, lying down skin-to-skin in the arms of your M-type (this last one is my favorite).

Mindful movement activities such as walking, hiking, or yoga can also help to promote clarity though self-reflection. Walking whilst talking with a trusted friend helps me to be open and feels good to my inner soul. I consider "walk-n-talks" a form of self-care both physically and mentally because I can express myself and be accepted while enjoying fresh air, getting exercise, and being social. Others find it easier to open up while they are side-by-side rather than looking directly at the person they are talking to, such as while swinging on swings, working next to each other in the garden, or taking a stroll. Even snuggling can be done without constant direct eye contact. If movement or side-by-side conversations help you, let your M-type know so they can decide if it is something they would like to put in their tool box.

To help you gain more clarity and insight, it is often beneficial to write some of your thoughts in a journal. This practice of writing can help reduce stress and anxiety, allow you to see your progress and growth, inspire creativity, and improve your communication. If you would like to write, but aren't sure where to begin, you can start with a stream of consciousness: quick, continuous writing of honest thoughts that pop into your mind without regard for grammar, spelling, organization, or anything else. It's a great way to "mind dump". Keep in mind that while journaling can be helpful for venting about worrisome thoughts, it is also important to include positive, hopeful thoughts and events. This helps you to have a more balanced point of view, stay hopeful, and not dwell in a place of despair or negativity. For example, you can include what you are grateful for, what you've recently learned, what you will do differently or better next time, what adventures you've recently had, and what you might like to do for fun in the future. You can even re-read your journal to see your growth and progress, and to remind you of important moments and learning experiences.

Even with reflection and self-awareness, it is not always easy to be completely transparent, honest, and open; and there may be times when it is a little daunting to begin a difficult conversation, especially at the beginning of a relationship, and sometimes even after years of being together. However, as an s-type, it's *really* important to be vulnerable and not hold back anything because of fear, including worries of what your M-type might think if you reveal your true feelings or difficult past experiences. Remember, the best way to overcome your fear is through your connection with your M-type, and open communication strengthens that connection and builds trust!

There may also be occasions when you want to communicate with your M-type that something is going on, but you don't feel that you can do so, either because of a tricky social situation (like being in the presence of certain family members or those that don't understand your dynamic), or because you are feeling overwhelmed. For me, there have been times when I was so overwhelmed that I could not verbally communicate without breaking down, so Master came up with a non-verbal method of communication: squeezing His pinky three times. This signal lets Him know that I am having an issue but can't bring myself to talk in that moment, and after I get His direct eye contact, He usually gives me a non-verbal signal that I have permission to retreat to a private space. He can then decide to give me some time or come in and find out what is going on.

Good communication can be challenging, especially if you have had significant negative experiences, and great communication can take a long time to build. However, if you want your relationship to grow and flourish, you need to do everything you can to make it work. This means reminding yourself to be fully open and honest, and working with your M-type to help you find ways to do so. For me, learning how to communicate was a long process and required a conscious commitment. Looking back, several things stand out as being exceptionally beneficial: mantras and affirmations, a positive mindset, my commitment to being "all in," obedience, logic, trust, and experience. (Some examples are included at the end of this essay.) Even though it was often uncomfortable, it was totally worth the effort! It has brought my Master and me closer, strengthened our relationship, and is such an essential part of our life together that I cannot imagine living without it.

Below are some mantras, positive thoughts, and affirmations that have helped me to remember why it's important to tell Master everything, and together they have given me the courage to do so when it has felt challenging. May they inspire you to develop your own reminders, based on the truth of your unique relationship, to help you better communicate.

1. I am His. I belong to Him. Even my thoughts belong to Him. It's only right that He knows what they are.

2. Master needs and requires me to always communicate and be open. I am not allowed to hide.

3. I must tell Him everything because I am His slave and promised to do so.

4. I want to be in our relationship, so I need to tell Master everything.

5. Master will accept me no matter what I share. He wants to know my thoughts and will be pleased that I tell him everything.

6. I care more about our relationship than I do about any embarrassment or shame.

7. Master has never been upset with me for what I have shared. It is safe to talk to Him.

8. I want to be able to tell Master everything!

9. There is no need to worry that I am sharing too much. Master will let me know if He doesn't want to hear something or wishes to hear it later.

10. Every time we talk about difficult things, I feel better afterwards!

11. Communicating always brings us closer and makes us stronger. Every time we have talked about something difficult, we have felt even more connected.

12. Master wants to be in our relationship, too!

13. Master has said that I need to give my best effort, but I don't have to do things perfectly.

14. If or when I make mistakes, it is a learning opportunity, and if I make them, Master will help me move forward.

15. I know Master has good intentions and I trust Him. I love Him.

16. Master trusts me, loves me, and knows I have good intentions.

17. Trying to "protect" myself by feeling indifferent doesn't work and doesn't feel good. I regret it afterwards. I need to feel my emotions and be honest about them. I need to be "all in", allow even sad and vulnerable feelings to surface, and share them with Master. Otherwise, the precious time we spend together is less than it could be.

18. Even though it feels hard right now, I know that I am going to tell Master everything. I always have. I may as well just go ahead and do it!

19. Master needs *all* of the information so He can best guide our relationship. I appreciate that He leads us, and my role is to give Him the information and trust him.

Joy is the property of Master Arend, and both are members of MAsT Massachusetts.

Communication Under Rules

Kyra of Mists

I am in a M/s poly relationship where there are three of us, two slaves and one Master. One of the most challenging aspects about our M/s relationship was learning to communicate and behave in the manner that my Lord expects. He has high expectations on how we are to communicate and behave with him, with each other, and with other people in general.

Alandra and I are not in a relationship where we have authority over when, where and how communication takes place with our Lord or in how we behave. He has outlined specific protocols on how we are to approach him to request permission to talk with him. Which protocol we are required to follow will depend on the situation. For example, when he has us on formal protocol, hand signals are required. However, the hand signals work so well and are so discreet that they can be used even in casual situations.

These protocols are specifically designed to create effective communication and appropriate behaviour, and this in turn allows us to have a calm, healthy, happy relationship between the three of us. However, that communication happens on his terms. We have to get his permission to ask a question, give him information or express an opinion. To some it may sound like this inhibits communication, but since he has ADHD and has trouble hearing, we could start talking to him and he would not even hear us or be paying attention. Asking permission to address him allows him time to focus on us, or even say "Not now, come back later."

Despite the restrictions, we are required to be transparent and completely open and honest with what is going on inside our heads. For him, transparency does not mean to say whatever you want to say, whenever you want to say it, no matter what the consequences might be. Honesty and transparency are as much about being honest and transparent with ourselves as it is with each other, and "ugly truths" are rarely about honesty.

Some of the other rules and protocols we follow are that we are not allowed to use absolutes when speaking, like "always" and "never".

We are to address him as "my Lord". We are not allowed to make assumptions. We have to correctly label whether something is a thought or a feeling, and self-pity is usually dealt with harshly. We are also to do his will with grace, which means without a negative attitude or passive-aggressive behaviour.

When I first became his, I was not required to meet all these expectations at once. It was a continual process of adjusting my behaviours one at a time to meet the bar he set, and it happened over months and years. Once one rule was achieved, another was introduced, until several years in when they had become second nature. It was through repetition and being held accountable that I slowly adjusted to what he wanted. Surprisingly, it is amazing how much easier it is to communicate and be understood when I follow his rules.

In this M/s relationship, I have developed good communication skills that have helped me in other areas of my life. I gained emotional self-regulation that improved my behaviour with everyone, not only here. It allows me to maintain control of my behaviour despite how I may be feeling. Controlling my speech helps me control my thoughts, which helps keep my feelings in check. Alandra and I are also required to behave in a certain way despite how we may feel at the time.

I may feel angry because of something that I perceive he has done, and if I have permission, I may express that in a way that he has decided is appropriate. What I can't do is be passive-aggressive, yell or curse at him, or say every little mean, hurtful, petty thing that goes through my head. Because even though they might be in my head in that moment, it doesn't make them truth, doesn't make them valid, and doesn't mean I would be realistically honest if I expressed them.

I cannot recall the last time I thought something mean, hurtful or petty regarding to him, but part of that is because he didn't tolerate it in action or thought. I imagine that if he allowed that kind of behavior or those thoughts to go unchecked, our relationship would not be near as serene and peaceful as it is.

In the beginning, when my behavior was inappropriate, he would shut down interaction until I could behave appropriately. (I cannot recall an instance where it took more than five to ten minutes for me to get my behavior under control.) Then we would talk about what was going on inside my head to create all the hurtful, mean things that I was doing. He would show me alternatives to the thoughts that created the feelings. He would point out different perspectives through which I could view an event, and that would change the thoughts, and therefore change the feelings. He taught me how to come from a place of certainty that he is doing what is best for the relationship, and that he would not intentionally harm me. It is amazing, the change that happened when I fully believed in that.

We are essentially practicing the skills I learned in Cognitive Behavioural Therapy. We are both well-versed in some of the techniques, and they helped improve our relationship immensely. Being held accountable for following these techniques, and the constant repetition of them, is what slowly changed my behaviour and communication style. To this day, it is something that is still practiced and expected.

Kyra of Mists is the slave of Knight of Mists. She lives in Canada with her master and his other slave, Alandra of Mists. Their two house mottoes are: We are one, and We do what is best for the family. Everything they do flows from those statements.

Nagging, Whining, and Complaining
katie

Everyone knows nagging is actually gentle reminders. Complaining is merely expressing a need for help. Whining is about seeking compassion and care.

How broken is that paragraph if you seek a satisfying Authority Transfer Relationship? How ineffective are those methods for pursuing satisfaction and accord? Removing nagging, complaining, and whining from your interactions has a consequence: a healthier relationship. That's what we wanted, but in the early years I had to learn new ways to navigate tough times and struggles. Actually, we both did, but this isn't a book about Leaders.

Let's start with nagging.

How could nagging even be an issue? Leaders are incredible, efficient, competent people who never forget anything right? Maybe usually, but they are also humans that get busy or distracted!

I have a fair amount of skill for tracking time, tasks, and responsibilities for both of us, so Kevin expects me to give him reminders. There have been uncomfortable occasions that I've reminded Kevin twice on some issue and everyone knows that three reminders become nagging, right? What am I to do if he forgets once again?

In the early years I would run face first into the nagging like Wile E Coyote when he forgot about that tunnel painted on the mountain. I needed to find my way to clarity and service. With some thought and exploration together, we found a solution that felt true to my Follower role but was still supportive of Kevin's needs:

The second time I give a reminder, I ask Kevin if he wants any further reminders. There are two possible outcomes. If he says, "No more reminders," I am absolved of my duty. He is responsible going forward. This is not a passive-aggressive dick move by me. (The only dick move I have perfected is the swirly hip one.) If Kevin says "No" to more prompting, he is either going to be more aware of the issue and attend to it, or he will forget again, not attend to it, and take responsibility.

The second possibility is that Kevin will say, "If I forget, come remind me again." In which case I cannot possibly be nagging. Not only do I have permission to remind him, but I have also been directed to do so. I am serving.

Another communication struggle I wanted to avoid was Whining and Complaining.

I loathe whining and complaining, from myself or others. Serving with a martyr's attitude is sucky service and nobody is fulfilled by it. But what about those times I've gotten worn out, overwhelmed or frustrated? What if Kevin hasn't noticed how busy, sweaty and sigh saturated I am each time I walk past?

Break out the whining and complaining! That's sure to have response and recognition! Also, it is sure to highlight discord and unpleasantness.

Let's take a quick recount of the situation:

❖ I have a leader.
❖ I have a struggle.
❖ It seems my leader is not aware that I am struggling.

Come on! This isn't hard! I tell him. I have a Leader who is a retired psychologist, and he still has not attained the Mind Reader skill. He still misses times I struggle.

So, I give Kevin the information he needs to make good decisions and keep his fingers on the pulse. (Sidenote: I love feeling the pulse as he hoses down my garage with his revved-up Hummer.) Instead of adding any attitude or negative emotion to the communication, I just calmly share that I am tired, or I feel overburdened, or that things are going poorly. At this point Kevin has what he needs to make some decisions. There are many ways he might chose to address the issue. He might:

❖ Help me.

- ❖ Take something off the list.
- ❖ Offer a solution.
- ❖ Tell me that I'm his fucking girl and I should step up and get that shit done and come kiss his feet and thank him afterwards.

All great tactics to get me through a tough spot.

Nagging and whining makes us both feel unsettled and frustrated. Seeking clarity and giving him information enhances our effectiveness and inner peace.

These early struggles with communication and frustration fell away quickly as we implemented some simple tools, some scripted interactions, and the self-discipline to consistently use them.

katie is a 20-year follower of Kevin, and they are both the 2017 International Power Exchange title holders. They travel and teach about discipline in power dynamic relationships, as well as many other useful subjects.

Conflict and Community

Dr. V

Part 1: Conflict

Please note that I will use "s-types" as an umbrella term for slaves, submissives, property and anyone identifying on the right side of the slash. Also, please note that I speak from a perspective of living as a slave 24/7 without a "break" at any time for any reason.

One of the biggest struggles I had as a new slave (during the first year) was going from being in a position of leadership at work then transitioning to a slave headspace when I came home. I struggled with the concept that at work I would make major decisions, run a nursing unit, course and classroom and then "turn it all off" (or so I thought) to come home and be a slave. I hear this struggle from s-types I mentor, and I have found that slaves (or s-types in general) can become very stressed about it because they (as I did) see this as two separate ways of being or two different worlds. I've also heard this struggle from slaves who have had to act as leader in their dynamic due to their Master's illness or absence; there can be stress when returning to life with Master back at the helm. In my experience s-types are generally strong people with problem-solving skills and many more skills to effectively get sh*t done!

I resolved my struggle by taking a step back to look at the bigger picture. My Master isn't only my Master at home; he is also my Master when I go out of the house, do my job for my employer, or take care of the house in his absence. No matter where I am and what I'm doing, I'm *always* in service to him. It was that reframing that resolved the internal struggle and brought all the facets of my life together as his slave. I am always his slave, whether I'm at work in a leadership position, in the community in a leadership position or at home serving him. When I looked at the bigger picture, I realized it's not a transition at all.

Something I still struggle with, is that there are very few models showing slaves to ask for what they need. I find that many slaves think, "If I tell my master what I need, I'll come across as [insert negative characteristic], or he'll think I'm [insert negative descriptor]." Usually it's a fear of being "un-slavey," or "un-submissive," or some other negative descriptor someone made up to make a comparison to a fictional character. Those negative feelings, insecurities and worries can be very hard for me, and for other s-types I know. My Master and I practice Nonviolent Communication, which includes "I feel [insert feeling] and I need [insert need]" statements. This form of mindful communication helps a lot, but it's not inherently easy for me. When I feel myself getting upset because I have an unmet need, I need to stop, take a breath and ask myself, "What do I need? or what need isn't getting met?" I think that's where most conflict comes from in relationships—people's needs aren't getting met. Whether in a poly relationship where someone is unhappy/ jealous, or an M/s relationship where someone is unhappy, these feelings generally indicate that someone's needs aren't getting met.

Another problem I see is when the Master and slave have different conflict management/ resolution styles. For example, one is an extrovert who wants to discuss everything *now*, and one is an introvert who wants some time to think and to discuss it later. It's been my experience that often the Master is the introvert and slave the extrovert; of course, the reversed exists too. The key to dealing with this is to talk about conflict management and communication styles in the beginning when things are going well. Put the systems in place before you need them. I find that people don't want to have these conversations when everything is new, exciting, and there's NRE (New Relationship Energy) going on; it's not sexy to plan for conflict resolution, is it? I hear, "Oh, we're great, there are no problems, we don't need to talk about that!" But that's the time to discuss how to handle conflict; do it before you're in the middle of it.

I find that M/s, is a very mindful practice. It helps me evolve and grow; it is definitely a spiritual discipline. Like Buddhism or any other spiritual discipline, it helps me know myself better, become more aware and more effective. And it's even got rituals! It's absolutely spiritual for us.

Part 2: Community

We were very lucky that when Master collared me, we were (and are) part of a community with a lot of strong M/s couples, we were able to get to know them and get guidance when we needed it. I don't think we would have come this far if we hadn't had community support. I don't think M/s dynamics work well without community! I see couples break up, over and over, because they are in their own little bubble/black hole, and they think "Oh, we're fine, we don't need to talk about or learn anything" but then they don't last.

So, I would say to new s-types: Look for community and open yourself to it. Be willing to be vulnerable and actually talk about the challenges you encounter. Whether that's through MAsT (Masters And slaves Together, mast.net) mentoring, or some other form of support, reach out and find people who are living the way you want to live.

I have, in the past, been in submissive groups who were mostly limited in their power dynamics (only at an event, on weekends or just in the bedroom); my Master and I have a 24/7 M/s dynamic that never turns off. I am his slave 100% of the time, and sometimes when I would talk about something required of me by my master, some group member would become horrified. I heard, "Oh, no, we would never do…" or, "When we have problems, we step out of the dynamic until they're resolved!" OK, fine, if that's what works for you – but we don't do that; I felt awkward and judged.

I spoke to my mentor about these comments and my feelings, and she said, "slaves need to get support from slaves." Yes, we're all here on the little-s side of the power dynamic, but once you're in a 24/7 dynamic as a slave with no "breaks," things happen which are different from part-time dynamics, and I agree that a slave should have healthy peer support from people who understand and have navigated similar situations. At the same time, I understand that finding peers can be difficult when you live in a rural area, have financial, transportation, or physical constraints. Here, in our large city, there are so many groups to get involved with; we have choices. We can also afford to travel to conferences and events, and I know not everyone can do that. But still,

I'd advise reaching out for peer support any way possible, because I believe s-types need that—and I believe M-types need that too.

So, if I have one last piece of advice for new s-types, it would be: Get a mentor. Get someone to help you through the first few years, someone who is an experienced s-type, has been there, and is where you want to be. When I started out, I found someone to mentor me, and they offered a structured program that included my Master's input on everything, which was great for me and supportive of our healthy dynamic. Find someone who is living in the way you want to live, vet them and of course, be sure your Master is involved since you are their slave. If you are developing yourself as a slave in preparation for a Master not yet in your life, then you and your mentor can design the mentorship to guide you towards the dynamic you're ultimately looking for.

An aspiring genie with a spotless, tilted halo and a dirty mind, Dr. V (and her boots) has been in the kinky lifestyle for more than 30 years. After adventures in New York, England, and Florida, Dr. V has found her place as a leader and active participant in the central Texas community and as Senor Jaime's slave. Dr. V identifies as: queer, poly, slave, bootblack, rope bottom, leather sister, friend, teacher, lifelong learner, and researcher.

Professionally, Dr. V has been an educator and nurse specializing in mental health/illness for more than 30 years. Dr. V assists Señor Jaime with running The WhatKnot, is a proud member of Bound by Desire, and is a co-producer of the HEaRT of TX conference (Hypnotic, Erotic and Recreational Trance). Dr. V was a co-founder of Austin BDSM (Bootblacks doing a Sunday Meetup), co-founder of Team Friendly Austin and was a co-director of MAsT Austin.

Looking Outward, Looking Inward
BellaVoce

Part 1: Community Opinions

I've been in an M/s relationship for eight years now. We consider it an Owner/property relationship, as we have a total authority transfer. We have a contract where I signed over all my rights when we started this, and that's how it's been ever since. It's worked out quite well for us, with all the work we have put into it. It helps that power imbalance is the primary orientation for both of us.

The biggest struggle that we've had in our relationship, in the beginning, was around looking owned versus being owned. I think that a lot of people in this community have an idea of what power exchange is supposed to look like, and when a relationship doesn't end up looking like that—even when the power is still there—it can be a little difficult. For example, my master isn't particularly fond of interacting with other people, and so when we go out—especially when we go out to eat or something like that—he has me order for him, because he knows I know what he likes. Sometimes he'll even have me choose the food, if he doesn't care about what he eats at that moment, as long as it keeps him from having to interact with anyone but me. So, for a long time, especially when it came to managing our calendars and making plans with others, I worried that other people thought that I was the one in charge because it looked from the outside like I was the one making all the decisions.

It turned out that this was just a lot of my own personal nonsense that I had to figure out, because it was all about my worries about being seen to be a "good enough" submissive/slave. That was not easy to get past. It took us a while, because I was having so much difficulty turning away from all of the things everyone else in the community said it should be, and working on what it actually is. I'm on many submissive-and-slave groups on the internet, and those people say a lot of things about how these relationships should be, using whatever works for their relationship. So really, it was all about my worry that when we were with other D/s and M/s couples, they would think that the power was going the wrong way, or that I was somehow "topping from the bottom".

At one point my master turned to me and said, "Would you rather it looked like you were owned, or would you rather be owned?" That was pretty much the turning point for this problem in our relationship because I realized, "Oh. How the power looks from the outside doesn't matter. The fact that the power *is there* is the key to all of this." That was really the end of that discussion.

Getting past this took a lot of time, a lot of me recognizing that it wasn't important. I'm usually pretty good about not caring what other people think about the rest of my life, and so it didn't make any sense for me to care about what they thought about this part of it, either. The power itself was exactly how and where we wanted it to be; whether or not they thought that it looked "correct" ultimately had no effect on what we actually did. Their judgment had no impact on the validity of our relationship and our authority transfer. So once that really sank in—once I had that chat with my master about looking owned versus being owned—I realized that how it looks to the outside world doesn't matter. Our authority transfer works well for us, and what other people think of us has nothing to do with it.

We have this idea that there are specific chores or activities that slaves really "should do" to be a good slave, to be ideally submissive. "Gosh, this slave doesn't know how to cook!" Well, does their master care? Does their master prefer to do the cooking? Do they just want to eat out all the time? Would they rather just eat raw vegetables? Who knows? Whatever works for them is what should be done.

I feel that this is one of the biggest stumbling blocks for every slave-identified person I've met. I call it the "fake internal master". It's the voice which says, "You should be doing the dishes, and you should be cleaning the house, and you should be mopping the floors all the time." That fake internal master has nothing to do with the master who is actually in front of you, who may be telling you to do other things, such as working outside the home, or scooping pig shit for that matter. Who cares? It's hard, because sometimes we can let that internal monologue get in the way of going with the flow and following orders.

If you're a submissive or slave who is struggling with this, you must focus on the fact that if you're not the one making that decision, and you're doing what you're told, then you're being a good follower! Look to SM play as an example: If he wants me to peg him, or smack him around in a dungeon, the fact that he's the one who is in control of it has everything to do with our authority transfer. How people perceive it has nothing to do with the way that it actually goes.

Leaning on that example: I've never topped him in public, but I've done it quite a bit in private, and we've talked about it to other people in the community. I think they find it a little confusing, because so many people have such a big problem in conflating topping with dominance and mastery, when they are such different things. The way that you perform the act determines where the power flows in any situation. I call this the "blowjob principle": There are a lot of dominants who might give their slaves a blowjob in a way that is completely different from the way a slave would give one to their master. They might be doing almost the exact same thing physically, but the energy around it, and the way it's being managed, whose pleasure it's for, are all completely different in that regard. So ultimately it must come down to whether you can accept your power dynamic looking "unusual" to folks from afar.

I like not being in charge, and I like being told what to do, so being told how to top him is fine with me. My master is trans, and he enjoys certain kinds of penetration, and some people really have a problem with that—especially the couples who are feminine bottoms and masculine tops. They tend to have weird and rigid ideas about what constitutes power and where it flows. The One-True-Wayers can get into your head if you're not careful, and it doesn't help that all the good porn I've seen ends up being about slaves who don't do service topping. They're always groveling, always naked and scrubbing the floor until it's clean enough to eat off. That would be terrible for me, though—I don't like the idea of trying to clean the barn naked. I'm glad my Master allows me boots and coveralls for that!

There's also the issue of reality. We live on a farm and part of our ethos is making as little waste as possible; we work regularly on taking ourselves out of the commercial food and supply chain, but there's no way I could keep the floor clean enough with a conventional mop. So, with my master's permission, I finally gave in and got a Swiffer mop, because I could not handle how dirty these floors were. We have an enormous drooly dog, and we've got people walking in and out from the back yard, and the pasture/barn where our livestock is. It's one of the few truly wasteful things that we have in the house, but it has helped my sanity so much. I feel very guilty every time I use it, but man, it works!

I think submissives or slaves who follow unconventional orders are likely to have a moment of "Oh, shit, am I really being a good slave because I'm doing XYZ?" But for me, the easiest thing has been to focus on is, "Did he tell me to do it? Did I follow orders? Then I'm fine." So, when I have my own little anxiety spiral about what other people think of me, that's what I turn to, because ultimately, a successful relationship is a successful relationship. Focusing on making your relationship as wonderful as possible is best, and maybe also spending less time on forums where people say things like, "All Doms/subs must be/do/like XYZ to be valid."

Ignore the One-True-Wayers. It's all about recognizing that if you're not the one making the rules, but you're following the rules, you're doing just fine. How other people perceive it doesn't matter. It has no effect on the relationship itself … unless you let it.

So you just can't let it.

Part 2: When Submission Feels Normal, and That Doesn't Feel Right.

In retrospect this issue is really funny, but at the time it felt like the worst thing that had ever happened. About three or four years into our relationship I sat down with my master because I was having a massive anxiety problem. I was feeling as if I wasn't really owned; as if the things we were doing weren't enough to make me feel owned and controlled. It felt like my life wasn't difficult enough for me to justify the ownership situation. It didn't feel like I was struggling enough to be a "real" slave. I sat down with him and said, "I feel like our power dynamic isn't really there anymore."

He looked at me and said, "Tell me more about that."

"Well, I just feel like there's no authority transfer any more in any of this."

He looked at me and nodded slowly, and asked, "OK. Who decided about your hairstyle?"

And I replied, "Well, I mean, you did, but I like it this way too."

"OK. The last time we went shopping, who decided what clothing you were allowed to buy?"

"Well, you did."

He pointed out, "You cook the food that I want. You keep the house the way that I want it. You interact with the people that I enjoy, and you do things that make me happy. All of your money is turned over to me, and you don't have access to it unless you get my permission. I'm the one who tells you how to cast your vote, choose your shoes, and whether or not you can have sweets after supper." He went on, listing a string of other points where I obey him.

I just kind of looked at him and said, "Well, yes, but that just feels normal now."

"Step back and look at that for a minute," he told me. "This is not normal. It is absolutely *not* a normal egalitarian relationship."

Now I look back on that and I laugh, and he laughs at me about it, but it did take him a while to get me over the idea that the way we had our relationship set up was somehow too egalitarian, even though it wasn't, in any way, shape, or form. For me, it had come to feel so normalized that until we sat down and really looked at all of the changes which had been made, it just felt ordinary. I realized I felt that if I wasn't struggling, the power dynamic wasn't there.

I think I associated power dynamics with struggle because it was a struggle with every other partner which I'd had—and in the beginning of our relationship, too, there was a lot of internal struggle when it came to me changing and adapting. This was especially true for big changes which involved learning new ways to think about things—that was constant work for me. It wasn't a negative thing; it just felt like it was hard work, but in a good way. So I had come to view the internal work I was doing regularly, and had to focus on intensely to make it happen, as what felt like "real" slavery and submission. That was about internalizing his values and his desires.

Now, it had come to a point where a lot of it was just ordinary. After all, I'd practiced it for four years, and a lot of it had become habit and preference on my part. Not everything is going to be that way, of course; some things take much longer to work on, but now it was just my normal interaction with him. I think he did a very good job of humoring my anxiety for a moment, but then he told me to shut it. "I can tell you to stop talking at any time, and you will."

No one in an egalitarian relationship would put up with this! Egalitarian partners don't have to ask every time they have to go get a drink of alcohol, even when they're in public with their family. They can make a Caesar salad for supper anyway, even if their partner would prefer a steak. If they want to dye their hair, or get implants, or have a child, they can, whether their partner wants it or not. I do not have that leeway in my life, and I love that fact. I wouldn't want it (which is why I gave it up).

So after that, we developed a regular practice of looking back on all the changes which had been made since the beginning, and pointing out small actions which had changed for the better, in ways he really wanted them to change. We started doing that regularly—maybe once a month, or if I was having a weird moment. If I was frustrated because the house wasn't clean, for example, he would point out, "Well, this is leaps and bounds away from where you were when we first started." Is it perfect? No. Will it ever be perfect? Probably not. But we can work on it, and get closer.

Doing these "reviews"—which makes it sound formal, but they really aren't—made it a lot easier for me to continuously recognize that what we were doing was still working, even if it wasn't hard for me anymore. We still do them now, four years later, and they help me so very much.

Part 3. But Speaking Of Stuff That's Still A Struggle...

This brings us to my next difficulty, which is housekeeping. I can clean a house just fine, and it will be spotless and delightful, but keeping it clean was very hard for me. Both of my parents are hoarders, and I grew up in that environment for my entire life. When you grow up like that, there are processes you just don't learn, which apparently other people learn when they're younger from parents who clean regularly. Like picking up as you go, and other small actions which add up constantly over time.

That has truthfully been my longest-running mental switch-over we've been working on in this relationship. He likes the house quite pristine—maybe "spartan" would even be a good way of labeling it— and it's taken me a long time. I still struggle with it. The house is fine now, but I could still definitely improve.

We do regular check-ins about it, and if I'm having a week where it's been particularly bad, we sit down and talk about it again. As we're going over it, he'll say, "So what was going through your mind when you cleaned up all that and totally forgot this thing over here?" And that makes me think about my process.

I didn't realize that hoarding was not a totally unusual thing for children to go through until about six years ago when I learned that there is something called "clutter-blindness". This happens when you grow up in a hoarding household and you just stop seeing things which are out of their places, because there's so much stuff everywhere that you cannot take it all in and still remain sane—so you just start blocking it out, for the most part. It took us a while to realize that this was a problem for me, and that was painful and unpleasant on both of our parts, I'm sure. Since then, it's been a slow tweak every single day, with me learning new skills and constantly applying myself to it, day after day after day. We've been living together for seven and a half years at this point, and been through two moves. It can take a long time to change ingrained habits.

I still have difficulties, for sure—the dog shredded a cardboard box a while back, and I picked up almost all of it, and missed one piece on the floor. I thought it was fine, and went off to do a lot of other things. My master came out and said, "Did you finish cleaning up the cardboard box?" I said, "Oh, yeah, I did, totally." Then, while I was making lunch, he said, "So what's that?" I turned around and groaned inwardly because there was the last piece of cardboard.

It's a matter of reprogramming me. I know that he must have a huge dedication to this relationship which I cannot fathom in its ambition, because—good grief—the amount of ongoing work he has put into this one thing with me is shocking, in my eyes. I've constantly gotten better, but it has been such a slow process, with a lot of setbacks I've had to move through. On the plus side, though, his house is much cleaner now, which he likes quite a bit.

What gets me through the process of learning to master a skill I wasn't raised to do is a practice of constant gratitude. When I end up getting overwhelmed with frustration, and it feels like nothing is ever going to be enough, or that no matter how hard I work it's never going to be right, I remember that every single time he gives me a correction, it's because he loves me, and he wants me to do better. We are both so dedicated to this relationship that he wouldn't bother giving me that correction if he wasn't invested in us for the long term. That's what it comes down to, really, with all my frustrations.

Looking back on the first year or two of a relationship, when being together is so new and you have crazy NRE (New Relationship Energy), and everything they ask you to do is the most exciting thing you've ever been asked to do in your entire life ... It's important to remember that early gratitude and embody it, to tell yourself, "Every single time they do this, this is the reason why I choose to follow."

On a more pragmatic level, there's a book called *Home Comforts: The Art and Science of Keeping House* (Cheryl Mendelsohn, Scribner Press) which is all about homemaking, including how to take stains out of clothing, and the best ways to get grease out of your carpet, and that was a big help for me as well.

Part 4. Slave Friends

When I first started out in this relationship, I'd had a friend for several years who was also a self-identified slave, and the way her master ran his harem was not something I was interested in being part of. (They were both heterosexual.) We were good friends for a long time, and she'd been a great mentor for me in many, many ways, especially in my earliest days of joining the kink community, and in wanting to see more long-term, successful M/s relationships. However, when Ty and I got together, she ended up having an extreme problem with the amount of authority transfer that I wanted in the relationship. She was especially concerned with how we were handling control over money, and the way he allowed me to spend my time with friends, or that he was in charge of how I vote. He had authority over the way that I dressed, the way that I ate, and the way I was managing myself as a whole.

She had a significant problem with that. She was very regularly upset by it, and she felt that it was abusive. I thought that was kind of silly, because the way that her relationship worked was not what I wanted, and mine was not the way she would want her relationship to be—we are different people. Everybody has a different idea of what works for them in their M/s relationship, and what doesn't. But boy howdy, she had a problem with it! She was upset for a good two years into our relationship. It was like nothing we did was right in her eyes. She had a lot of specific ideas about what M/s should look like, and she felt that what worked for her family should be the standard for everyone. He didn't live with his girls; he stayed with them in rotation. They were all polyamorous, and all lived separately. They all retained their own paychecks, and most other decisions. The setup he had was extremely different from the ways I've seen other M/s folks do it.

Eventually—no shock—we stopped talking to each other. But it was hard to give that up, and to recognize that if this M/s relationship is what I want and need, then no matter how she felt about it, I had to do what felt right. I'd also had a couple of other friends who were in M/s relationships who were also nervous about it, as they also had different types of relationships. I was part of a local poly community for a long time, and in a lot of the M/s relationships in that community, people didn't live together, and they had a lot of partners in varying levels of authority transfer with each other, but few with as much authority transfer as ours. Which was fine, but I think it was very difficult for them to see us settle into it so quickly—and, honestly, easily—because once we sat down, outlined our contract, we signed it and he collared me...that was it. It wasn't the last decision I ever made, but it was the last free decision I ever made. I think a lot of our friends uninterested in total authority transfer had difficulty with that.

Anyway, my slave friend made a lot of assumptions about how much he cared about me based on the way we managed our dynamic, and everything about it was hard for her to hear, so we ended up not talking to each other anymore. That sucked, but it was ultimately better for both of us.

It wouldn't surprise me if she felt that her own dynamic was reproached by ours, honestly. I don't think she would have wanted to do anything as extreme as handing over her paycheck, for example. I think that really scared her, on a fundamental level—the idea of not having that control over her life. Her master could tell her to buy things for him and she would buy them, so there was definitely power exchange in that regard, but he didn't pay her bills—she did. Eventually, once we decided that I wasn't going to be working outside the home anymore, and obviously I wasn't going to be making any more money, I think that was especially scary for her to see ... and she had difficulty parsing out what was right for her versus what was right for everyone else. I tried setting up boundaries with her—"Let's just not talk about this," which is difficult when it's your main relationship—but it didn't help.

If you have a very high level of authority transfer, it's possible you will lose friends, even M/s friends who do things differently, if they feel challenged by your relationship. But ultimately, if any relationship is damaging to the goals you want most in your life, and it doesn't look like that damage is going to stop, there's really no reason to keep it. I genuinely believe that every relationship has a time and a place, and sometimes that means endings. The relationship I had with her was wonderful and helpful for my growth and education in a lot of ways, and it was hard to say goodbye to that. But I also recognize that I'm going to be with my master for as long as he'll have me, or until he's dead. So having somebody constantly nagging in my ear, creating problems where there are none, wasn't healthy. It's sad and it's painful, but sometimes doing the right thing is painful and unpleasant. So, if you have a friendship where the conflict is not going to manage itself, you have to graciously bow out and say goodbye, because not everything is meant to last forever.

BellaVoce lives on a small 3-acre farm with her master and a lot of livestock; working the farm is her job, as well as attempting to keep the house in some semblance of order. She runs a monthly Owner/property discussion group in Spokane, WA.

Feeding Your Slave Heart
dee tealover

What kind of submission, surrender, speaks to your slave/ submissive heart? What makes your soul sing? For many in the Master/slave community, it is a service-oriented surrender. For others, it is an obedience-oriented surrender. I do both of these things, and they feed my dynamic, they feed my M/s, but they don't feed my slave heart or make my soul sing. Through struggling to understand my slavery, my submission, I came to realize I am a devotional pleasure slave, and I've learned to embrace that aspect of myself. But the road to this realization and accepting myself for who I am was not easy for me. I struggled a lot, believing that perhaps I did not fit in, thinking maybe I didn't quite belong. In many cases, the terminology being used was a struggle, in other cases, the struggle stemmed from my heart simply not being fed by what I was seeing around me. My vision at first was narrow, and my understanding as someone new was incomplete. I am writing this essay about my experiences because I want to share the information I now know, but that I wished was more easily visible when I first began my authority exchange journey.

I believe that it is important for s-types to explore what feeds our slave hearts, our submissive souls—to understand what kind of submission or surrender speaks to us on a deep level. I don't mean the things we willingly do, or even necessarily things we enjoy doing. All of that is genuinely wonderful; anything that comes from a place of positivity, I believe, strengthens our dynamics. But what I really want us to think about is: What makes your soul sing? What nourishes your heart and feeds you in such a way that you almost feel invincible? Or maybe nourishes you to a sense of safety where you feel happily vulnerable? Or, to put it another way: What about these dynamics really works for you, and perhaps is even the reason you get up in the morning? I'm pretty sure the answer is slightly different for each and every one of us.

Words matter. The words we use, the definitions they hold, and the baggage they carry, impact our experiences. As a lover of words, I want to start our exploration of authentically feeding our slave hearts by exploring the definitions of some words I find relevant to our topic. (Just as an FYI, I used the Merriam-Webster dictionary for my definitions.)

I personally appreciate the word *submission* and resonate with the idea of being a *submissive*. I know many strong and self-actualized s-types balk at these two words, and I deeply respect that. But for a moment, if you will, let's think about this word and its dictionary definition shares with us a meaning that we can, on our own terms, tie into the idea of feeding our slave hearts. The relevant definitions of *submission* are:

❖ *The condition of being submissive, humble, or compliant.*
❖ *An act of submitting to the authority or control of another.*

I'll add the definition of *submissive:*

❖ *Willing to obey someone else.*

In addition, because the word comes up in the definitions, I feel the need to look up the word *compliant* and the word *comply:*

❖ *To conform, submit, or adapt (as to a regulation or to another's wishes) as required or requested.*

And to me, the most fun definition is the one the dictionary calls obsolete, but I think perhaps is alive and well in our community:

❖ *To be ceremoniously courteous.*

Another word that is relevant to authority exchange dynamics is *surrender:*

❖ *To yield to the power, control, or possession of another.*
❖ *To give up completely or agree to forgo especially in favor of another.*
❖ *To give (oneself) up into the power of another.*

Now let's think about the definitions of these words: *submissive, submission, compliant,* and *surrender*. When I read through these definitions, I see a lot of the concepts that are part of many of the dynamics in our community:

- ❖ Following the lead of an authority.
- ❖ The willingness of many s-types to obey that person.
- ❖ For many, an element of humility pervades their behaviors.
- ❖ To conform, adapt or submit to that authority are ways of following the M or D type in the dynamic.
- ❖ To be ceremoniously courteous calls to my mind some of the higher protocols many embrace in their dynamic.

The truth is that for some people, these words will resonate, either the word itself or the definition. And for these people, even if the word has cultural baggage, the baggage is either irrelevant or can be overcome, allowing the s-type to claim the words on their own terms. For example, for me, as I mentioned, I have always resonated with the word *submissive,* and the definition also works for me: submitting to the authority of another. However, the word *surrender* did not originally appeal to me. At first, I interpreted surrender as giving up something of my core Self. But that isn't an inherent part of the definition: *Willing to forgo for another.* That definition does appeal and resonate, so I can appreciate the word *surrender,* and claim it for my own.

For some people, our words won't resonate at all. Not the word itself. Not the definition. Perhaps they won't be able or willing to deal with the cultural baggage. I don't have a personal example for this experience with words, but maybe you do. If you don't like a word, perhaps because of the definition itself or because the word has too much "cultural baggage," then I ask you to think about:

- ❖ What definitions match you?
- ❖ What words are you choosing to inhabit?
- ❖ What words enrich yourself and your dynamic?

Because the words you do choose to embrace and inhabit matter. They enrich your experience of your slave/submissive heart—and maybe speaking your words out loud, sharing your words, will touch the heart of another slave/submissive in ways they didn't expect. Understand that s-types are a diverse and unique group of wonderful people. It is important to recognize that what feeds one person's slave heart might not feed another, and yet it is all beautiful.

Feeding our s-hearts, nourishing them, is vital and keeps the energy alive for our dynamics. As I mentioned, I wanted to write this essay because I wanted to share different ways of thinking about our words and about what feeds our slave hearts. After all, what feeds my slave heart I couldn't see in those early days. I now know that what feeds me was always there in others in the community, but I just couldn't see it. Partly because it's visually subtle, partly because it was less talked about. And in those early days, looking around the spaces of the community I was beginning to inhabit, I felt unsure. I was starting to define myself by what I saw that I was *not*, and that made it hard to figure out what I *am*. I had trouble seeing where I fit in this world. I didn't yet see or understand the beautiful diversity I was just mentioning. I spent a lot of time trying to understand different styles of being an s-type and what most resonated with others around me ... and with me.

As I looked around, I don't think it will surprise you that the first s-type orientation I noticed was service. After all, service-oriented s-types are often the most visible because they are often the ones on the front lines doing "all the things" in our groups and at our events. There are a multitude of definitions for *service*, but I will share those that are the most relevant for our purposes, and the definitions are quite beautiful:

❖ *A helpful act, useful, beneficial.*
❖ *Contribution to the welfare of others.*
❖ *To be favorable, opportune, or convenient.*
❖ *To be worthy of reliance or trust.*
❖ *To comply with commands or demands and to gratify.*

As far as I have noticed, service can take a multitude of forms and the limits are only the limits of the imagination. I remember at a conference in the early days of my M/s dynamic going to a class on service. The class was small, which allowed the participants and presenters to have a comfortable and lively discussion about service and what service could be. The presenters challenged me, saying that even if I don't think I am doing service, I probably am. They suggested that if I were mindful, I might recognize the service I was already performing. They were right; I was already doing a lot of service for my Master, I just didn't recognize it until challenged to really "notice". Most s-types do service of one kind or another in their dynamics or within their communities. For many s-types, these acts of service resonate with them deeply; service is an element that feeds and nourishes them. But some of us do service, even if, as in the case of myself, we don't realize it. And many of us do it well, perhaps with good humor. Even so, service doesn't resonate on a deeper level within everyone's heart.

In my local community, in the "before COVID" times, my Master and I attended many formal dinner parties. The hosts of these dinner parties are quite adept at putting on these events and this service they provide our community resonates feeds the s-type's slave heart. The parties are always beautiful, simply elegant—a choreographed dance of food preparation, elegant meal plating, and table service, course by course, executed according to their house protocols. The s-types all fulfill their various roles quietly and gracefully as the M and D-types converse and socialize. Objectively, the evening is usually one of beauty and elegance, grace and near precision, nervous tension, excitement, and fun. And yes, I love formal dinner parties, but while I do enjoy the formality and the elegance, my slave heart is not fed as I know the hearts of some of the other s-types that help at these parties are fed.

Another commonly seen way of being an s-type is *obedience oriented*. There aren't as many definitions for *obedience*, but as you'll see, it ties in powerfully with what it is we do.

❖ *Submissive to the command of authority.*
❖ *Willing to obey authority.*

Though the definition is short, obedience comes in multiple flavors from highly micro-managed (and the surrender and beauty in that), to the macro-managed level of obedience where the details are open, but the broad brushstrokes are defined. Sometimes the obedience comes in the form of the s-type always knowing that they are expected to behave as "Master Would Want" whether their M or D- type is with them or not. For fun, this is sometimes called: What Would Master Want, or W W M W. Different s-types obey with varying degrees of speed, accuracy, and joy, but for some, whether they are in a good mood or not, something about obedience speaks to them. Feeds their slave heart. Nourishes their soul on a deeper level.

I do my best to *obey*, which for me is trying to "just do" when commanded. I have sometimes failed at the first-instance response. Failed is a harsh word, and my Master says there is no failure, there is only trying your best. He always assumes my best intentions. But I struggle with the first-instance response. I try not to ask too many questions, but I can't help myself; I ask a million questions. If I can't ask out loud, the noise of the questions is all I hear in my head. I need to have clarity, to know "why", even if the clarity is "Because I said so." Not having answers often derails me from the whole "obedience" piece. And regardless of my skill at it, it's not the fact of obedience that resonates in my heart.

As I mentioned, when I entered the scene, I noticed these two ways of being an s-type most frequently—and the truth is, I do both things. I *serve* my Master in a multitude of ways, but it's not the service in and of itself that feeds me. I do my best to *obey*, but it's not obedience in and of itself that feeds me. Both service and obedience feed our dynamic and nourish our M/s, but neither of these feeds my slave heart. They don't make my soul sing, and at the beginning of our journey, this fact caused me to struggle. I heard service and obedience talked about from people I met in classes at multiple venues. I started to ask myself: Where do I fit in? *Do* I fit in?

If my slave heart wasn't singing with any of these ways of being, am I a slave or a submissive at all? Or am I something else? Are service and obedience the only way? Is there another way? I saw obedience and service truly feed the hearts of s-types I knew, and I saw that as beautiful. I wanted beauty, but those paths were not authentic for me. I wanted to understand myself better, understand what feeds my slave heart, what makes my soul sing, why I am doing this thing we do anyway. I thought about my dynamic and what makes me want to follow my Master's will—why I try to obey him, though I often falter. Why I do acts of service, though receiving and not giving is my love language. As I tried to understand myself better, I realized that I *am* a submissive. The truth could be seen in our definition from earlier. I follow the lead of my Master; he is my authority. I surrender, I forgo my desires, for those of another, of my Master. And I further realized that some of the fuel feeding all of this for me is the mere fact that I *worship* my master. I *adore* my master.

We've all heard this one. The question is sometimes asked hypothetically: Would you obey your master in all things, knowing he had your best interests at heart? Would you jump off a bridge if he asked you to? For me, the answer to that version of the question is *F%*# no*. But if the question was posed as: How much do you adore and worship your master? Do you trust in his leadership and worship and revere him so much that you would follow him into a burning building or jump off a bridge with him? The answer to the question posed that way is: *Why yes, I think I would.* But no one has ever asked me the question that way; it's always been asked from the perspective of obedience. A sense of obedience to my master wouldn't move me to any extreme action. My adoration of him could.

And so I learned to add to *Service-oriented* and *Obedience-oriented* s-types a new category of *Worship -oriented* or *Devotion-oriented* s-types.

- ❖ **Worship**: *To regard with great or extravagant respect, honor, or devotion.*
- ❖ **Devotion**: *The fact or state of being ardently dedicated and loyal.*
- ❖ **Adore**: *To regard with loving admiration and devotion.*

And once again an obsolete definition is quite relevant! **Remember** *the object of one's devotion?* My Master is the object of my devotion, I regard him with great respect, honor, and adoration. My reverence for him feeds my heart and nourishes my soul This. This right here, this is a driving force for why I do what I do. This is what feeds my soul. This is what gets me back on track when I feel derailed. To go back to the Formal Dinner Parties I mentioned earlier, I shared with you that the service aspect is fun but doesn't feed my heart. Why do I like them, then? Because Formal Dinner Parties give me an opportunity, with grace, and compliance (and specifically compliance as described in the obsolete definition of *with ceremonious courtesy*), to show my Master my devotion.

Of course, there are even more things that feed the slave heart, even more types of surrender. We s-types are complex, and our souls can be fed in multiple ways. Another one for me, to be honest as I blush, is sensuality, sex, and pleasure. I love MAsT Meetings, as you might imagine. A discussion group on authority exchange topics? What's not to love for someone like me who always needs to understand things and ask "why?" One of the people in my MAsT chapter Andrew James, and I resonate with the words spoken by him and his s-type, and how they talk about their own dynamic. In 2019, Andrew James published a great book: *The Way of the Pleasure Slave: Erotic Slavehood for the Submissive Woman.** This book captured my attention. A lot of what he writes about matches being worship-and-devotion oriented, but takes a slightly different focus with pleasure and joy being important. The book describes this kind of s-type being a sort of "consort" who brings ease and comfort into the life of her M or D-type.

Because of this, I want to add to our list of ways to feed our slave hearts the category of *Pleasure-oriented.*

- ❖ **Pleasure:** *to give pleasure to, gratify, to give sexual pleasure to.*
- ❖ *Frivolous amusement, a source of delight or joy.*
- ❖ *From Shakespeare: "…wait upon his pleasure".*

---

* https://alfredpress.com/the-way-of-the-pleasure-slave/

"What is a Pleasure Slave? A pleasure slave is a specialized s-type whose primary role is to provide erotic pleasure to her M-type. She strives to increase her M-type's physical and emotional well-being, and her own, through their shared experience of pleasure." –Andrew James, The Way of the Pleasure Slave

The author points out that not all M/s relationships include sex, or even if they do, it might not be a particularly important component of the dynamic. But he also points out that: "...*for the pleasure slave, it is central to her identity and the focus of her service.*" And "*The pleasure slave's motivation lies in a desire for personal growth through the cultivation of intimacy with a specific individual (or individuals if she is polyamorous) ... her orientation is relational at heart.*"

Oh, how I can relate to this. Pleasure can be seen as a service. For me, it is something else as well; the focus on personal growth within the relationship, erotic pleasure, and emotional well-being all dovetails nicely with being devotion-oriented. Another factor of the pleasure-oriented s-type I resonate with is the frivolity and gaiety such an s-type might bring to the table. I call it being "the Keeper of my Master's Whimsy". I provide frivolous amusement for my often-too-serious Master. That's definitely a service, but it is pleasure-oriented.

Recognizing and embracing the elements that feed my slave heart—worship, devotion, pleasure—strengthened both my sense of self as an s-type as well as my M/s dynamic. This self-awareness, once shared with my Master, was a game-changer that allowed for a deeper level of surrender.

I hope you found something to feed your slave heart in this essay, but what I discovered for myself doesn't exhaust the possibilities. There are no doubt other ways to feed one's slave heart beyond those mentioned. Because of my journey, it's important to me that all voices are heard. If you did not find an orientation that matches your truth in this essay, I hope you feel inspired to explore your inner self to come to a better understanding of how your s-heart is nourished. My main takeaway, more important than a list of definitions: figuring out what feeds your slave heart is personal. It does not matter if anyone else has ever had their heart fed by a similar thing. All that matters is that you explore and discover what makes *your* slave heart sing.

Losing the No
sparkle

I fell into this dynamic. Well, not literally, which is unusual for me, but figuratively. Like many others I came for the kinky fun stuff; then he happened. I'm not sure how he captured me; it was either rope or cookies, but there I was asking to be more than a play partner and bottom … asking to be his submissive.

I was new. I was so new I didn't know what polyamory was, so he explained it to me. He introduced me to another partner and answered every question I had. I wasn't planning any kind of long-term relationship with this guy, so I was cool with it.

Then we caught the feels for each other. Maybe we'd had them from that first meeting and finally acknowledged them, but there they were. Feels. Big Feels. Suddenly, that polyamory thing was A Thing for my mono brain and heart to learn to handle.

I want to tell you all the funny moments that we have experienced—the moments where I realized I wasn't thinking about what I wanted, but what he would want. I want to tell you all of the little nuances of "I own you" that make my surrender to this man so fulfilling and so frustrating. I love those moments because they are the fun part of our dynamic. When I'm completing a task exactly the way he wants it done while muttering "This is stupid!" and then handing him exactly what he wants, done the way he wants it. I want to tell you about the moments where I'm doing something and I think "We talked about this months ago, and then he dropped it and we haven't talked about it since," to his "Programming complete!" grin. He doesn't even have to say the words anymore, because I can read that grin on his face. I want you to know all of those easy, fun times that make me smile because those are the ones that I experience most often these days. Once, at a coffee social, I was talking to friends, and he caught my eye and just turned his empty coffee cup upside down. Moments like that which build our happiness in our dynamic are what I want to share when I talk about my journey into surrender and being owned.

But those are the easy things, and getting there isn't always easy.

Just Breathe

In case I didn't make it clear, he's poly and I'm not. So of course, it was over polyamory that he took his swan dive off the pedestal of perfection that I had put him, my dominant, on. You know that moment when you realize that the person you serve, the person you love and submit to, isn't perfect? Yes, it happened. I had that moment. It was, I thought as I sobbed into my pillow, the one thing that was going to break me, break us. (This was more than ten years ago, so clearly it didn't.) As I look back at that moment, I think it was one of the times I saw not only how strong he is, but how strong I am and how much stronger we are together.

He apologized and understood why I was so angry. He's not a tyrant who says, "I'm the dominant, I'll do what I want and you'll deal with it." He promised to help me get my footing again, to trust him and trust in us to get past this. "Just trust me."

I had to decide. Did I need him to re-earn my trust? What did I need to move forward? Was this one moment going to define our relationship's beginning or end?

It was the beginning. I looked at him and said, "I will trust you," and I did. Deciding to trust someone after you've been hurt by them isn't always easy. You can't keep bringing up the transgression. The wound won't heal if you keep picking off the scab. When you decide to trust someone after being hurt, you must forgive the hurt. You can't keep beating them over the head with it, because both of you will become resentful. When you decide to move forward, looking back over your shoulder only keeps you from growth and healing. So, I did; I put it behind me.

No, it was not just that easy. I struggled ... but then it was over. It was an event that happened in the past which we can look back on and see how far we've come. That is not to say I don't still have struggles and challenges, but I look ahead to new struggles and challenges instead of dredging up old ones.

But my struggles both as his collared property and as the "mono" in a mono/poly relationship are different. I've learned things along the way. I recall one conversation in which we were discussing something that he had said, and I had grasped it like it was a life jacket thrown to me while I tried to stay afloat in the deepest of stormy seas. I held on to that life jacket as if it was going to save me; I made it my safety handle. Then, one day, it was gone. I honestly don't remember what we were talking about, but it was gone. I did what I do best: I panicked. The calm voice over the phone reminded me that he was my safety handle. Holding onto things and words that may change as our lives change was not going to work; I needed to hold onto him.

I've learned that when he says, "Just breathe," he means it. It's kind of like telling someone to calm down. It used to be gasoline on a fire—"I am breathing, dammit!" Sometimes I tell myself in my head (in his voice of course), "Just breathe!" and it works. Stop, breathe, listen to what is bothering me, and breathe. Learning to acknowledge feelings, especially negative ones, and give them space, was hard. Sometimes the words about the feelings just need to be said, poured out in the light of day and heard so that they can be released. There's not always something to fix, there is only a feeling to be acknowledged and heard.

You Will Lose Your No.

While the mono/poly relationship was hard, it wasn't and still isn't the only hard thing about being his collared property. When I first asked about moving from the satisfying but not quite right D/s dynamic to M/s, I asked him what changes that would bring to our life, what I would experience as his slave that I didn't experience as his submissive.

"You will lose your No," he said.

I shrugged. Big deal. What was he going to do, make ridiculous decisions that would cause me to change my life? He wasn't the micromanaging type of dominant. He didn't need me to account for every minute of my day, choose my clothing, hair color and length, or nail polish. So, I shrugged and said, "I can live with that," and I trusted in his honor and integrity to keep me safe.

About a year later, I knelt in front of him before our chosen family and he put his collar around my neck. I gave him my No. But there was no magical line to step across into the land of being a perfect slave who never questioned him. In a community where slavery seemed to be represented by a high-protocol micromanaged dynamics, we were low-key. He gave a lot of suggestions, a lot of hint-structions, and I followed them. He was in charge, right? It never really felt like I had given up anything and gained everything.

Doesn't that sound perfect? It is, at times. Sometimes there is nothing bothering me, nothing I'm worried about, and everything is calm. I want to capture those moments and preserve them for the next storm as a way to reassure myself that the storm will pass.

I don't remember the first No that I faced. At the time, it was probably catastrophic in my mind. I don't really remember any of them, although I'm sure he does as they were likely accompanied by challenge, by struggle, by tears and anger. And he did what he has always done, both then and now; he stood there beside me holding me up, supporting me, and helping me stand beside him.

Other times I struggle. I struggle with my own fears, my own insecurities ... and to be honest, I struggle with the decisions he's made for me, for us. Not all of them, of course, just the ones I don't like. I struggle against things I can't change—and when I can't carry them alone, I take them to him. He is my greatest cheerleader, my biggest supporter, and my rock.

How Did We Get Here?

Time. Consistency. Determination. We love each other but as I've told so many over the years, the Beatles had it wrong: you need more than love. Sometimes you can love someone who is not good for you. People often say that "We are two sides of the same coin," or "He/she/they complete me," to describe their connection to their partner. No. I'm a complete person on my own. He is a complete person on his own. Together, however, we are a complete *us*, more than the sum of our parts. We complement each other's strengths and weaknesses. When my fight-or-flight reactions cause a desire for flight, his stubbornness and determination hold on to me, knowing that this is just a hiccup. This mountain I am trying to climb is a bump in the road. Every single time.

And communication. If one didn't grow up in a home where communication, healthy communication, was practiced, one didn't learn how to communicate when things were tough. I learned growing up that anger removed love, and that is a hard one to unlearn. But it can be done; therapy helped. I learned how to communicate, but at the time I was in a relationship with someone who refused to communicate anger as well, so there was really no reason to practice those tools. They sat dusty and unused in the corner until this relationship.

Suddenly, I was in that place where I was owned. Every thought, every feeling, every action was available to him to review, discuss, and change. That "You will lose your No" was suddenly right there in my face. I pulled out those tools I'd so painstakingly learned in therapy. With the 100% transparency that I'd learned was expected, I learned to communicate again. I learned it was OK, and in fact required, to share the ugly feelings. I learned that he already knew that anger didn't erase love, and I learned that my anger wouldn't erase his love for me.

It was a gradual slide into the surrender that I desired as his slave. He didn't just step up and say, "I am in charge of everything," as we rode off into the sunset after he collared me. He's smarter than that; he waited. He knew I had said that he had 100% authority over every part of my life, but the smart man said, "You handle that; I don't need to."

I think it may have been his decades (I like to say that because it makes him sound old and sometimes poking the bear makes me giggle) in the US Army as a senior NCO that helped him fine-tune those leadership skills he uses on me. He doesn't often give specific orders or directions. He gives me a goal, points me in that direction, and lets me figure out how to handle it. He's a resource, a support network of one, and my biggest cheerleader. It's so rare that he tells me how to do something that it takes me by surprise. He doesn't make me a better person; he makes me want to be a better person. And that, I think, is one of the reasons our dynamic has lasted. He doesn't set me up to fail; there is no benefit to him in that. He sets me up for growth and lets me find my way as long as my way aligns with his goals.

And that is a stumbling block sometimes. I've been known to mutter, "Who died and made you God?" under my breath just loud enough for him to hear, or he just reads it on my face as I stop what I'm doing to hear what he's telling me he wants me to do.

Was I born to be submissive? To be a slave? No. I don't have a submissive hair on my body. I'm one of those driven, could-be-a-Type-A-person-if-I-cared-to-make-the-effort, people. Surrendering to him does not always come easily. There are times when I'm fighting tooth and nail to keep up with him, to stand beside him where he wants me to be … and there are times when I must let him carry me, because, well, I just need him to. He leads this relationship and moves it in the direction he wants us to go. Sometimes I try to grab the wheel and steer things my way a little bit. I will tell you now, if you grab the wheel while someone else is driving, the crash is probably going to hurt. Surrender, that moment when my brain, my thoughts, and my actions feel so in tune with Master's direction, is an amazing feeling and it makes me crave more.

I am this man's slave and property. I submit to this man and surrender to him because it fulfills me. It is where I want to be.

> "Sometimes what seems like surrender isn't surrender at all. It's about what's going on in our hearts. About seeing clearly the way life is and accepting it and being true to it, whatever the pain, because the pain of not being true to it is far, far greater."
>
> - Nicholas Evans, The Horse Whisperer

I discovered kink through erotica and soon wanted to find out more. After a 27-year vanilla relationship I traded in my white picket fence for a collar and haven't looked back. "Submissive" didn't fit me well, there wasn't enough given for what I felt I was getting. I asked for more. And got it. As collared property I have surrendered my No and am valued for my independence and ability to be his majordomo and right hand. For us, it is about authority, not control. And it works.

Thirty Years as Property: Growing and Changing Over Time

jessie

I have been my Owner's property for almost thirty years, so there have been plenty of issues to struggle over in that time. Here are some examples that come to mind.

Bathrooms

In the first few years, he had issued a standing order that I needed to ask permission to use the bathroom when we were together. He was reasonable; I could be discreet if other people were there. At first the whole thing was super-hot. I loved the slight humiliation of asking; I loved the shared secret naughtiness of excusing myself in company and looking to him for a nod. As the months and years went on, though, I began to find it less sexy and more of an annoyance. I didn't want to hurt his feelings, so I didn't bring that up. But occasionally I would break the rule (usually with some legalistic rationalization). I felt bad after breaking the rule, and I would confess and be punished—and that was nice. I would feel bad about having messed up, and recommit to the rule.

Then we got married and I got pregnant, and suddenly I was going to the bathroom a lot. I was fed up with my body, and fed up with asking permission, so I stopped. But I didn't talk to him about it; I just stopped, and he didn't ask what happened. And I thought that meant he was done with our M/s relationship, and maybe sick of me entirely. I got really depressed, and eventually he asked me what was wrong, and I spilled everything out. By now I hated the bathroom rule, but I hated even more that he didn't care about enforcing his rule. Or maybe he hadn't even noticed that I wasn't asking any more. He heard me out, and said that he had figured out that the rule wasn't working anymore, and he had decided to just let it go. But our conversation led him to end the rule explicitly, and to put in a new rule that I had to communicate when I was upset about a rule. I won't say that new rule fixed all my communication issues, but it was helpful. And the whole experience was helpful in nudging us towards caution and communication before he makes any rule permanent.

Touching

When our babies were infants and nursing, I felt very "touched out", and I asked him for a break from him grabbing me and fondling me all the time. (That had been something I enjoyed, until the babies came along). He granted me the break I asked for, but apparently my brain was overloaded at the time, because I forgot that I'd asked him for a break. A year or so later, I went to him, upset that he no longer found me sexy enough to grab and fondle—was our dynamic over? He simply reminded me that I had been the one to ask for the break, and ended it, and went back to grabbing and fondling me. We learned a lesson from that experience to write down our agreements rather than rely on me to remember them, especially during stressful periods.

Polyamory

Ten years later, we faced an even bigger issue. He came to me and told me that he had had some sort of one-night stand, six months earlier. Now, we had never made an explicit promise of monogamy. In fact, one time, the first year we were dating, he let me know that he wanted to spend the night with an ex who was in town, and—although it was emotionally difficult for me—I didn't tell him he couldn't do it. I felt proud of myself for accepting that my Owner had that right. We had also fooled around together with other people at sexy parties, but then with our new focus on kids and careers, we had stopped going to sexy parties and we slid into what looked a lot like a monogamous relationship. So, it came as a shock that he had done something and not told me about it until much later.

I'm not proud of how I reacted. I cried a lot; I accused him of dishonesty. I wanted new rules in place so I could read his emails and texts whenever I wanted to. (As my Owner, he already could read my emails and texts.) He agreed to the new rules, and I agreed to explore non-monogamy with him. I came up with more rules: we needed to go out together on date nights as often as he went out with other people. And no bringing dates over to our house, as I didn't want our kids to find out. That first year, he let me set the pace and the rules. Gradually,

I learned from reading and talking to more experienced polyamorous people that my rules were counterproductive. My Owner's compassion for me helped him be patient as I learned from those more experienced people, and his commitment to the privacy of his other partners helped me learn that I didn't need to know everything he was doing all the time. There was a difference between what I wanted to know out of curiosity or insecurity, and what I needed to know.

Expanding Sex

Once my Owner was exploring with other people, he discovered an interest in bottoming. It was emotionally difficult for me to accept that my Owner wanted to bottom—that desire didn't seem very dominant to me. On the other hand, I had known him a long time, and I didn't have any doubt that he was a dominant person, aware of what he wanted and good at getting it. I started reading about dominant bottoms, and I learned that it's not that uncommon for people who enjoy being in charge to also enjoy being beaten, or whipped, or teased. My Owner began seeing someone else—an experienced top—and I saw how pleased he was with the marks he came home with. After a while, I got over my prejudices, and I asked if I could try spanking him. He was still clearly in charge of our scenes, but he was using me for his pleasure in a new way. It felt good, to grow past my misconceptions and provide my Owner with a new form of service. Years later, when my Owner thought it might be fun to wear a chastity cage, I was able to see that in a similar way. My Owner is still fundamentally in charge, and having the fun he wants to have—it's just that sometimes his fun involves me teasing him and telling him "No," for the sake of the game. We both know who is really in charge: when he's wearing the chastity cage and he wants out, he tells me firmly and I let him out. But if he wants me to play at being a stern domme, I can offer him that just as I can offer him a spanking.

Interruptions

Another persistent issue is that I am prone to interrupting. There will probably never be a permanent fix to this, but I have found that meditation practice provides some help. During my daily fifteen-minute meditation, I practice experiencing an itchy nose without immediately scratching it. I practice keeping my hands in my lap when I want to check my phone. I practice putting my tongue on the roof of my mouth when I want to ask, "What was that noise?" All that practice comes in handy in my regular life, especially when my Owner is talking. I'm far from perfect, but I'm better than I used to be at holding my tongue, listening to what he's saying, and thinking before speaking.

Body Image

Another issue which has surfaced over the years is my Owner's love of large breasts. I resisted the idea of surgery, but we had a breakthrough when he encouraged me to wear falsies. Over the years, he got me larger and larger inserts. I had a lot of insecurity going out wearing them, worrying that I looked ridiculous, trying to be sexy. Then one day I went to a class on dollification and that was truly transformative. I started identifying as a doll—that helped me feel it was no longer my concern whether I looked sexy in the outfit my Owner chose for me, whatever the size of my fake boobs. If I was just a doll, then I could relax and wear any outfit without feeling insecure. The lesson there was that one can always learn a new approach, and taking classes and talking to other s-types has helped me learn what has worked for other people facing related challenges.

Maintenance

One area where I feel our approach might be able to help other s-types is our "Sunday smiting." My Owner has always encouraged me to think about what I crave and to let him know. I don't always get what I crave, but I'm always allowed to ask for it. That process led me to realize that I function best when I get regular beatings (like putting gas in the car). Sometimes people talk about "maintenance spankings," but that term felt like a chore to my Owner. Then I ran across someone else's fetish on Fetlife: "Since it's Sunday, I will smite you." Aha! We workshopped the hell out of that fetish, until we settled on a protocol that worked for us. Each Sunday, I ask my Owner about scheduling the smiting; when should I present myself? At the appointed time, I present myself with an implement of my choosing. Then my Owner does whatever he wants with the implement, for however long he

158 JOSHUA TENPENNY

wants. Then I thank him, and I put the implement away again. My Owner finds it entertaining, and I find it helpful to know I have a fun weekly scene to look forward to.

jessie has been participating in online kink discussions since the 1990s and has been active in the San Francisco Bay Area kink community since 2010.

Serving Through Past and Future
The Musings of a Long-Term Slave
Slave Gaia Amor

I grew up in South Africa with a dad who never understood love. He was singularly focused on never having a woman tell him what to do. In his mind his own father was abused and bossed around, and he would never go through that. Thus, he took control of his wife and his three daughters in a way that was not healthy. He screamed, punished, used gaslighting, and never acknowledged accomplishments, except for a single occasion when he praised me at my master's degree graduation ceremony. He was an absent father who never celebrated his family much. He excelled at making me feel less than and not good enough.

When I was five years old, my grandfather started molesting me, and my father did not believe me or my sister when we told him. My mom did, but he refused to, until my grandfather apologized to him on his deathbed. My mom took us out of the situation, but my father failed to protect me.

I went on to marry an abusive alcoholic who excelled at verbally breaking me down, humiliating me in front of others and when we were alone. I would regularly hear how bad I was at parenting, cooking, cleaning, sex, and more. He also had a bad temper and would start screaming when I tried to defend myself. He often left me to go drinking when I needed him in times of crisis. At first, I tried to make him happy, but nothing was ever good enough. All I ever wanted was to serve and please someone, to be acknowledged and loved.

I was in a cycle of being attracted to abusers like my father, but eventually came to understand there is an enormous difference between *serving* someone who is self-aware in their authority and someone who gives themselves the *illusion* of being powerful at the expense of another. By this time, I equated this type of bullying, with men in general. I wanted to avoid intimacy with them altogether and thought I would be happier serving a woman. After years of therapy, I learned that my attraction to domineering personalities was a misplaced aching for intentional structure, for someone strong enough to look after me and keep my tender slave heart safe. Despite being a man, when I met Master Dante there was undeniable recognition. I knew I had finally met someone who would provide a space for me to succeed in my calling to serve, and I have been collared to him for seventeen years now.

He changed everything. No, he didn't take away the triggers, the trauma, the loss of faith in myself and humanity all at once or even swiftly. There are still stumbling blocks we are discovering on our path. As a result of all the abusive history with other men, and the resulting protective walls, I still struggle to be vulnerable and take direction well. I crave acknowledgement, but often don't ask out of a fear of sounding needy. Even though he is very generous with praise, I struggle to even *hear* praise, let alone internalize it. Because of all my insecurities, I often don't have enough compassion for myself, and don't love myself enough.

But that is changing.

When Correction Hurts

Face your challenges when they come, and find a way to face them with love.

It is hard for me to handle correction with grace. It's hard for me to hear, "You did this wrong," because what I hear is, "You are useless. You are a bad cook. You are a bad slave." I don't hear "Just fix this part. The rest of it was great." I have a tool now, to help me fulfil this fundamental requirement in our dynamic. When my owner wants to talk to me about something, I ask myself what he needs from me right now. Master Dante wants to ensure that I do the best I can and that I am the best I can be. He wants me to celebrate my achievements and he wants me to grow and improve in those things which make our lives easier and more loving. He needs to be heard. The tool is to actively listen and acknowledge exactly what he has said. That's what I try to do now. So instead of hearing my evil inner construct "Darth Dante", I hear the actual man before me say, "You know what? This meal was delicious, but the salad could use a little more dressing," instead of "You can't cook worth a damn." Baby steps, and remembering that he is fulfilling his responsibility of giving me a safe structure to blossom within, makes this a little easier at times.

This also helps me to be more vulnerable. It helps me to say, "Master, would you please repeat the correction, because what I just heard you say is that I'm a bad cook." At this point he would look at me, affirm me and remind me that his goal is to help me serve him better. Transparently sharing the inner voice of terrible judgment has helped him Master me better, and helped me have more compassion for myself. I also am starting to finally have more compassion for him when his voice raises. I am finally coming to understand that his need to be heard is as critical as my need to be safe.

All this work leads to the next question: How do I love and serve better? By doing more self-care. By working on what's inside of me. Through therapy, I have now discovered what my actual needs, wants, boundaries, desires are. I've also discovered what my features and my flaws are. I understand that I come out fighting and that I hurt him when he tries to do his job because I still don't recognize that I am safe and loved. Accepting love was foreign to me, and has been a long journey. Thankfully, I have my adoring Master and loving slave sisters to show me the splendor of its many-colored coat. Self-care and self-love are teaching me that I am worthy of love. Correction helps me grow. Correction is a gift. Correction and being held accountable are part of the process. Self-care has taught me to reframe things in the only way that matters. How does this improve our dynamic and what part of his commitment is he fulfilling when he offers it?

Compassion is taking responsibility for actions I have taken that might not be great, but without judgement. Compassion is finding a way to reframe it as an opportunity to grow and to love more.

All of this is seventeen years in! It takes as long as it takes, but it's such a freeing thing to realize that you are not "less than" because you are serving someone. It's just fulfilling a different role and interpersonal need. For years I thought I was less than the person who had authority, because I've always been told that I am. Now I realize that his responsibility as my owner is to care of me and our dynamic. My responsibility is to obey and serve him in the way he wishes to be served. We have different roles, but he's not better than I am, and I'm not worse than he is, because the roles are complimentary. It takes a lot of strength to be in an M/s dynamic. He must be strong enough to lead and to take responsibility. I must be strong enough to put my demons to rest, hear him clearly, and remain focused on our goals.

Advice From the Inner Sanctum of My Heart

> *One does not just tell people what to do, one leads by example. All the work I have been doing has shown me what I probably should have done from the start.*

If you are going to be a healthy s-type, you need to know who you are. You need to know the difference between needs, wants, and desires, and you need to be able to communicate these clearly to one that you serve. Write your very own "Instruction Manual" that helps them see the lay of the land, helps them find the places where angels would fear to tread, and helps them understand what makes you tick. Release this information slowly and see what they do with it.

You also need to know what your boundaries are. Boundaries exist for a reason. Don't give them up before you trust another with your life and your surrender. These can be renegotiated when you are ready to have them removed, and someone worth trusting with your life and well-being will support you in that. Know that slaves in fiction aren't supposed to have any limits, but that's not the way it always works in real life, especially before trust is built.

In addition, you need to know the M-type's boundaries, needs, wants, and desires. What are they going to want you to do? How do they envision their dynamic with you in practical terms? M/s is not necessarily about comfort, but being seriously uncomfortable with their answers about areas of core alignment when you're just getting to started is a serious red flag. Don't take someone's offered collar just because you think you need-a-collar-right-now. That's how you wind up in a situation with someone who may not necessarily have your best interest at heart.

In BDSM play you need to take responsibility for who you play with. If you're a complete newbie and you want to get tied up, it's your responsibility to find out what bondage is all about, what the risks are, and what someone skilled will do in preparation and during the scene. When it becomes clear that you are not in good hands use your safe word, leave, and get support.

If a scene requires this level of preparation, then surrendering yourself to another needs your due diligence and your commitment to discuss and remove red flags when you see them. If you don't feel safe sharing your needs, wants, desires, and boundaries with someone, that is not someone you should be with. That path leads to destruction. You need compatibility, safety, honor, trust, and respect.

Settling Out

This brings us to another point that very few people talk about and is the reason why compatibility is so critical. As time goes on, things can settle in just like they do in a vanilla relationship. With NRE (New Relationship Energy) every day is filled with play, sex, and kinky fun times. You can't wait to be with them, and your body responds to their voice, a text, a message, even a look. When NRE passes play and sex may become less frequent. The same experience curve can happen even if your dynamic was never focused on sex or play, but with rituals, protocols, and areas of active service. Whatever the components, the M/s dynamic that you negotiated is still there and you need to ensure that your protocols, interactions, roles continue to function in the structures set by both of you. That's why the sharing of wants, needs, desires, requirements, and boundaries is so important. That is why it is important to go back to the basics every so often to prevent or address dynamic drift and complacency.

In the end our bodies age and things become a little more challenging. Yes, it's hot in the beginning when Master says "Kneel, slut!". Your body reacts to that command, and you are ready to go. When you're fifty you may not be able to kneel quite as elegantly or for as long because it hurts too much. Your body also might need some extra lube even though the person in front of you is still the most handsome being on earth. You start looking for alternatives to make sure the intent of the ritual is still honored. You might get a pillow or little chair that ensures that you can sit at his feet. When you both start to forget things, you might have to get creative. The most important thing for me is that our dynamic is continuing to thrive because our hearts and minds seem to get more connected as we grow older.

Fantasies Dashed

I had this marvelous fantasy that I was going to be held in a little stone room with bars, and I would be pulled out and used, and then stuck back in there. I thought it would be cool to be a complete object with no rights. When I got into M/s, I realized that would not have worked, since I personally do need the love and the affection of my owner.

I also thought M/s would be a life of never having fights or miscommunication, because there would be a structure where if you do something wrong, you get punished and then everything's fine. I thought that processing would be much quicker, and resolution would be reached much sooner. He thought he would have a relationship with no power struggles. It should come as no surprise that we were both wrong. Just because there is a transfer of authority doesn't mean it isn't very much a relationship in many ordinary ways. It doesn't make you less human.

I thought that he was always going to be in control and steer us faultlessly, that I would always be submissive and super-slave all the time. In real life, we get sick, we have bad days, we mourn. We never expected how often we would need to correct drift and realign with our core dynamic principles. You must work at it, and there's way more work involved in M/s than I ever thought possible. It's worth it, though! If I had to choose again, I would choose my life with Master Dante over and over again. In fact, I do exactly that, every day when I kneel and ask, "Would it please you to accept my service today, Master?"

Our goals keep us focused, and this is the most satisfying work I've ever done in a relationship.

Go Slow

It's important to take your time when you go into a dynamic. You don't have to be collared after six months, or even after a year. The best relationships take time, and it's often those s-types who have been in service for two to three years before they get a committed collar who maintain long term dynamics that inspire others. You need to have some say in how things develop *before* that collar goes on, so going slow empowers the shared dynamic.

It is also important to know that a collar is heavy. It comes with a lot of responsibilities that aren't always easy to bear. It's worth it, but it takes a lot of work, so *take your time.*

Self-Care

Self-care is not just bubble baths and candles. It's hard work. It might be seeing a therapist, or reading self-help books, and constantly figuring out how to improve your service. How do I become a more centered, happy, loving person? For me, that has been a seventeen-year-long journey. I am still learning more about myself, but now I find myself wanting to say no far more often in various areas of my life. Being a woman in your late forties makes you want to say "No!" a lot more for physical reasons, and sometimes it just slips out. That's human, but can sometimes have undesirable consequences in this type of dynamic!

A big part of my self-care consists of internal work. It also involves lots of time on my knees being vulnerable with Master. Somewhere along the line, I realized that I am a strong and loved person who can give love to others, but only when I take care of myself. I have new boundaries with others now. Self-care does mean saying no sometimes because you can't do everything for everybody. As an s-type, you're probably going to be inclined to say yes too often, and to think you can do *all* the things, but you only have twenty-four hours in the day. When you find the right person, be honest about when your spoons are very low, and ask for help managing that.

The Graceful Exit

When setting goals with your M/s partner, remember to include exit goals, because not every relationship is meant to last a lifetime. Some relationships are only for a reason or a season. I learned a lot from the two owners I served before Master Dante, and I will always be grateful for that. An exit strategy needs to be actionable under the worst of circumstances, agreed upon, and ideally written down, because there's nothing worse than a very negative public break-up. Take responsibility for yourself, love yourself, love the partner that you're with even if you don't want to be with them anymore.

Homecoming

As a slave, I think one of the most important things is making your master feel at home and that their home is filled with harmony and peace. Building a home when you have had to relearn loving is hard, but I am finally getting there. Master is *my* home. We are passionate about giving back to our community and we both serve where we can. This is a calling. Like any other true calling, it isn't easy, but it offers more joy, awareness of self and place than most can comprehend. Seventeen years in, I've still only scratched the surface, but one thing I am certain of… it is truly home.

Slave Gaia has been in service to Master Dante Amor for seventeen years as of 2022. She believes in community service, is an associate member of Onyx Pearls Northeast, the secretary of MAsT Metro NY and member of The Poly Exchange. She is also the Master/slave Conference workshop coordinator as and the Education Liaison for MsC Worldwide. She supports her chosen family, House Amor, which includes her beloved slave sisters Sarah and Coco, in all its endeavors. In everything that she does, her focus is Love, because service for her is love in action.

Meet Them Where They Are
MonsignorX

For the record, I have been in a power exchange relationship with my M-type since 2012. During the time of COVID and recent political issues in the United States, along with just aging, things have been challenging at times. This essay is an attempt to explain how to move things along and keep them together when the M-type is having trouble leading the way they did in the past. I will be addressing three challenges we have dealt with over the years, the hardest one last.

By way of introduction, I call myself MonsignorX, and I am a male bisexual using he/him pronouns. My owner, who I will refer to as Daddy, uses she/her. I have known I am some kind of s-type most of my life, but Daddy was the one who introduced me to M/s and showed me things I both loved and thought impossible. Our first contract was in 2012, with an annual review until COVID happened, when everything became very complex and not quite what it had been. But I will address that in Challenge #3.

As an s-type, I have always been attracted to female bodied/energied persons for submission. My experiences with men and others have generally been more egalitarian. I had a previous D/s relationship with unnegotiated M/s elements that went poorly, and those scars led to some deal-breakers for my relationship with Daddy. (To quote Daddy: "Like not telling you that you were in an M/s relationship, and having unvoiced expectations.") Daddy considers my former relationship an emotionally abusive one with unfairly moving goalposts. I frequently suffered massive anxiety and intense feelings of failure for minor offenses which were simply resolved by talking it out in our new relationship. In one case, not being able to find the collar we had used previously affected me deeply, as in the previous relationship I was constantly castigated for misplacing one. Daddy solved this by just buying a bit of chain and a lock at a home improvement store. To her, the symbol should never take the place of what it represents.

For many of these discussions, several key issues are important:

❖ A major element of all of our agreements is that I am subject to my Owner's whims. While these were often sexual, and she was generally the sexual lead, they could involve all sorts of other variations from putting a long piercing needle through my face for one event, what boots I should wear with a kilt, the use of ordeal for our annual "re-up" (new contract), reversing certain gender assumptions, controlling what I might order for dinner (lobster) and many other things. This was a formal line in our agreement for many years.

❖ Daddy has another M/s relationship with her own owner, but it has no transitive properties, although there have been jokes about it.

❖ I have a family and child, which is completely separate from any dynamic.

❖ We are both polyamorous, and all relationships are open and honest.

❖ I am ex-military and she comes from a military family. This affected our use of concepts like "chain of command" in our relationship. For me, it also ties to a saying from my time in the Army of: "Lead, Follow or Get the Hell Out of the Way!" I will return to this later in the essay.

I have chosen to use a Far Past, Past and Current approach to this essay, as this is a long-term relationship and I feel that viewing M/s that way has great value.

Challenge #1: Early Issues: My Loyal, Protective Nature (Dog)

I came from a previous relationship which had strong D/s elements, but also had many major communication flaws and changing expectations. While it turns out that an M/s or O/p relationship was something that would work for me, in the beginning I had false ideas of what one entailed. I have heard a master I know refer to M/s in the context of being a ship captain—you have to know your vessel inside and out, and everyone has the right to expect that of you.

One element that Daddy helped me find at a Leather event was Dog, which is what I call my "pup" side for lack of a better term. This side of me, like any loyal dog would be, is *deeply* protective of Master to the point that I start growling without even thinking of it. This became a challenge in a situation where Daddy was pushing too hard and broke down, and I went into full protective mode and would no longer take commands—and was fetching water and food and keeping people away. Here my M-type felt that it was because she could not focus on command, but I realized in the moment (and later) that I *need* to make sure that the person I serve is safe. My previous relationship had blocked that, which led to massive anxiety.

As a former military executive officer, I expect my commander to be a human being and have frailties, and to be prepared to step in when those frailties make it impossible for the commander to lead in that moment. That in *no* way changes the chain of command; it just changes what I need to take care of in that moment. My owner is still a human being; imperfection and vulnerability is allowed. As a person who loves them, I *need* to know that I can be protective, so long as it is according to previously established protocols. Not being able to protect the people I love creates massive amounts of discord in my psyche.

Daddy insisted on a formal contract because she knew that my previous relationship had included moving goal posts, and a contract would help eliminate many sources of anxiety for me. (My titles in the agreement vary between Boy/Dog/Beast/Bitch). After lengthy discussion of the above, we made the following change to the contract:

> *Boy's first duty is to maintain the physical health of Sir and himself. Any and all other duties, tasks, and orders shall be secondary to this one. If a duty, task, or order is in jeopardy of countermanding this first duty, it is Boy's responsibility to bring it to Sir's attention as soon as the potential conflict is discovered. The ability to communicate this will never be limited, though he shall use all due respect if it is in a public forum. If Boy needs to move, he shall move unless Sir is actively restraining/pushing him. If Boy believes he is experiencing unintentional pain, he shall say something.*

An important realization in our discussions was that, despite many fantasies to the contrary, the commander is human and imperfect. If my owner is having a meltdown due to overwhelming events, I should step in with whatever is needed to let them rest and recuperate. Sometimes that means being ready to feed her cheese due to a sugar crash. Sometimes that means stepping in to finish tasks we were both working on for others because she is exhausted.

Finding what was in my nature was critical to solving this problem.

Challenge #2: Continual Issues: Spiritual Matters

Here we need to talk about my spirituality and religion. I am a practicing Norse Heathen with some internal mystical elements to my practice, a number of pieces of body art, and various connections to spiritual communities. Daddy is an atheist materialist who accepts such practices, but generally has no personal belief in them. She is extremely protective of my interests and safety, however, and some of my spiritual practices do tie into ordeal work. This has been handled in two primary ways:

1) Daddy is in charge of any major ordeals and took charge of a major rage rite that I needed (involving the Norse God Fenrir) and coming to terms with my own anger issues. She has also handled a number of smaller rage and ordeal rites. (I am leaving out the longer story of this as it is something we cover in a class I sometimes teach.)

2) For any spiritual matter that might in some way touch on our relationship, she is fully available and sometimes attends if she thinks that is appropriate. She has stepped in a time or two when someone was trying to use my faith in play to make sure I was safe. Over time, this approach has worked very well.

Challenge 3: Recent Issues: COVID, Politics and Aging -

Obviously, between politics and COVID-19, America since 2016 has been extremely stressful. Some relationships with our communities changed when elements tied to COVID and human rights made themselves known, and issues of personal safety (and the safety of others) came to the forefront. Additionally, we are both getting older, and this has also affected our health, sexual desire and other elements that were originally core to our dynamic.

In the interest of clarity, Daddy and I met when her sex drive was peaking, and some of our dynamic was almost the reverse of classic male/female dynamics, up to and including a literal cave-man-style scene where I was dragged away by my hair to another room from a nearly dead sleep and mounted for her pleasure. I made sure to stay healthy to be able to be able to function to please her, and actually adjusted my workouts to accommodate those needs. Anxiety, age, existential dread and other factors changed this dynamic, and I have had to learn to adapt. We have found that she still finds pleasure in owning me and hurting me, but it is less directly sexual. We now need to set aside time for pleasure and deal with things more deliberately than we used to. While things are not as simple in some ways, I can still find my role, and learn how to behave in ways that nurture and support her while we explore the changes that life brings.

Conclusion

When you are used to only following the desire of your owner and they are unsure of themselves, support often requires thought. For this and other relationships, I think it is critical for both sides to "Meet Them Where They Are". Whether you think of yourself as a vessel, an animal, or a role, a good leader should know your capabilities and how best to use you. It is still your responsibility to know yourself and advise your leader on where you are. They cannot read minds and should not be expected to. You also have to accept—whichever metaphor you use for your relationship—that they will change as well, and that the initial halcyon days will fade, and your relationship will grow in different directions. I have found this to be true both with Daddy and with other things I have faced in life. We have found putting the relationship before the dynamic to be vitally important to our success.

I wish anyone reading this luck in finding the path that works for both of you.

MonsignorX considers himself a bisexual switch male philosopher with strong interests in rage work, male submission, ethics, ordeal, helping the abused, strength and vulnerability. He has been in an owner/property relationship for 8 years. More recently, he has been drawn more to poetry, storytelling and working to help others find their voices, especially submissives who have trouble finding a strong and functional path where their needs are met and strengths recognized.

Followers With Control Issues? That's Me!
dawn

Hi, my name is dawn and I'm a slave/follower with control issues. (This is where you respond with "Hi, dawn!")

There are many situations in my life where people have no clue that I'm a follower. I help produce events. I create and produce my own events like the "Subs in Service Intensive". I'm a Reiki Master and I produce spiritual/energy weekends. I've created vending weekends. I was a director at the local BDSM club. The list goes on and on.

Hell, in my vanilla life before finding kink, the school my sons went to didn't have a Scout group and I couldn't find parent volunteers, so I created and ran a whole Scout pack on my own. Tiger Scouts through Webelos. Since I couldn't find help, I just did it myself.

Before that, at the age of 16, I was the youngest leader in the women's auxiliary of my parents' lodge, nationwide. I was also the youngest leader in the Keyette organization in high school. When I saw something that needed a leader, I ran for it. I feel like I did a great job with these—and I will tie it into my power exchange relationship, because there is a connection. The problem was that at the beginning, once I was in charge, I tended to do great in these positions until I burnt out. I didn't know how to, or want to, delegate anything. I didn't trust people.

I think the reason I wanted to be in charge of things is simply so that I could be in charge. Growing up, terrible things happened to me that I had no control over, and it taught me not to trust those who were "in charge" or "in authority" over me. (And sometimes to not trust people in general.) So if I was in charge, no one could hurt me— and if I did everything myself, I didn't have to trust anyone else.

This attitude worked its way into my first marriage. I wanted someone who could be there for me so that I wouldn't have to be in charge all the time, but it really didn't work out that way. I had to be in charge so that the kids got fed and we had a roof over our head. I hated it. Did I draw that man into my life because I was in a mode of wanting to be in control of situations? Or did I think he had the qualities to be in control, or at least part of the team, and he just let me down? I'm not sure. Anyway, I learned over time that I could be in charge and delegate some items, but I still checked constantly on the person to whom I had delegated a job. (My trust issues again.) I slowly started delegating to the husband ... and realized that was a mistake.

Then I found Internet chat rooms, and as someone who has always had naughtiness trapped inside, I was able to explore a little bit, and found BDSM and power exchange. As I spent time in the chat rooms, it struck me that I had no interest in being a Top or a Domme. Funny—I thought I would have fallen right into one of those positions. But I found that I was drawn to something else: Someone else in charge. Someone else to take care of me. Someone that had my best interest at heart.

I had taken on so much responsibility so young and for so long with no enjoyment, only doing it because it needed to be done, and it fulfilled my mode not trusting people. But here was a role I could take on that was different ... a role where I would *have* to trust the other person and they would be in charge. How scary! How thrilling! But I realized that if I was going to embrace the role of sub/bottom, I was going to have to work on my trust issues and my control issues. That was even more scary.

And that's how I found power exchange at the same time I started on my healing journey. They worked hand in hand. Hell, power exchange was and is part of my healing journey.

The idea of surrendering to someone I could trust? The kinky and slutty part of BDSM was hot as well, but for me it was all about the power exchange. I had to give up this need to control everything around me. Instead, I wanted to surrender all that need, all that mistrust. I wanted to move beyond that. I craved that.

I shared that with Dan—and he had a craving as well, a craving to be responsible for someone, to be in charge. (And the kinky/sexy part was hot for him as well.) It clicked and our friendship turned into something magical. We danced a magic dance, and continue to dance after twenty years.

The thing is, though, I still have to battle that urge to be in control. Dan uses that skill of mine as an extension of his will, and supported me when I decided to become clergy and a Reiki Master and get my college degree—all that stuff is of great benefit to me/us/him. That's not the problem. The problem is when I want to do things my way, even after twenty years. Even after experiencing full surrender, even after discussing how it's what I want and need for my growth and healing, it can still be difficult. Even knowing Dan always has my/our best interests at heart, I still have those moments where I think my way is the best way.

So, I still have control issues … and it still boils down to trust. When I want to do things my way, sometimes Dan lets me, sometimes he puts his foot down and we'll be doing it his way.

I've learned to delegate, and delegate correctly. When we put together our staff for BTL and PXS, it took a couple of years, but I finally heard them when they were saying, "Let us do our jobs which you brought us in here to do." I had to trust that they had it and didn't need me leaning over their shoulder to check on everything. When Dan tells me to do something and it's not how I would do it, I have to trust that he has my/our best interest at heart, and let my fear go.

Now that we've sold the condo and are full-time RVing, I'm seeing my control issues pop up over and over again … and over and over again I have to look at them, and tell myself that we'll be OK. If Dan makes a mistake, he's the type of Leader who will admit to it and fix the problem.

Breathe. Let it go.

This morning, I have my lists out so that I can control as much of tomorrow's move as possible to make it less scary. There is a list on a huge post-it in front of me about prepping for changing campgrounds tomorrow. A list of the food we have in the cabinet and what we still need to buy. A list of what I'm supposed to get done today … laundry is at the top. I'm trying to control as much as possible. Dan is more of a fly-by-the-seat-of-your-pants type of person, so we balance out pretty well. But I imagine some days are harder than others. I know they are for me. Like when I have the departure list all figured out, or any project for that matter, and he says "Nope, we are doing it a different way," and I'm like, "But, but, but…" and he constantly has to rein me in and remind me he's in charge and I agreed to this. After twenty years, I still have to take that breath and make the decision to let go of whatever I had in mind.

To be clear: Yes, Dan and I are a team. Yes, he listens to what I have to say and what my thoughts are on matters. Yes, he gives me space to express my fears and why I think things should be done a certain way ... and because of our power exchange, sometimes he doesn't.

Like I said, it's a lot of work for a Dom who leads someone that has control issues based on fears. I don't want to be in charge, I just want things done my way so that I don't have to worry so much. But, when I turn those fears over and just trust my leader, healing happens. *One day at a time.*

I express those ideas and thoughts and then I choose to step back. And when I can step back and give him the power to make the decisions as we agreed upon so many years ago ... that's when I feel free. That's when I can breathe. The times that I forget to do that— and those times still happen—I don't feel good. I'm not living up to my side of the bargain. I'm not living up to what I agreed to. I'm not being my best self. I'm stepping in the way of the power exchange dance that works so well for us.

When I work at surrendering and get to the point of surrender, I'm sitting in my seat of power—and when I sit in my seat of power, Dan sits in his seat of power. Sometimes it takes a moment to get back to that place of peace, but the work is worth it. The reward is the beautiful dance and the overall feeling of peace.

And then I stumble with my control issues, and I work on it again, and surrender again.

Beauty. Peace. Strength. Empowerment.

dawn is a follower of Daniel Belum's leadership, and has been collared to him for more than twenty years. He has gifted her with the title of belet, and they have worked hard to co-create the magical life they have together. She is a priestess and a Qadishti witch, and her passion is healing, sacred sexuality, and sacred touch. She is also the co-author of Living M/s: A Book for Masters, Slaves, and Their Relationships, *and* Sex, Stories, and Power Exchange.

Surrendering My Sword

slave Rhiannon

I have always been what I would consider a service-oriented submissive. I entered the BDSM lifestyle and soon realized that I was craving a deeper, more complete power exchange. It was suggested to me by my first Dominant partner that I might be a slave, because I assumed that role very naturally in many ways. For example, slave poses were instinctual, though I didn't know what they were called. My body just seemed to position itself in certain ways. Honorifics were second nature, having grown up in the southern U.S., and I immediately understood the benefits of structure and routine. I enjoyed asking for permission to do just about anything.

Indeed, being a slave quelled quite a few of my anxiety issues. With permission from a higher power, I no longer found myself uncertain of social situations or activities. I felt empowered, suddenly held accountable to someone other than myself. I found it easier to set boundaries with other people and to even say "No," which had always been a struggle for me in the past.

I enjoyed challenging myself to push my own limits. I appreciated the self-discipline it took to be a slave, and the introspection it required. Being a psychology major and working in the field of mental health, I understood the benefits of many training techniques that slaves go through and enjoyed the mental gymnastics of behavior modification.

Though I desperately wanted to be a good and obedient slave, though I had spent many years in therapy working on my defense mechanisms and triggers, nothing prepared me for some of the challenges that I would endure during my journey. It is easy to be obedient when one is doing the dishes or sucking cock. It is harder to do so when it requires you to share some of the more intimate inner workings of your mind—things you have never admitted to anyone, or even yourself. Challenges you may have avoided, or accountabilities you have never taken. Patterns of behavior that you do not want to admit are problematic, or bad habits that you aren't keen on breaking.

When one of these issues would arise, it seemed that I would immediately offer a challenge to my Master, of the sort that some would consider it "bratty" behavior. It was as though I would not give in without a fight. Whenever I hit a mental wall, instead of breaking it down, I expected my Master to know how to remove it and if he did not, well then, I guess he wouldn't get what he wanted. After all, just because I was a slave did not mean I was a doormat. I am a strong, incredibly independent single mother. I was fierce and at times, even aggressive when I felt pushed. I could dig my heels in and outright demand that my Master either overpower me, or let it go and let me be "myself". I would give him devotion, loyalty, respect, but I would not depend on him, and I would not do anything that I felt might make me lose my identity as an individual.

One request that comes to mind was his desire for me to beg for sex. This triggered a deep anger in me, and I refused. In my eyes, begging was pathetic. It meant that I was helpless, and at his mercy. It was something that "weaker submissive" people do. It was akin to groveling, in my opinion, and I refused to grovel. I would be vulnerable enough to share my desires, and even ask for what I wanted. But if he did not want to give it to me freely, then I would take his answer with grace. I would not give in to humiliation. I would rather go without. I gave my submission because I *wanted* to, not because I *needed* to. Or so I thought.

Over time, this caused more issues within the dynamic. I was frustrated. His constant rejection of my attempts to engage with him sexually hurt my feelings. Why didn't he want me? Was I just a kink dispenser and if I didn't perform the way he wanted me to, then he was not interested in me? Did he not love me? How could I be so hungry for his touch, time, and attention and yet he was so cold and distant?

I began to give attitude, and I started having emotional outbursts. I started shirking my chores and abandoning my daily routines. I half-assed my writing assignments and stopped doing tasks. I wanted attention, and if he would not give it to me, then I would act out until he punished me. When this didn't work and he didn't give in, I grew more and more agitated. I began to feel like he didn't care about the dynamic. Finally, I broke down. In a puddle of tears and snot, I asked him the questions that had been haunting me for weeks. "Why don't you want me? Is this just a game to you? I thought we were in a relationship."

He all but laughed at the absurdity of the questions. He sat quietly for a moment, letting me sit in my discomfort. And then he said simply, "It is because you are too proud to surrender to me."

This angered me further. I had been obedient. I had worked hard to learn his likes and dislikes; I journaled every day. I expressed to him deep personal thoughts and feelings that I had never told anyone. I created paintings and art at his request. I kept the house tidy and neat, as he expected. I never questioned him. Until recently, I had never given him attitude or showed any disrespect. I trusted him more than I had ever trusted any other man in my life. Did that mean nothing to him? All because I would not grant just one request, did he no longer consider me a worthy slave? Did my boundaries not matter? Had he not been teaching me to stand up for myself, to not give in to others' demands when I did not want to? Did this rule not apply to him as well?

At this outburst of emotion, he shook his head. He said, "You do not know what it means to surrender."

"Is there a difference?" I asked.

"Yes."

Over the next few days, I collected myself. I processed what he said. I began to ask myself what the difference between submission and surrender was. I thought about him saying I was "too proud to surrender," and I asked myself what other things I might have been too proud to do. I knew that begging would not actually harm me in any way, and yet I did not want to do it.

And then I asked myself: *Where does my pride even come from?*

The fact is, that I did not want to be seen as weak, although I knew very well that my Master did not consider me weak at all. He knew, and often reassured me, that I was strong. He taught me that submissives and slaves are some of the strongest people one might ever meet. I knew the strength it took to force myself to be honest when I did not want to be, to do my chores even though I was tired from a long day at work. I knew self-discipline and the pain that can come with it.

Finally, I was able to put a word to the feeling: *Fear*.

I was afraid of being rejected, which ironically, was causing me to be rejected constantly. I feared being vulnerable, helpless, or needy. I knew that if I showed my soft underbelly, that if I took off all my armor, I was exposed and defenseless. And what would I do if I exposed myself in that way, and he took advantage of me? What if he laughed at me? What if I made a fool of myself? He might be able to hurt me in the worst way possible. And worse yet, what if I grew to depend on him, his praise and guidance, his reassurance, his affection, and he left me? I would truly be broken. I did not think I could emotionally or mentally recover from such a blow. I would be humiliated and devastated, all because I humbled myself and did something that made me so vulnerable that I had no choice but to trust him not to hurt me.

Then I thought about that word: *humble*.

Was this way of thinking humble, as a slave should be? Certainly, it was not. In fact, I realized that this fear was nothing but my ego talking. The ego fears being made a fool of. The ego fears what it cannot control. The ego is self-serving—everything that a slave is not. Did I want fear and pride to rule my life? Perhaps this is what surrender means. Giving up what you want to control, deeper than your daily life. Deeper than your secret fantasies. Giving up your fears to someone else, which enables you to overcome them. Giving absolute trust, which I realized I had not done. I was too afraid.

I thought about everything I had been through. I had grown up with incredibly abusive parents who beat me, called me names, and told me that my dreams were unachievable. I had boyfriends that had cheated on me, hit me, and lied to me. I was abandoned by my son's father and forced to raise a child alone at the age of 20. My heart had been broken too many times to count.

Despite it all, I was still standing. I was working through the trauma to give myself and my son a better life. I worked two jobs and put myself through college. I was pursuing my dreams and desires. I had depended on people who had disappointed me, failed me, or abandoned me. I always dusted off, got back up again, and accomplished my goals regardless. I was strong. My *spirit* was not broken.

That was the point when I realized that my spirit *could not* be broken. No matter what happened to me, I would rise from the ashes like a phoenix and carry on, better than before. So, if that was really the case, what was there to fear?

In realizing the depth of my personal strength, I was able to let go of my pride. I no longer had a use for it, as it was a hindrance to my development as a person, not just a slave. I found that it was easier to surrender my heart and mind without fear holding me back from blossoming.

When the dynamic with my Master ended six years later, I was sad. I mourned him for a few months. I considered leaving the lifestyle. Then I remembered this lesson, and I dusted off and tried again. When I found myself in another dynamic, I was not afraid to trust again. I was not afraid to be vulnerable.

I knew that no matter what happened within that dynamic, though it might not last forever, I would recover—and I was not afraid to serve or love again. Through surrender, I realized my personal power. The lesson my Master had been trying to teach me all along.

slave Rhiannon is 31 years old. Her journey into the lifestyle began 7 years ago. Currently she is co-director of the Rochester NY MAsT chapter (Masters and slaves Together International, an educational organization for Authority based relationships). Rhiannon now identifies as a House pet and resides with her Handler in Upstate NY. She is a registered Choctaw Tribal member and considers herself an Indigenous Occultist and sexual healer.

Trusting a Flawed Master

Joshua Tenpenny

How did I develop trust in my master? Well, trust is a funny concept for me. I see it more as a process of observing someone's track record, and making logical predictions of likely future behavior. What's most important to me when it comes to trust is that I know what to expect from someone, whether good or bad. I can trust my master to be himself, and that created the first layer of trust.

I got to know him, and I became increasingly confident in knowing what I could expect from him. There are some things that from very early on, I was very confident of. I was confident from the start that he was a decent guy, that he absolutely no intention of deliberately harming me, or recklessly disregarding my well-being. And he was clearly someone who made consistently better and more responsible life decisions than me, so I trusted him in that way.

I was also very clear from early on that he's got a lot on his plate, and I wasn't going to be his number one priority. He had other responsibilities and commitments that are super important to him, that take a lot of his time and resources, so there were going to be times when he wasn't going to come through on something for me because a higher priority thing came up.

He also made it clear from the start that while he'd done D/s relationships, he had no experience with the type of heavy power dynamic we were pursuing, and honestly, he was skeptical that it could work. It meant I wasn't going to trust his *ability* to master me correctly or effectively, because he was genuinely not sure whether he could do it, whether it could be done at all. But he was committed to trying, and working into it gradually, making sure both of us were comfortable with what was happening. On the other hand, I was confident the basic structure was workable. I trusted the plan, and I was not hesitant to wholeheartedly try to implement the plan under his inexpert direction.

It was not at all hard for me to trust his good intentions and his basic integrity as a human being. Developing trust in his ability to implement those good intentions ... that came more slowly, as he *developed* his ability to implement those good intentions. It was a process assessment and evaluation, of learning what he could do and what he couldn't do, not a process of "learning to trust" in an abstract emotional way.

From the start of our relationship, I was clear on what role I was suited to and what role he expected of me. I had periods later on when I seriously doubted that I'd be especially good at this role, and how close we would get to the relationship I had hoped for, but I knew that we could make *something* work where he was basically in charge.

It did take me a while to come to that point. I was fairly rebellious growing up. I got into my first M/s relationship almost by accident, and I came out of it thinking, "Well, that was an educational experience, at least. I learned I *never* want to do that again!" My first master tried very hard to make it work, but I just wasn't ready. I needed more time to explore my options. I was a kinky switch for some years, primarily a top, but maybe a year or two before I met my present master, I started to realize that there was something about service and surrender and obedience that really called to me. (Thank you, "Miss Abernathy"!) I started bottoming more seriously, exploring control and service, rather than just sensation play. I was actively seeking some type of live-in service relationship prior to meeting my present master, and by the time we got involved I was confident that this was what I wanted.

My master is a total communication whore in ninety per cent of things, coming from a feminist consensus nonviolence background as well as the polyamory community, so he expected to *talk* about *everything* in excruciating detail. And he's a writer, so while we were still living many hours away from each other, he'd write me long things, and give me writing assignments, to work through my thoughts on various topics. This developed a level of mutual understanding that made a solid foundation for trust.

I'd say he initiated most of the heavy intimate discussion type stuff, but I was an enthusiastic participant once I believed he wanted to hear real answers from me, even if they were messy and awful, rather than polite scripted answers. Once we realized we could both be brutally honest with each other, we were both all in. It was an intense and turbulent period, but cracked us both open in ways we had never anticipated being with anyone. That was another milestone of trust—I discovered that I could communicate even difficult subjects and ugly parts of myself to him, and he listened and didn't reject me because I wasn't a perfect slave all the time. Being able to show my whole self without penalty meant I could give my whole self to him.

Another consequence of this mutual openness is that I understood very clearly what he wanted out of the relationship. I knew what parts of the relationship delighted him, and which parts frustrated him, and which parts scared him. It was reassuring to know with some certainty how well his needs were getting met. There was no reason to fear he was secretly resenting something, or dissatisfied with me, because he never showed much hesitance to just tell me. Again, this helped me feel like I knew what I could expect from him.

The most important consequence of this, though, wasn't trusting him but learning to trust myself. During the first few years, we had a lot of arguments. Turning over all your decisions to another person who will inevitably make mistakes with them can be terrifying. Being a slave is a very vulnerable thing. When he would screw up, even on small things, I would freak out. These weren't huge injurious screwups—honestly, his judgment is better than mine on important subjects—but a raft of little things. Spending more money on plumbing fixtures than I would. (What did that say about his judgement and his ability to budget?) Leaving his gardening tools in the rain until they rusted. (What did that say about what he might do to me, also his possession?) These small things became so charged with emotion in the context of this relationship, and the process of working through that taught me how to master my own fears and insecurities.

It was another slave who give me the best advice on this issue. She told me that she trusted herself to be able to handle whatever mistakes her master might make. She was reasonably confident he was unlikely to make terrible and life-destroying blunders, due to his track record. But primarily, she came to believe that she was resilient and strong enough to manage if some plans went sideways. It helped that her master was willing to acknowledge his failures and clean up the mess, including when the mistake was something to do with the slave.

She knew she would not be left alone with the cleanup of the error. I know that my master would do the same thing—he does acknowledge mistakes, apologize, and attempt to find ways to do better next time.

This leaves the final piece of work to me—trusting myself to be sturdy enough to endure whatever errors of information or judgment my master may commit. If his decisions or actions upset me, hurt me, or even harm me, I will endure to the best of my ability. He will assess the situation, with my input, and he will decide what (if anything) should be done (by either of us) to avoid this in the future. If I'm really upset about a situation, no matter who or what caused the situation, the first question is whether I can do anything to be less upset. If we think I need assistance with that, who is the best source of that assistance? If he decides one of us needs to do something to repair the damage, or prevent this sort of thing from happening again, that isn't related to deciding whose "fault" it is, or who was in the wrong. That isn't relevant. We are a team, and no matter what happens, we will work as a team to make this relationship mutually fulfilling. In our nineteen years together, I have never found it productive for either of us to focus on blame and forgiveness. He'll apologize when he thinks he's in the wrong, but from my perspective, there is nothing to forgive. Both of us are likely to regret what happened. Both of us are motivated to help prevent either of us from causing or coming to harm in the future. Both of us are committed to a relationship where he is in charge, and I do what he says. That, more than anything, is where we need to be for our relationship to weather anything that is thrown against it.

Submission Story
Twuntalope ksst

My Master and I met in high school in 1986. My parents required me to do some extra-curricular activities, and being an extremely shy, nerdy introvert, I chose the Dungeons and Dragons club. My Master was the president of the club, and I was attracted to him from the first sight. I know this because I wrote it in my (very cringeworthy) diary that day. We became friends. It was about a year later that this other guy I was dating happened to ask me, as we were breaking up, "Is there anyone else at school you 'like'?"

I said yes, and told him who it was. He later went to my future Master and said, "You should ask her out; she really likes you." He did, and that was pretty much that. My Master went away to college, but we kept up a constant flow of letters back and forth; eventually he graduated, and we moved in together, and a few years later we got married. Years passed, moves happened, children came along. I was a stay-at-home mom and he was a veterinarian. We bought a small farm and a lot of animals. It was a very good life, but one thing that caused friction between us, and not the sexy kind of friction, was sex. He always had a much higher drive for it than me, and I went through several periods of extreme slumpage in the sexual desire area. I think part of it was caused by hormonal birth control, but I'm not sure that was the whole explanation. It's very hard to become interested when you just ... aren't. We even went to a marriage counselor at his insistence, but I felt like they were just ganging up on me to harangue me into doing things I didn't want to do, and I refused to go back for a second session.

If only the marriage counselor had said "You just need to tie her up and beat her ass to get her in the mood," but of course they don't say things like that. BDSM wasn't on our radar at all. I didn't consider myself a masochist at all, which makes me wonder if masochists are born or made? My Master would make occasional comments like "We should become Baptists or (insert other patriarchal religion here) so that you would have to obey me." As a strong feminist married to an atheist, I would always laugh it off.

When the internet came along, I would occasionally look up stories about bondage, and I read novels which had some fairly strong subjugation/ownership themes with waaayyy too much interest. Finally, I found a BBS message site which had people who talked about living D/s lifestyles and I was really intrigued. They made it seem like it wasn't just a fantasy, but could fit into reality. I went to my Master and asked if I could be his submissive, and if he would tie me up and spank me. He agreed to try it, thinking it was just a short-term fantasy thing, but the more we "played", the more I wanted, and the more he asked for. I began calling him Master almost right away; it just seemed right to me, and he liked it. It really was falling down the rabbit hole, as people describe frequently.

The First Hurdle: Acclimating to my extremely intense feelings about this, and my fears that he wouldn't want it as much as I did. It's hard to admit, but this led to some temper tantrums on my part (what am I, five?) and that led to some punishments from him. A lot of the work on this issue was done in my head, on my own recognition that I wasn't as sanguine or accepting as I wanted to be of his wishes and desires. I talked to other submissives online and learned about mantras, and how to be a better submissive in my head.

On his end, one of the issues was that he wasn't extremely sadistic, but he did like the effect that certain methods of playing hard had on me. He didn't want to *hurt*-hurt me, and he felt a little bad about it, being raised as most men are not to hurt women, ever. But I reassured him several times that I liked and wanted it, and my body's reaction certainly encouraged him, and he was completely thrilled by getting to finally have all the sex he wanted, any time and in any way that he wanted it. I thought being submissive meant never saying no, so I just stopped saying no to anything he wanted, even if it was things that I'd been saying no about for the past twenty years. Together we gradually grew in a sadism-masochism dance until neither of us felt weird or uncomfortable about it all. But it wasn't just about the beatings, it was every part of life that I became agreeable about, including things like him getting a gun or new video game systems, or sex with other women.

In some cases, it was hard for me to get over what I wanted and become accepting of what he wanted. The first challenge was a simple order to go grocery shopping and take the kids with me so he could stay peacefully at home by himself. All I felt like doing that day was sitting at his feet. But I went grocery shopping, which was the easy part. The hard part was changing my own mind around so I didn't feel like I was put upon to do an unpleasant chore, but came around to feeling like I was happy and doing a good thing in serving. It was a mental challenge that I overcame, and once one hurdle is overcome, it makes the next hurdle and the one after that easier and easier until they don't feel like hurdles and obedience becomes natural. Some of that was my own internal work, but we did have some punishments also. The first time I refused an order, we'd only be sort of D/s for a couple of months. The dishes, through long tradition in our marriage, belonged to whoever didn't cook. Since I was cooking all the time, he was doing the dishes—but one night he told me that I had to wash the dishes. I refused, and received a punishment, which wasn't terribly heavy but emotionally felt terrible to me in that I hadn't lived up to our standard of obedience. So I washed the dishes, and kept washing them. (Although I still hate dishwashing.)

It was about five months into a D/s relationship when I asked him if I was more of a submissive or more of a slave. He said he thought I was more of a slave, but if I really wanted to be a slave, he had a couple of conditions he wanted me to agree to. One, that he could have sex with anyone else. Two, that I would have sex with anyone else that he chose (assuming those people consented, of course). I agreed to those conditions, but in the back of my mind all I could think was, "Who is going to want to have sex with a couple of middle-aged married folks?"

Plenty of people, as it turns out.

I don't recommend this approach to other people, this kind of ultimatum, because it tends to go wrong in several different directions. But sometimes you do things the wrong way and it works out OK anyway. One of the useful things he did to make sure it worked out for both of us was that before we had played with any other people, he told me to make a list of all the things that might make me feel jealous, and to put them in order of from least to most jealousy-inducing for me. That way he could get a feel of what was going on in my mind and not just assume he knew what activities would bother me. (Which he didn't do before he asked because it wasn't something that had ever come up before.) He began with the easy end of my scale, and didn't really go through all the way to the hard end. In case you are curious, the most jealousy-inducing thing I could think of was that he had another girlfriend that he took out to dinner, leaving me at home alone. I guess I most feared being left out—and also, eating at restaurants was a rare treat for us then. It turned out for me that watching him fuck others was better than having my own private porn show, and induced no jealousy.

There were lots of times that we played with other people when it was simply a good time, and no unpleasant emotions or jealousies came up. There were times when I needed reassurance and he always gave it to me. After the first time he told me to fuck another man, I felt a bit nervous the next day thinking about what I had done (slut shaming myself, just a little bit). But his reassurance made all the difference, and soon it was all good. Other times, I feared that I had become boring, and he would prefer new people to me, but he always reassured me and called me his "First Choice Cunt", which I really liked.

I had a hard time with doing things that didn't feel very submissive to me. At times he wanted me to tie him up do pleasurable things to him (he was never into pain). It felt all wrong and topsy-turvy in my head, but he continued to work on my mindset and insist that I do those things until I was able to do it (and I even enjoyed it). I wasn't *being* dominant; I was putting on a performance to entertain and give pleasure to my Master.

The Second to Last Hurdle: One time I decided I'd had enough of being a slave. I had been feeling major angst about all kinds of service for at least nine months, and I hadn't really brought it up as a serious problem. I may have mentioned it as a problem in not feeling very slavey, but usually a caning or flogging would sort that out. I feel badly that when I told him I didn't want to be a slave, it hurt him; but I also feel no regret because it was that short break, just a few weeks, of trying not to be a slave that made me realize that I didn't really want to be anything else. I was his slave, and it ran too deep to change. I appreciated everything a lot more after that short break. Some minor things were changed, but all the important bits of our M/s relationship were left intact.

The Last Hurdle: In July of 2020 my Master was diagnosed with cancer and our emotional resources were tested in every way possible. It made all my previous struggles look like a minor stumble on the playground of childhood. As treatment after treatment failed to work, the most important person in my life was doomed to pain, suffering, and eventually death.

The doctors didn't give us much hope, and with each passing month the slim hopes we had were repeatedly dashed. I felt that if he died, I only wanted to fling myself into his funeral pyre. I couldn't face life without him. He told me that I was not allowed to kill myself, that I had to be strong and to go on. I am grateful for that now, because there is a lot to live for even after part of you dies. There were many times I had to find resources within myself and outside of myself, simply to go on. I drew upon spirituality and therapy and revelation from the Universe. I had to become my Master's strength at times because of what the disease was taking from him. I had to make decisions, and near the end, completely take over because he had become confused and disoriented. The last hurdle of our relationship was taking care of him to the best of my ability as he passed.

My pseudonym is ksst, or Twuntalope ksst on Fetlife (how that name came about from my Master is another story I won't go into). I became interested in BDSM in 2011 and then shortly after that in M/s. I was a stay-at-home mom/sheep farmer for many years and currently I'm still raising sheep in the Midwest of the USA, training sheep herding dogs and working almost full time in a clinic.

Recapturing A Fallen Dynamic

Anne Campbell

Drew and I have been together for twenty-five years, and while we played a bit with a power dynamic when we first started, we put that aside after we had a child and during the period she was growing up. When she got old enough to be more or less independent, we started turning our focus back to each other, and we started our M/s relationship in earnest about ten years ago.

At the beginning, we had the honeymoon period like everyone does. Even though we weren't new to each other, we were new to this style of relationship, so we had a crazy, wonderful first few months. We created lots of rules and protocols, many of which we later ended up dropping because they got to be onerous, which I also think everyone does when they first start an M/s relationship. We had some of the usual bumps in the road, including miscommunications, insecurities, rules that were too intense or not intense enough, but where we really hit the roughest part of our relationship was when Drew became disabled.

We came back from a trip to California, and Drew felt flu-ish and under the weather, thinking they had maybe picked up some bug, but they ended up diagnosed with fibromyalgia after a few months of extreme fatigue and pain. They then suffered through several years of bad fibro flares, including bad exhaustion where they slept up to sixteen or eighteen hours a day. That really put a strain on our relationship—as it would on any relationship—but from my point of view, the hardest part was just feeling like we were barely getting through each day in survival mode. We didn't really have the bandwidth to put anything into our relationship, and it felt like the M/s just fell off. I wasn't feeling any dominance from Drew because they were just focused on getting through the day, trying to feed themself and stay alive and not be in horrible pain.

It's difficult to say what improved the situation, because while we were struggling to figure it out, they did begin to feel physically better and recover. They still have fibro flares occasionally, but it's more or less in remission now. That was a turning point in our relationship, but it wasn't something we did on purpose. But as we look back on it and talk about it now, we both believe that there were things we could have done better.

I was often saying, "I don't feel any dominance from you anymore—you're just sort of here, and we just have a vanilla relationship at this point because there isn't any vestige left of the protocols we set up, or any more of the emotional intimacy of dominance and submission. It's all disappeared." And Drew's point of view while they were still very sick was that they were just trying to survive it, so how could I ask them to do more than that? They felt it was an unreasonable demand, and that I was putting undue pressure on them to do things they were not physically capable of doing. We had a lot of difficult discussions about what we could have done differently which could have given us the feeling we'd had of our M/s relationship still being intact, even though we didn't have very much energy to spend on each other.

As we look at it now, there were a lot of things we could have been doing that we didn't do. I had to do a certain amount of physical care for them—for example, bringing them whatever they needed when they were in bed for so many hours in the day—and I could have done that with more of a mindset of service. I could have seen that as a manifestation of what my submission to them was at the time. No, it's not very glamorous to be bringing ibuprofen or ice packs or snacks to someone in bed, but that was something I could have framed in a way that fed my submission a little bit more.

From their point of view, they think that while they may not have been physically capable of doing much kinky play or sex or physical romance-stuff, they could have—without expending any more energy than he otherwise would—asked for these simple things in a way that used my title as their s-type, or incorporated some gesture that reminded us both of our dynamic together. When we look back now, we can see in hindsight that we could have done things differently, and that would have cut down on the resentment we both had for each other.

I thought I was not feeling their dominance, and they thought I was being demanding—and we were both right, and both wrong. We could have worked together against the problem instead of working against each other, because I think that's when we're at our best. I believe that holds true for any type of relationship, but even more so for M/s dynamics. It felt like we had both slipped into being each other's adversary, even though that was not conducive to love and affection and closeness. If we had it to do over, that's the main thing we would change—looking at it as the two of us against the problem, and how we could solve it together, rather than fighting with each other about what the other one was doing wrong.

Lots of couples end up with someone having a temporary or permanent disability or illness—someone's had surgery, someone's had a baby. These situations come up, and they may be temporary or long-term, and either way, if you want to stay together, the idea is to team up against it.

Anne Campbell is a queer switch who has been partnered with her favorite person for over 25 years. She lives in Orlando, Florida, but is a New Englander at heart and an expatriate member of MAsT Mass.

Serving Through Trouble with Grace
Railen Panther

I started out reading the Gor books, which I'm sure a lot of people from my era were familiar with. I read the Gor fantasy about what a "slave" is—all the positions and the abject submission and the "no will" and the "no self" and all that. I wanted that fantasy—to be chained to the bedpost and to sleep in a cage and to have no will of my own. And that's great for a role-play scene; it's acceptable for short periods, like a Saturday morning or a weekend. It's part of what spices up a relationship.

But any relationship, whether it's D/s or full-time M/s, has to live in reality. It's got to be a conversation between two people who start out as equals. It's one person saying, "I have needs and wants," speaking to another person who also has needs and wants. Those needs and wants may be coming from different perspectives, but ideally, they interconnect. "I enjoy and get pleasure from subjugating someone." "I enjoy being subjugated." When those two people can come to an understanding that makes the relationship work, they can make great things together. It's that synergy between the two of them which makes a D/s or M/s relationship really click. But both need to come to the table with the understanding that the other person has true value— that's what makes these relationships really shine, and work long-term. I think that's something that new people going into a relationship may not have the perspective or longevity to understand fully.

I think that a lot of new people get into this, and they think they know what they want, and they find someone else who thinks they know what they want, but they really don't know how this works. They may thrash around until they figure out how it works, or they may end up working with someone who has the perspective to tell them how it works. It takes a while to figure out what makes both you and your partner tick, where the yin and yang lies between you that makes you fit together well.

It's certainly easy to find porn, and to watch a lot of scenes of BDSM play, of people being whipped or beaten (or doing the whipping and beating), and think, "God, that's hot! I'd like to do that." But you need to understand that's a performance, and it doesn't tell you about the dynamics that go into a long-term relationship. There are consequences for every one of those acts. Mistress and I have gotten to a point where as much as we enjoy a sexualized or pain-based scene, we value even more the cuddling that we do afterwards. That's really just as good as anything we do in sex swings or bondage, because of the closeness it brings to us. In a lot of ways, it's like the scene is the foreplay for the physical and emotional connection of the cuddling. Obviously, this will be different for everyone, but it's the intimacy of the whole set of acts which drive it for us.

When entering a relationship, some people desire that closeness and some people don't, but it's important that when someone is first coming into this lifestyle and is starting to investigate these things, they start with baby steps in order to figure out whether it's the acts or the closeness which follows that they really want. One of my mantras is: There's always tomorrow. You don't have to do everything today. You don't have to push harder than you feel comfortable doing. You don't have to hit milestones on a regular schedule. If you're doing these things with someone who isn't going to disappear tomorrow, you don't have to explore every boundary tonight. If you try to push yourself or them to go further and faster, you may go one boundary too far, for either yourself or them. When that happens, it's very common for the other person to pull back, and then you feel ghosted and wonder what happened. Leave things at a comfortable place, because then you can always start again and pick up where you left off. Build on what the two of you have made solid rather than bolting ahead too fast.

Negotiation can be very difficult, because you don't know what you don't know. You may have no idea what is going to feel good until you've experienced it. You may cruise along in the early stages, thinking, "Yeah! This is hot!" and then you might do the emotional equivalent of "More, more! Push it in hard!" Then suddenly somebody's hurt, and somebody feels bad for hurting them, and even if you say, "Nah, it was OK, I healed up after a couple of days," the other person may still say, "I don't want to do that anymore." And now two people are hurt because of overenthusiasm. You need to remember that your partner may find emotionally difficult limits the hard way as well. It's better to have good boundaries, and to have said, "I feel kind of bad because you didn't push this harder," and let them say, "Well, maybe next time we can," or "I'm not comfortable with that." I think it's important for new people to recognize that it's harder to go back than to go on.

My biggest struggle as a slave is coping with my Mistress's disabilities. I do a lot of anticipatory service, and I like to solve problems, and it's hard when I want to find solutions for situations where there don't seem to be any solutions. Sometimes there might be medical solutions, but I'm not the person who can fix that.

I know that with her chronic illnesses, sometimes the best solution is sleep, and I have to be OK with that. Lately her sleep pattern has been to go to bed around 11 p.m. or so and sleep until noon. I bring her morning medicine at 8 a.m., and then she goes back to bed, and I go to work. I eat lunch with her when she gets up at noon, and then I go back to work while she putters around the house; we watch a movie together in the evening, and then go to bed again. On the weekends, of course, we can spend more time together. But as someone who does anticipatory service, being able to step back and not attempt to find a solution to this issue is hard for me. I'll think to myself, "Well, if I brought your medication to you at 6 a.m. instead of 8 a.m., would you be able to get up earlier?" And I have to step back, because it's not my job to design her day around what I think would suit her better.

She is doing better and has been more stable during this past year than she's been in quite some time, and I have to remember that if this is working, don't try to fix it. Coming to that understanding has been kind of a revelation. There have been times over the past many years when I have been challenged to figure out a solution in the moment, where Mistress has been in a real health crisis. Being both her husband and her devoted slave, the person who cares for her more than anyone, I was driven to coax her down. "Look, I care about you so deeply! We can get through this together!" For me, that was a service to her, because I do care about her that deeply, and because that's part of my expression of who I am. I don't know if all or many husband or boyfriend-types feel that way—maybe they do, maybe they don't –but we met as Mistress and slave, and that's who I am to her. I'm her Panther, and she is my Queen and my Goddess, and I don't want to see anything bad happen to her.

Sometimes my service to her is to work with her on steps to get to the resolution of the problem—to remind her that she has tools she can use, or to talk through options with her in the moment. She's been through a lot of medications, as many people with these disabilities have been, but the current best one is medical marijuana to manage symptoms. Part of my service to her is to remind her that it's not as big a crisis as it feels like to her in the moment of pain. We've developed a lot of emotional intelligence quotient around communicating about her disabilities. I can describe the familiar symptoms that I see, and in reflecting that back to her, she is much better able to recognize symptoms in herself, and to intercept them and do what is necessary to help herself. We've been together for seventeen years, and we're finally getting this down to a science.

How I cope with this emotionally is to focus on successes, even the small ones. It can be really frustrating when life circumstances make everything seem like failures, but if you can find little successes and joys to focus on, that can pull you through. As a slave in this situation, it's important to me that my Mistress acknowledges that I did something right. If you're with a partner who is always focused on your failures, that can be extraordinarily demoralizing, but a partner who can regularly recognize your successes can make the relationship a lot stronger. Yes, you'll both have failures, but if you both recognize each other's positive actions, you can keep your heads above water. As an example, Mistress said this morning that she really appreciates how neat and tidy the kitchen looks, despite all the hours I've been spending at my paying job, which made me happy to hear. On the other side, she's been trying to spend more time up on her feet during the day, and she managed to vacuum the carpet and cook us a great dinner, so I expressed my appreciation for that.

Recognizing each other's successes builds confidence, and gives you a daily foundation to keep the relationship more stable. Yeah, shit happens, and yeah, we'll both make mistakes, but we'll do good things too. I'm naturally more of a pessimist—at my day job, stuff goes to shit all the time, and if I were to focus on that, I would never turn on the computer in the morning! Mistress taught me another mantra: We did the best we could, knowing what we knew. If we knew then what we know now, we might have done something different, but it's OK—we're still on the right track.

When it comes to obedience, one of the qualities both Mistress and I think is important is respect, and I will obey out of respect. Mistress and I sometimes have discussions about decisions, and they may tend to be disagreements, but they are never arguments. She'll say, "I'm going to do this," and I'll say, "Well, you probably should do this." "No, I'm doing this." "Well, if you do it like this, it will probably be better in XYZ way." "No, I'd rather do it like this." That's the point where I remember that I respect her and I say, "OK." Mistress gets her way, and I will obey her. I don't often lay down the "Only if it pleases you, Mistress," line, which some slaves use to communicate that they really don't want to go along with an order—or rather, it's usually sarcastic. "Let's watch the Kardashians!" "Only if it pleases you, Mistress."

I am pleased to obey her, but I know that's not easy for everyone. Obedience is an emotional contract that requires respect on both sides. You need to pay into the relationship to be able to withdraw from it, so if you're asking someone to do something which is against their grain, the cost will be higher. If you're always withdrawing from the relationship and not giving back enough to cover it, the well is going to run dry eventually and the other person will be unable to give more. That's a difficult position to put somebody in. You can't ask and ask without paying a lot back.

As a final piece of advice: You can't sleep chained to a bed all the time, because it's inherently unsafe—and those safety issues have sometimes frustrated my "fantasy heart". We have some psychiatric cuffs, nice leather padding and post with a slide lock and a key, and Mistress always made sure to clip the key to the cuffs when I was in long-term bondage, where I could reach them. And I wanted to be absolutely helpless, because that's what should be happening, right? But she would always leave a key within reach. At one point I got a set of four locks that were keyed alike so that I could be chained spread-eagled, and again she would always clip the keys within reach. I realized finally that she was wise to do that, because if she had a problem that she couldn't control, she wanted to make sure that somebody was able to unlock me—and since we were the only two people in the house, that was going to be me.

So when it came to play, she was the "sane" in Safe, Sane, and Consensual. In spite of how it defeated my fantasy of helplessness, she was smarter about it than I was. There's always got to be somebody watching out for you, and if it's not you, it's got to be your partner. So pick a partner who will watch out for you ... even when you don't want them to.

Railen Panther is the president of the New England Dungeon Society, and past director of MAsT Massachusetts. He cares very deeply for people who engage in this lifestyle. He values education, but at the same time he appreciates the social aspects of this lifestyle, and he and his Mistress have a special spot in their hearts for newcomers.

Dreaming of Genie: The Collar-Spaced-Out Nightmare Who Broke My Brain

Reiver Scott

"... *Excellent! The brat just disappears with the collar. Look at that, the mighty Reiver is just my little subby. Let's see you in that submission pose. That's it. Arch your back a little more. Legs a little wider. Oh, you were listening. Good girl.*"

There's an imperceptible tug on the D-ring of the collar, correcting my form. A haze of subspace pulls me in and under, my body replicating his desires. "Thank you for taking your time with me," *I murmur.*

He has this toppy chuckle, a sound I'll never tire of hearing. "It's beautiful."

"Beautiful?"

"*All this anticipatory, natural protocol you have. I don't even have to teach you it. You know exactly what to do, what to say, because this is who you truly are, right? Who'd have thought it was all in there under the snark and reiving?*"

Warning: Contains Nuts

Every Bard is given a *tuath*, a tribe, and you, good kinky friends, are it, for me.

As a storyteller of course I want to tell you the funny and the nice, hot tales of kinkery. But this is no happy-ending story. It's a cautionary tale of star-crossed lovers, a tragedy, in which I'm both the storyteller and the damsel-in-distress. It features frank discussion about collar wreckage and a terrible ordeal prior to, and following, release. So, before we begin, there are a few cautions.

The first version of this essay was placed in my blog in our internet community commons, where I managed to worry my friends, and, not coincidentally, a few Serious Leather Masters™, who stumbled into the discussion, read it, and were horrified, and started writing to me with deep and well-intentioned (and gratefully received) Opinions. You will doubtless form opinions too. Masters and Charges—in this essay I'll use the terms Master and Charge, and I'm using the term Master in a gender-neutral sense—read my writing and then opened up, in the discussion and privately to me by email and direct message, about how release from their collars affected them, both at the time, and in subsequent dynamics.

This essay in its shorter form triggered a lot of people. It's a dark story, folks. It could get you somewhere soft. So, it probably goes without saying that this is a vulnerable piece of writing that carries with it discussion of mental health, and the agony of collar wreckage. If you're needing to take care of yourself today, that's the content advisory. These pages will be here for you on a better day.

There's another caveat and perhaps a more complicated one, and that has to do with blame, and shame, and why it's the antithesis to real growth. Here in Scotland, at least, we're trying as a *tuath* to normalize incident reports to allow for no-blame reflection on scenes or even dynamics which go awry, so we can learn and revise our practice, if necessary, rather than just live in denial, shame, or self-flagellation. My former Master and I have discussed this, and he's had sight of drafts, of the things I've written about our dynamic. There are times and places in the Bardic traditions for the blistering satires that unseat the unjust kings—but this is not one of them, and he is not one of those kings. I hold no grudge or grievance against him. I have no wish to shame him, degenerate him, or disrespect him. Quite the opposite. In my heart and soul, this flawed and beautiful man is kept in a place of deep respect, and high honor. Show me the "master" who claims they've never erred in the dance of power, and I will show you a bullshit-merchant with smoking underwear.

Reflection is a necessary part of what we do and who we are, or it should be. He could have demanded I remain silent. It would have made him an epic cockwomble, but he could have, and I have strong views about kiss-and-tells. and respecting people's privacy. It would have made healing harder, but I'd have kept my silence. Specifically, he told me I had the absolute right to my own story and to my memories. He let me—no, enabled me—to stand in my truth, and in my power, despite what it cost him. For that, he deserves, and has, my full respect. (Also, I took no lasting harm, I'm healing in love and power, but if you're worried, my inbox is open to most.) The mettle and measure of Mastery is the ability to respect the sovereignty, integrity and honor of your current and former partners. That takes courage, and anyone who has that courage deserves my respect.

The style of M/s that I'm writing about here could be more rightly termed "Owner/property" in which the Master had a vast degree of control over nearly every area of my life for the duration of the contract. All in, boots wet. That's what "the collar" means in this essay, but it also means the literal collar, the fetishistic symbol of all the power sunk behind it. Going in, I knew that this was edge work: a completely new area of BDSM for me, one in which I had no idea how I would respond to the things he would do. M/s educators will advise s-types and M-types considering this form of deep power exchange or transfer to focus hard on compatibility and values—and not just sexual compatibility. If Shit Happens, that's what's going to get you through the bad times.

But one of the things which makes this cautionary story so terribly sad is the degree of compatibility my Master and I had. The collar didn't wreck for want of compatibility.

The cruelest twist of fate here is that my Master and I hit every beat which should have made us, damn it, a near-perfect match. We had everything going in our favor. We were perfectly aligned in our leftist, anarchic politics. We got on extremely well (and still do), both of us activists in the same political movements for Scottish sovereignty. We aligned even just as friends with the same taste in books, poetry, and music, and where we differed were points for deep and fulfilling discussion and exchange of ideas. We were compatible in that we both practiced adjacent, animistic forms of earth-based spirituality. We genuinely liked one another. And hoooooooooah boy. Us, together in an SM scene? We're talking nuclear fission level heat, folks. Deep, wild passion, a full tilt fucking beautiful dance of trust and power, each of us moving in the perfect steps of erotic resonance. A tango of tangos. Rigger to bunny, Master to Charge, Sadist to masochist. Right now, there are kinksters all over the world lighting candles to the love gods, praying for the sort of compatibility and connection we had (careful there, Eros is a Needle Top and does so love His hook-sports). For the love of the ancestors, we even had the same sun and moon signs—

though oftentimes I do wonder what dark aspects crossed in our fixed and silent stars.

And although we'd been practicing very different styles of kink (in my usual modes I'm an egalitarian bedroom-only slap-and-tickle anarchokinkster and he is a man keyed to heavy conquest, control, receipt of sexual and domestic service, in every way what we'd term a Master) we both were adults who adhered to the Consensual, Risk-Aware, Shit Happens ideas of edgy kink. We both knew we were running risks and trusted our genuine regard for one another and commitment to the principles of kinky consent to weather what storms we were risking.

As I described it to someone who was alarmed for my wellbeing in the discussion to the first version of this essay, it's best to think of what happened to me like a peanut allergy. What if someone makes you a peanut butter sandwich, a sandwich you found otherwise delectable, and you don't know you have a peanut allergy? Now let's suppose no one knows about peanut allergies. Let's suppose there are no patient accounts, no medical literature, no peer-reviewed immunology studies, no guidance in cookbooks, nothing in the Sandwich-Chefs-and-Munchers-Together classes. Let's suppose peanut butter is the main ingredient in nearly everything you make, everyone says that peanut butter is the best way to make a sandwich, and no one has told you, nor have you ever observed, this could be a problem?

Can the chef be blamed or derided for giving you the sandwich if neither he nor you knew about the allergy? If neither they, nor you, knew peanut allergies were a thing, and you did actually like peanut butter right up until the point of anaphylaxis?

We were consensual and risk-aware (or we thought we were). And Shit Happened, folks. As it turns out, I have a psychic "nut allergy". This is what Shit Happens looks like. This is your heads-up, sandwich connoisseurs, that allergies can be a thing.

It goes without saying that I'm not placing my Master in the stocks here. I bear bone-deep loving respect for this man. He danced edges with me that he'd done with no other. I'm grateful to him for the time he took with me, and that will never change.

Even though our dynamic . . . contained nuts?

We're standing in the holy place of pre-Christian worship where he'd collared me. The wind whips light weals over my bare neck, the full Samhain moon arching high above the mountains over our heads, the heavens strewn with stars. He's all shadow, his voice a soft susurration of light, and dark as he speaks the formal words of release. The sound of running water from the river cutting through the glen below us swirls all around us. I kiss his hands. The little band of leather he's just removed lies limp in my fingers.

"Thank you for taking your time with me."

"Thank you for your service, Reiver. I'm so sorry it went the way it did."

"Ach, don't be." I quip, trying to hide the shake in my voice. "You're the best Master I've ever had."

He barks a bitter laugh and pulls me into a huge bear hug. "You've no standard to measure me against." There's wetness on my cheek. I've brought my Mast—no, my companion—to tears. And the tears are also mine.

Could the Shit Happens have been avoided? Maybe. But only, perhaps, if he or I had come across accounts when researching our kinky inclinations like the one I'm giving here. Yet for that, there's a degree of vulnerability required that's truly daunting for an s-type trying to swim, bleeding, in a community that still has its fair share of sharks. Maybe that's a reason why accounts surrounding collar wreckage are so scant, or else inarticulate, trauma-filled emotional spews where no sense can be made besides acknowledgement of the terrible pain the s-type is in. The D-types and M-types are notably, notoriously silent in the "Recovery After Release" groups, their missing self-reflection vaster than Space, a gaping void between the lines of an s-type's howling pain.

When I got over the drop enough to start writing about my beautiful and terrifying excursions into heavy power-exchange, I truly "swithered" (a Scots word for which there's no real translation which indicates being in two-or many-minds about doing something)—aye, I swithered—over writing about the effect the collar had on me because of the real stigma surrounding frank discussion of mental health. And, even now, I still worry a wee bit that the collar broke something in me that can't really be fixed, or else exposed a fatal weakness, indicating my architecture-award-winning Mind Palace just isn't up to code.

For a while—though clarity comes with time—I had no idea what had happened to my brain, and nowhere, but nowhere in The Discourse™ on M/s or power exchange had I read an account of a reaction to a Master's collar even remotely similar to mine. I checked my kinky library. I trawled the pages in the internet power-exchange groups. I read every Most Masterly Master book by Master McMasterson, Expert Master, I could find.

And I couldn't find a single, solitary account of what happened to me happening to anyone else. Maybe it's one of those things we just don't talk about, hmmm? Until someone goes first, and her Fetlife inbox fills up with letters from s-types with similar experiences.

Theater Prop or Spirit Fetish?

The Master whose collar I was wearing, if you asked him (and I did) would tell you that his collar was pure theater, pure semiotics, a mere prop to get the sub in the right headspace and most importantly, quell defiance. Or, if you asked him in his darker, more sadistic modes, quell any sense of agency. Private theater, with all its archetypal masks. Yet my Master reacted very strongly, and negatively, to the idea that a s-type could own their own collar, and turn it over the Master for the duration of the M/s Arrangement. That visceral emotional reaction was a little extreme for a mere "theater prop". Probing a little deeper, my Master revealed in countless ways that the collar to him was a sacred thing, something imbued with deep mysticism and power.

And what is magic, if it's not changing consciousness at will (as English Occultist Dion Fortune wrote)? That wasn't a piece of fetish fashionwear he had around my neck; it was almost as if it had a spirit all its own, and in the old myths the gods of theater—the drama gods—are also the gods of shifting consciousness and the means by which we reach those altered states. And boy oh boy, did they take me on one hell of a trip.

My brain loved the altered state of collar space and also simultaneously hated it. With the collar on I was not the keen analyst and mistress of my fate with a mind that shines like justice and a wit to slay the pleather-masters and fake internet "dumminants". I'm not the dark brat of brats. I'm not the smart-ass challenging my top to beat me until I was bothered (she broke a wooden spoon over my arse). I'm not the blistering satirist and consent writer with Unicorn Poachers in her pistol sites.

No. I'm Genie—a vulnerable sylph bottled up in my own psychosexual being.

Genie's the name I give myself here so as not to expose my legal name, but she's also an archetype. Growing up through the "Satanic panics" of the 80s and 90s, my Xian parents deemed TV shows like *Buffy the Vampire Slayer* inappropriate for their daughters to watch, but were perfectly fine with us watching re-runs of wholesome 1960s family entertainment sit-coms where a woman pranced around in harem pants taking instructions literally and calling her husband "Master". Who'd have thought my kinky magical self would manifest like that?

Aye. Apparently, I'm Genie in a bottle, on a beach somewhere, waiting for some space cadet to crash-land, rub her the right way and uncork her. I had no idea she was even there, until the day he collared me. At which point the M/s contract and the associated collar stopped being theater props, and became something far more akin to baneful, transformative magic. Something which functioned more like a boot code for a systems override initiating the conversion to .slave protocols.

This is in no way a slight or disparagement of the Master. He had no idea how his collar would affect me (and never having taken a collar, neither did I). He told me he'd not treat me any differently from any of his other girls, and as far as I know, he didn't. Entering service, I knew what his style of kink was. He was nothing but honest with me; I knew he was an edge player and a guy who got off on control. Facing the fear of control was one of the (stupendously dark and complicated) reasons why I was kneeling on the floor of his tricked-out lair and in his collar in the first place.

Ahead of the collaring, though, he told me he wouldn't work with my brat side— the Reiver, Queen of Snark.

"Okay, no bratting, no snark, no use of the imperative mood, and I am, Reiver, absolutely going to take the wheel."

"That's okay, I'm sure I'm fun to drive. I'm going to be the worst slave in the history of BDSM, probably, but I'll put my back into it. I'll try my hardest for you. I mean, how difficult can it be just to do as I'm told for a bit without the whole Objection, Your Honor thing, eh?"

(You see it, don't you? As in the first of Act of a Shakespearean tragedy, this was the first crack, the first hint of the fatal flaw that undoes the protagonists in the story.)

It's not uncommon for Masters to strictly state the sub will have to "keep their brat under control". Or to write, view and advise one another on techniques for removing or training out "the brat" from their dynamics. My master had read that discourse; had had those discussions. His brat-phobic outlook seems, to me, fairly normalized, baked-in to certain modes of power exchange, at least here in the UK. And bratting does require negotiation and boundaries—an essay for another time. I know and understand why brats and smart-ass masochists are frustrating to many M-types, who might be tempted to see those sides of the personality as flaws to be corrected, ignored, or otherwise erased. Much ink has been spilled on the methods of doing precisely that. So let me tell you what that involves, what you're risking, and then we'll talk about whether you still want to do it.

My Master didn't want to work with the smart-ass, so, as he requested, I dutifully benched that entire side of my personality. I can do that, apparently, all on my own, turning my fierce will inward. He didn't even have to take her down, put her in her place, take her surrender. He just got my consent, and buckled a hideous engine of slavery and sorcery around my neck, and as if by magic, it worked.

The collar on, and he got the cool effect of quelling the "Reiver" part of me. The Spirit in the Fetish, having its way. It worked perfectly.

And it turns out that once the smart-ass is locked away, all that's left is a bad man's good girl.

Doin' My Hagel Exercises

The contract had stated he owned me for the Duration. But my Master hadn't thought about what the parts of my personality didn't want to engage with were doing in my brain. I think, in his own mind, he felt that the defiant resister, the smart ass "Reiver", would just go to sleep—and would always remain asleep around him. Or perhaps he thought that the brat-side wasn't really the true me, a fake or false mask only there for the brave front put up for the benefit of the community, and the 'real me' was someone else. Maybe so did I. But that's not what happened.

When I was with him, for two days out of the week, it wasn't so bad. In fact, much of it felt so bloody wonderful. Nothing to concern me, except delighting my master. And if things were wrong? No problem. All he had to do was tug on the collar and the swirling pool of subspace would drag me sweetly under. All I had to do was delight him a little more. Anticipate his needs, relax into service ... it felt peaceful. It felt right. At times it felt fucking amazing.

But in the days in between, without the physical pull on the collar, without the psychological direction, those two distinct voices in my head pushed me closer and closer to a full mental break.

"Reiver" —not so much a brat, really but a resister, a mutineer— wasn't happy. She was angry, spitting, hostile, and locked down so far that she only came out at me when the master wasn't around, in a terrifying cacophony. It wasn't quite a split personality, but I swear it got close: because the collar hived off an entire part of myself and that part became a separated but ever-present extreme voice in my head.

The Master got "Genie", the internal squish of submissive vulnerability. And every other part of me that wasn't the squish? The parts he wouldn't interact with—the parts he "owned" but had rejected— became monsters in my mind.

Unbeknownst—don't you just love that word, I've been waiting to use it for years— unbeknownst to the Master, this was the hellscape of my mind as that glorious bastard was having his masterly way:

Reiver: Gorean slave positions? Are you fucking kidding me? You can't just keep me chained up like this! Look at you. Look at you! You can't just roll over. Fight him! Fight, dammit! Genie? Genie, listen to me—

Genie: I made a promise. The contract. Hmmmm. He owns my body and spirit. And this feels so good.

Reiver: For fucks sake, Kick-me McDoormat! I'm not supposed to be this separate voice in your head! Our head. My head! Let me out, please. This is insanity. Let me take it off! I can't keep you safe like this!

Genie [high on collar space, giggling drunkenly]: I can't touch anything tied by my master. Not his ropes and not his collar … not the rope on the gate … I have to stand and wait … all I have to do is feel … all I have to do is kneel … hey … everything rhymes, y'know?

Reiver: Of course you can take it off! We can. I–I can. I can. Please just unbuckle it and safe word out of this now. Please. The buckle's right there. Get ahold of yourself.

Genie: I can't. And you're not allowed out, Reiver. It's only for a few weeks. Just to see. This just feels so … so … amazing … I expected to hate this, but I don't, why does this feel so good…

Reiver: Listen to me, you little oxytocin junkie. Genie, listen. You have to snap out of this. He's a white cisgender heterosexual sadistic dom. What are you even thinking? We—no, I— don't do this anymore. I don't do men anymore.

Genie: Oh relax, silly. Master will make sure I'm okay.

Reiver: You think you can trust him? I wouldn't trust him to top you with a mink mitten in a room full of Lesbian Leather daddies!

Genie: You don't trust anyone, Reiver. Your trust issues need to sign NDAs before they talk to your other trust issues. And you're so dramatic. Oh fuck. This feels incredible.

Reiver: So does shooting up. It doesn't mean it's good for you. Freya's holy cats, he's chained you to the sodding wall, you fool. What even *is* this? What the fuck *is* this?

Genie: Something character forming? Ooooooh, what's coming out of the drawer?

Reiver: Have you even seen the shit he's got in that drawer? This isn't safe. No one should control you. No one is meant to have this much control over another human being. You are literally fucking the patriarchy!

Genie: So good ... hmmm, his command is my wish ... this just feels so...

Reiver: Let me out. Let me go. Genie! Genie? C'mon, Genie, this isn't funny—

And all the while, all the Master saw was Genie's doe-eyed, shining devotion. Genie had been flawless in her service, a thing which both delighted and surprised the Master. Flawless. Not a single misstep. I went into it thinking I'd be the crappiest kink-slave in the universe. But—to my absolute horror and chagrin—my "Genie" side is pretty much your porn-standard Masterly wank-fantasy, harem pants and all. Every whim anticipated, sweetly and crisply attended to. Your command is my wish, I only live to serve you.

A dark, reiving terror stalked under that little band of my leather day-collar.

Such a light little thing, to bear such weight.

But where does the dirt go?

When I was about eleven or twelve, my science teacher did this experiment with alum and a test tube of dirty water. In went the alum, and as if by magic, hey presto, the water became clear, and the dirt disappeared.

"But, Miss," I asked. "Where does the dirt go? It can't just disappear?"

The teacher couldn't tell me, so I went home and asked my Dad, who, being my Dad, directed me to his study (basically the spare room from where he ran his engineering business) and to an ancient textbook called *Metals in the Service of Man*, from his technical college days. Therein I learned, before my educators deemed it was the right time to learn of such things, about the conservation of mass and energy, and how the alum made the dirt "disappear".

"I found out, Miss," I said, the next time I was in science class. "It's molecular flocculation. The dirt didn't go anywhere. It sank to the bottom of the test tube after sticking to the alum. That's why the water above it was clear." (If you think I was an annoying brat in science class, you should have seen me in Religious Education).

I wish my Master had asked a similar question about my brat side, my resister, my reiving warrior self, when it disappeared. He didn't. The collar worked as it was supposed to. As it always did. Why question something that, from your point of view, is working perfectly and getting the results you need?

And there's nothing about this in the Discourse™ that I can see.

Magic words

We know of course that BDSM contracts are another theater prop, right? I've even helped a few folks stuff them full of legalese for effect. But we also know that BDSM contracts are also not legally enforceable in Real Life. It's illegal—and this is a good thing, folks—to own another human being. This is why, like many, I don't like the term M/s or Master/slave. In my halcyon days as an egalitarian feminist anarchokinkster, where I resolutely refused to buy in to the labels, I thought the terms of the art of M/s were stupid. Derivative, appropriative of the experiences of oppressed peoples. Aye, the BDSM contact, the Master/charge contract? It's just a piece of theater. Fetsish-fashion. A prop. Like a collar, right?

Wrong.

In the beginning were the words, and the words have a power all their own:

> [8] . . . aside from the exceptions noted above, Reiver shall acknowledge that her whole self, body and spirit, belong to [the Master].

It's a big thing to take ownership of—and responsibility for—someone's body and spirit. And it was an implacable clause. Body and spirit in its totality, in finality. I've wondered from time to time why he chose this particular phrasing of all the clauses he could have chosen to signify ownership and power exchange.

Where does the spirit go, the parts of it you don't want to engage with? Would it have helped if he'd asked, when he saw the utter shift in consciousness and personality, where the rest of me had gone? What those unsurrendered parts of me were doing all that time? Would it have even mattered?

Putting me in a collar was experimental. I couldn't have predicted the internal conflict. But if only one or either of us had asked, before it went on, if these magic words make Reiver disappear, will she just sink to the bottom of the test tube?

Conservation of energy. Conservation of mass. As above, so below. What is the brain but matter and energy? Nothing ever truly disappears.

The worst of it was that Genie, who just wanted to please her Master, couldn't actually tell him what was wrong, couldn't even articulate the hellscape of internal conflict her mind had become. Because when she was with him, the effect of the collar was to place all her energy and drive into obedience, service, delighting him. When with him, the collar itself functioned as a gag. Once or twice, she tried to use the well-crafted protect-the-property clause in the contract (this is a clause which allows the Charge to respectfully, and within protocol, raise with the Master any issue which they believe may result in harm). She found though, she couldn't articulate to him what was truly happening (you can't be objective while you're an object). And all the while, the "Reiver" part of her, sunk to the bottom of her mind like the alum and dirt, grew more and more frantic and distressed. Eventually, it got to be too much. I safe worded out, and my beautiful Master released me.

Genie was devastated. The Reiver snarled and howled in the true joy of liberation. I swear that girl drinks *wode* for kicks.

So.

Still want to erase or ignore entire sides of your Charges' nature, M-types?

S-types, how do you feel now about your Master telling you to bench entire aspects of your being?

Know what risks you run.

You need to think about release before you collar.

Once more for those at the back. Think about release before you collar. Aye, even if you're perfectly compatible, lifetime partners. Even if you're only doing it for a few weeks to try it. Even if it's a "consideration" collar. Collars can wreck or end for all kinds of reasons. Illness. Disability. Psychological "allergy". Death herself, who comes calling for us all. Collars can also profoundly affect the wearer, even if they're only on a few weeks, including messing with their internal sense of time. Life happens. Death happens. Shit happens. The plan you make for your collar, if it's to be rooted in risk-awareness and informed consent, needs to include sober and frank consideration of these eventualities, even while you are still in the first sexy steps of the dance.

And if this seems too dark and difficult and scary? Power-exchange is neither the gold standard of kink nor the only mode around. There are others. You're not less of a kinkster to know this isn't for you. Even at the time of writing this, I'm swithering—though I'm grateful, so very grateful to my Master and the gods for the time he took with me and all the things I learned in service—whether to ever do this again. (And even if I do, there will have to be a sticky conversation along the lines of "Hey, Master Doe, you're an edge player, right? Wanna play with my brain at the weekend and see if it breaks this time around?")

Collars are very sexy things, and are a staple of the pornutopia-view of BDSM. They're present in nearly every piece of kinky erotica around, my own included, and as an erotica writer, I have them in there because I know marks and symbols of ownership light people's kinky fires, and as a courtesan in the house of literary sex-work, I want to get you off, and you to pay me for my time. A real-life power-exchange or power-transfer dynamic, however, is not a pornutopia. Even though I've always intellectually known that, there's nothing like the visceral practical experience to back up the theory. I can think of a million ways I would have negotiated the collar differently, now I have that 20/20 hindsight vision.

LEARNING SUBMISSION | 213

I thought my brain would be the same during the collar, and the same afterwards as it was going in. It wasn't, and I don't think it is for anyone. I'm happy with the person I am coming out, but I'm definitely not the same. I was never fully on board with the sugary fallacy of "the sub has all the power, really" and "they give their gift of submission" bullshit. The Master has real power, and if they are worth their salt, their power will be used. Choose wisely. Do you know how you respond to control? To being micro or macro-managed? Asked to do things you don't want to do, which will happen? I learned, very quickly, that my servant-self would absolutely do things for her Master she didn't want to do, things I'd never consider doing for a top without that collar on, things I would have scoffed at in my anarchokinking days, probably with a few choice Scots insults.

We had a control experience for the experiment, you see. A week before the collar went on and he was feeling out my levels, he asked me to take his horrible muddy boots off. *You are not compelled yet, but please take my boots off.* I stood there, outraged, for about five minutes. Eventually, gingerly, struggling, I knelt and took them off, outrage and fury all over my face and him laughing gently the whole time. Two weeks later, post-collaring, and I'd done the same action, automatically. He came in from the fields, sat down, and before I knew it, I was on my knees, at his feet unlacing the cowshit-covered nightmares, mid-way through the action before I remembered how hard that request had been to follow without the collar. He hadn't asked me to do it. I looked up at him, to see him absolutely delighted with me. The collar had changed me. And of course, the side of me that hated what was happening fumed in internal, chained-up mutiny, with my Master none the wiser. He viewed my beautiful, crisp, anticipatory service as a sign of the success of his methods.

And it would have been if my whole self had been involved in the act.

M-types, are you on-the-ball enough to detect when your s-type is struggling in their service? To have the congruence and empathy to detect when your Charge's mind has become an emotional hellscape? S-types, are there protocols you can negotiate in advance, warning lights that beep to alert you and your partner to a critical overload or breach? Are you self-aware enough to know when this is happening? How about in an altered state?

M-types, if you use protocols or contract clauses which "protect the property", have you given a thought to what you'll do if your Charge invokes it? Be aware that the collar itself may fuck with your s-type's ability to communicate what's wrong or to the degree to which it's wrong. Collar space is not like subspace. It's an altered state which is far more powerful … but also subtler in its presentation. What if you give the order anyway? Let me clue you in: you're responsible for the emotional aftermath of overriding your s-type's alert with your Awesome Domliness. Choose wisely, and if disaster ensues following your Masterly override, make sure you lay the responsibility where it should lie, and not with your damaged Charge.

Too (the Gorean too!), have you thought about how this person you're "remaking" is going to function if you're not around? On release? Do they have a community they can turn to? Do you? M-types, just as you're not immortal, you're not invulnerable. Do you have support for your own vulnerabilities somewhere other than your s-type? It's folly to underestimate your own emotional needs or well-being. I've watched a man I care about tear himself apart with guilt. Not a single day goes by when I don't wonder if he's okay, or whether he'll ever be okay again. And, speaking as a Switch, a million, trillion times over, no matter how much it hurts, I would far rather be on the bottom of a collar wreck than the top. There's no way around the proportional relationship between power and responsibility.

And afterwards, do you, M-type and s-type, actively unpack your dynamics, your scenes, your relationships when they end, and review what went wrong or what you could do better? Can you give and receive feedback with grace? Do you take time to reflect, before jumping to the next shiny bunny that hops across your path?

Or is the rasp of Velcro more your style?

An Insight Into Velcro Collars

I've seen a lot of whinging from M-types, writing as I do on the intersections of social justice and consent, about "Velcro collars", complaints over the slavey-types who take off one collar and the next second are collared to someone else. The Discourse™, nearly always written from the Master's perspective, is often contemptuous, as if this is a sign their Charge's commitment to the original dynamic wasn't real in the first place.

When I heard these M-types complain about it, I shrugged. Internally, I thought "this sounds like a 'you' problem". Power Exchange was so far outside my range of kink practice—or intent-to-practice—that it didn't seem important what a bunch of Masters were moaning in their Ye Olde Guarde rants like Monty Python's Four Yorkshiremen. *Subs these days don't know they're born! When I were a lad, they showed us some respect! None of that namby-pamby Velcro-collar Dom-hopping bullshit! A collar wasn't a fashion accessory, it meant something back in my day!* I'm sure you've heard it, friends. I know I have, despite my best efforts to avoid M/s circles, back in my halcyon days as subcommandante Reiver of the Anarchokink Revolution.

Now, I've other thinky thoughts. They're not pleasant ones.

My collar wrecked, and it wrecked despite my compatibility with the Master. Shit happened and I safe worded out. Even Genie the I-only-live-to-serve-you-Master fuckdoll figured out—despite not being the sharpest whip on the rail— that having raging agonized voices in her head wasn't healthy. My Master released me, and the collar came off. The parts he didn't want to engage with, the part I was forced to put away for the duration, the part of me the collar was so effective at keeping at bay, rushed back to life.

My personality had exploded under that collar—there's no other way to put it—with each block or piece anchored by a thread to my soul blown apart, spinning in space on the thinnest and most fragile of tethers to my being. In my journal throughout the period I'd been collared, to stop myself going (completely) crazy, I'd written out the internal conflict as conversations between storybook characters. Between "Reiver", trapped and snarling and angry, and "Genie", who just wanted to be a pleasure slut for her Master. Using my skills as a storyteller, I could pretend they were just characters in a story, not the screaming, maddening aspects of my own internal, unresolved dialectic.

But once the collar came off? The pieces of my psyche the collar had blown apart crashed back down to earth under implacable gravity, landing with painful thuds, never quite in the same places they'd been before the collar went on. It was hell. My pieces were burred and chipped. They didn't quite fit any more. My head was a terrified, jumbled mess of a psychic jigsaw. The Reiver rushed in to repair, shore up the boundaries, reclaim her psychic space, and reintegrate. Survey the wreckage and order in the repair crews.

Genie wept out her grief every night for over two months. Reiver took her bokken out and did a lot of counting in Japanese while slicing imaginary foes crown to crotch. (They say if you feel angry, counting helps?)

Suffice it to say, the collar drop was truly epic. Reintegration of the parts of my soul the collar had separated was like knitting back the pieces of broken bones sans anesthesia, emotional and spiritual agony on unimaginable levels. It hurt, like hell, in all the ways, folks. All the ways. And I couldn't tell the Master what had happened, either. How do you even broach a subject like that? "Hiya, luv, how's it going? Um, just to let you know, I think your collar broke my brain?"

The psychological shift during that period was so physically and emotionally brutal that I think if another Master had come along and offered their collar while I was in the thick of that interminable drop, the never-ending drop, the drop from the drop, the feelings that wouldn't go away no matter how much I wanted them to? I'd have said yes without hesitation.

Velcro, shmelcro. Anything to stop it hurting.

Is that why there's so much Velcro around? What if all that Velcro is because release from a collar just hurts too much, too much to handle, too much to take, and you have to go through it alone? Unlike the other sorts of kinky-drop around, where the players' mutual responsibility is to nurture one another through the emotional troughs, your former Master can't be there for the most epic drop of all—not if their very presence would prevent the psychological process of release from working.

In the end, my ex-girlfriend came to visit, and beat the queer back into me with a ritual birch rod collected on a cold January morning and dedicated to the Goddess. Birch, the tree of purification, of health, of purging, of new beginnings. Before she brought the rod down on my flesh for the first of the nigh-on 400 strikes I took that day, I wondered all over again: why are safe exit strategies from D/s dynamics never really talked about? Rarely considered?

What does it mean, really, to own someone, body and spirit?

The Wall

There's a joke in my kinky circle that my hard limits list isn't so much a list but the proverbial Wall of China. I'd taken down quite a bit of that Wall to enter service, and my Master's having some thinky thoughts of his own about it, even as it's clear to both of us the collar is going to have to come off.

"Okay, Genie," he says. (Reiver can't come to the phone right now, can I take a message?). "I think, once you're out of the collar, you need to review your Wall. Everything on it—bar one or two things I completely understand—seems to be a barrier to your own pleasure? Why deny this side of you? Just find the right Master, and let him do what he wants."

Genie thinks this is a fabulous idea.

Under the band of the collar, Reiver snarls, silently; "Don't listen to him, you daft wee fuckmuppet. That's first-rate, barking-at-the-moon lunacy."

When the collar came off, Genie wasn't in charge of the ship anymore. The "Reiver" part of me set out to shore up the boundaries around the "daft wee fuckmuppet". My friends and community—community I could not have done without and who pretty much got me through it, leatherfolk, anarchokinksters, my former Master's other girl, even my vanilla witchy friend—rallied around with actual and metaphorical hugs. I found my kinky connections much stronger when I came out. That's what community is for. Not for endless drama, gossip, and blame, and not as a shallow pool to hunt for your fetishes, but a deep abundant ocean of connected human beings, being there for one another when for whatever Shit Happens reason, we're dropping alone. That is family. *Tuath.* Tribe.

Collar drop is not like sub drop. It's a million times worse. The pain of it was nearly unendurable. If you're released, the person who got you through the sub-drop all those other times isn't going to be there. Plan for that. Some of my pathetic planning worked—the practice of journaling through the dynamic, which I thought was useless at the time, provided an important tool for analysis and healing afterwards. However, on reflection, had my Master had access to (and committed himself to reading) that horrific jumbly mental space where I was speaking freely to my own spirit, he might have detected that all was not well.

And, even if you make the plan, be prepared for the collar itself to throw you curve-balls. You may find you have to adapt that plan. You almost certainly will.

M-types, who will take care of your released Charge? Do they have friends and community, people who know they're kinky and to whom they can talk frankly? Have you not only allowed them friends but actually gone out of your way to facilitate our community in your Charge's life? Or have you isolated them from the *tuath*?

S-types, has your M-type not just become the master of your universe, but the only person in it? Can you function without your M-type, financially, physically, and socially? Who will you turn to for solace and comfort and a listening ear if they're not there? Hint: Make sure that person isn't holding a collar made of Velcro for your bared and naked throat. Heal your open ground before allowing someone else to camp there. In most cases, land needs recovery, a fallow period, before it can bear a new crop. Sometimes we have to be our own Guardians.

As a community, we are responsible for guarding and supporting and loving one another during those vulnerable, high-risk emotional times. I don't believe power exchange can safely be done without the *tuath*, a healthy community and support network. Friends, if you know of someone coming out of collar drop? Support them, protect them, hold space for them. Masters among you, make sure your prospective Charge is out of drop from their last collar before you consider them for yours—and make sure you do your own brutal, unflinching self-reflection when you exit a relationship. Be the community for others you'd want if Shit were to Happen to you. The presence of lots of Velcro in a community is a sign the *tuath* is broken.

I had support. I had my beautiful *tuath*. I can't imagine what this would have been like if I'd had to do it completely alone.

———————◗○◖———————

Show me who you really are.

A different day, a different Dom. The Bealtaine bluebells are still blooming, the collar-drop from my last dynamic long gone—but never forgotten. I've quelled my social anxiety enough to accept this man's invitation. This, of course, is just coffee, not Just Coffee. A first meeting.

He's interesting, this Master, and even though this is just coffee, there's still the little tick of calculation—he hides it well—as he assesses the woman before him. He removes a rope of silver from his neck.

"You made this?"

"Yes. I'll wear it every day until I find the woman for whom this will fit as a collar. Then I'll size it for her." He drops the heavy, serpentine silver rope into my hand, still warm from his skin. The smithcrafting's exquisite, byzantine links forged one by one, soldered and braided in complex, intricate twists. Days, weeks, of labor have gone into the making of it. I close my eyes and read the energy of those links. Light from shadow. Longing from loss. All the love. All the yearning. Frank desire, rather than flakey fantasy. Links that tell a story of one who has faced the Deep, a story that braids a map, for him, to his personal Holy Grail, the sought chalice. A holy thing, a needful thing. A dear and dangerous article of power like the forged treasure of an Icelandic saga. It's a privilege to hold; this heft of the magical silver coiled on my palm.

We go a little quiet, he and I, as is proper in the contemplation of the sacred.

I return it to him and we talk more. He's Old School, only a fool wouldn't see it. Maybe it takes one to know one. Maybe my school is ancient too.

"To be honest, I don't know where I fit, Mr. L, in the sort of M/s community you describe."

He sits back. "Really?" He sounds skeptical.

"Aye. Aside from the switchiness, where would my s-type side belong? Except—except maybe I'm the Auriga, the slave of Ancient Rome. The community property who held the laurels over the head of the Dux at his moment of conquering glory, receiving his accolades before an adoring crowd. All the time, whispering in his ear, "Remember thou art but mortal.""

My companion pales a little. "*Memento mori.* I—I have that tattooed on my arm."

I take a sip of my tea.

There's a very common, damaging idea—so common in fact that few question it when it surfaces in countless discussions—that the fetishistic displays of protocol are there to "strip away the ego and reveal who the sub truly is inside". Or—a darker, heavier under-melody—to break down the Charge and rebuild them in the Master's image. The s-type here is seen as a blank slate, or someone whose slate can be erased, to get to, or fabricate, the bits the Master is interested in. This is a pornutopic, sexy fantasy, right? *I only wish to serve you, Master,* and *Behold, I shall remake you in Mine image, slave.*

Master, remember thou art but mortal. Charge, remember the Dux is only human. Speak it in your heart, lipstick it on your bathroom mirror, tattoo it on your arm—as my coffee companion did—if you must. You're not gods, M-types. You're not omniscient. You cannot read minds, and you especially cannot read minds which are bound to the altered states induced by a collar. I hope, should you ever be tempted to intentionally embark on paths of erasing any part of your S-type's personhood, you learn the definition of hubris, STAT.

No sub is a blank slate, and there's no such thing as the "big reveal" of the s-type's "true self". And s-types? The god-like power wielded in the thick of a scene or dynamic by the Master is a paradox of implacable reality, and perilous illusion. Communication, emotional regulation, and the ability to convey what's going on under duress, in agony, when things are really, really bad, when we're being torn apart by something our M-type has asked of us but still desperate for the Master's approval—all of that is necessary, and, I believe, necessary to consider as much a possible before entering the dance of power. I'm the first to admit I didn't have communication skills developed enough for this, going in.

Power exposes. Power changes. When you strip down an s-type's defenses and egos—and doing this is pretty dark edge work, folks— then what you may find is not their truth, but your mirror. The conscious exercise of power will reveal much about you, M-type. Who are you, when you exercise Power? What is your truth? Where is your honor? When you ask for the body and spirit of your s-type, that's exactly what you're getting, and what you're taking responsibility for. Your Charge's true self is not "the parts of them you like". Their true self is equally the parts you don't—or the parts you're scared of working with. The parts you can't deal with. The parts of them that are in pain. The parts that tempt that inner monster you're ashamed of and are trying to ignore. The parts that are a pain in the arse. The fallacy, oft-repeated even by otherwise sound BDSM practitioners, that we can somehow "cancel the brat" is a recipe for disaster.

If the s-type is a brat/smart-ass/resister and a servant, both their sides are equally, and all, part of who they are. I can't speak for others, but my bratty, resister-self is an essential part of my personality, the part that evolved to defend and protect the more vulnerable squishy bits. She's not a fixable flaw or an irreparable break. She deserves to be honored as the hero and warrior that she is—and believe me, she's earned her stripes. It was our folly—my Master's, and most especially mine—to think that she could be erased, or put down, shut away or simply silenced. Nothing ever truly disappears.

If I had it to do again, when the Master said "I won't work with the brat," I know enough now to say "Then we can't do this, because she's not a flaw, she's essential," or advise that I would need to go toe-to-toe, resist and surrender at least once, just at the start, for that side of me to be satisfied in her honor and fully engaged, not just stuffed down and cut off, from the relationship. Or, possibly, direct the M-type to this writing or others on the emotional folly and risk involved with erasing or locking away people's personhood, and invite them to reflect seriously on their practice. Though I haven't tested this theory out, my instinct tells me that a service-oriented s-type's more resisting, bratty sides are also protective to the Charge and the dynamic, and prevent the full obliteration of their boundaries during power-exchange. And we need those boundaries, Masters come all ye, to effectively serve you. Boundaries are the only way you know that your dynamic is an exchange, a transfer of power and not outright larceny.

Taking on the responsibility of an s-type in a power-exchange arrangement means not just taking on the bits of them you're interested in, the parts that are useful to you, the stuff you wish to hone, or the parts which appeal to your wank-fantasies. You get a whole person, who is more than the sum of their parts and life experiences. That whole person has the absolute right to their personal sovereignty, to their boundaries, to their own soul even if they give you, the Master, control of it. All aspects of their being deserve respect, even as they honor and respect all parts of you. There, you must not only be the master of your own sovereignty but the guardian of your s-type's.

Are you ready for that call? Can you take on that level of responsibility?

S-types, be wary of the M-type who asks you to bench or strap down or lock away any part of who you are. I don't believe Service can be a thing done with anything other than one's whole self. At the very least, if your Master is seeking to erase any part of your personality, it's a sign they are not aware of the risks, and power exchange even at the lightest end can touch some implacable edges. All of your parts are your true and real self, and you are more, far more, than the mere sum of them. You're no tabula rasa. You're holy ground, a garden to be tended, not crushed over with a concrete parking lot of rigid ideas on what power exchange should look like.

Besides, sometimes the "slave" you need to be is the Auriga.

My Wall of China is as strong and high and implacable as it's ever been, an impenetrable fortress around my squishy vulnerabilities. The mortar is fresh. Some things have changed in the construction, but the vulnerabilities in the ramparts are repaired. On it, I hang a Master's collar—it looks exactly like his did, battered leather with nickel findings that inflamed my skin and fucked with my brain—on a nice new shiny hook, bolted into the stone. Some things need to be a hard limit. At least until you can figure stuff out.

I relax, looking out from the battlements across my sacred Land, knowing this doesn't need to happen again. No one needs to see Genie again. My nice feminist anarchokink can go back to where it was, birched back into place, and I'll call no man my Master, right?

Right?

Something troubles me, as nice as all this healing and reintegration is. The alum in the water. The genie in the bottle. Where, oh where, has she gone? Conservation of matter. Conservation of energy. Conservation of spirit.

Just because I can't hear her doesn't mean that she's just disappeared. Nothing ever truly disappears.

If the Reiver is real, then the Genie is too. Every bit as real. All my parts, complete, are reintegrated, like cracks in Japanese pottery repaired with gold. And all those pieces, my whole self which is more than the sum of its parts, deserve to be recognised and honored, not benched or ignored or fled. None can be ignored, or silenced, or beaten down or locked away. Including the vulnerable service-sylph who betrayed all the other parts of herself.

I still dream of Genie, sometimes.

Villanelle on Release

I contemplate the complex twists of fate,
The pebbles hard beneath my frozen feet—
Your collar's off, but still I feel the weight.

A sabbat-span to hold me in your sway,
One foot in harsh the other sunk in sweet—
We waded through those complex twists of fate.

The hours you kept me shaded through the day,
And bound me hard where pain and passion meet—
The collar's off. But still I need to wait

For what, exactly? My throat lies bared, like prey
To famished creatures 'til they loll, replete:
My marrow sucked in gnaws of twisted fate.

I'm deep in the red—I don't know how to pay?
You'll take no cash, nor kind, nor faith's surfeit,
The bonds are canceled: still I feel their weight.

I've said too much, there's so much more to say—
Released and yet still bound, the trick and treat.
I contemplate the complex twists of fate:
The collar's off: and yet I feel its weight.

Reiver Scott *is the pseudonym of a writer, poet, Switch, and Pagan Bard from Southern Scotland. A practitioner of native Scots-Irish spirituality and magic, she's been learning about kink and permaculture for a wee while, and mostly writes about the intersection between kink, spiritual sovereignty, and anti-fascism. Her writings can be found in print and online, and as of time of writing she writes regularly at Fetlife.com, where she can be followed @Reiver_Scott.*

Feminism, Authenticity, and Power Exchange
dee tealover

My Master and I have been married for over thirty years. About twenty years into our marriage, we transitioned our relationship from a "more-or-less" egalitarian dynamic to a power exchange. The journey we had together, creating the wonderful M/s dynamic we enjoy today, was one filled with personal growth, trials and tribulations, and much joy. Honoring our authentic selves strengthened our relationship and provided a powerful sense of felicity. Before we got to the felicity, however, were those trials. One trial for me in my personal growth into my authentic self as a slave to my Master was my self-identity as a feminist.

I was born in 1969, which means I am a child of the '70s. During that era, the Feminist Movement was spreading across America. My mother was an at-home mom with a philosopher's mind and an artist's passion, and her personal growth through what many in hindsight call the "second wave" of feminism was palpable. There were, of course, other famous women championing the equal-rights-for-women movement, but Gloria Steinem was so popular in my childhood home that she felt like a famous distant relative. We were early subscribers to Ms. magazine, the first national women's magazine on feminism. Our house was decorated with "women's tokens" made of clay by an artisan friend of my mother's. The tokens were marked with "59¢" and represented how much money women were paid (at that time) on the dollar compared to men. Valuing equal rights, opportunities, and greater personal freedom for women was a message my siblings and I received from not just my mother, but also from my father. So, in many ways, feminism was the background of my childhood.

I came into my relationship with my Master having been raised on feminism. I knew every word to every poem, song, and story on the soundtrack from the feminist children's book *Free to Be You and Me* which was conceived of by Marlo Thomas and created in collaboration with Gloria Steinem and several other writers, poets, musicians, and actors. Though a product of its time, and therefore not gender-inclusive by modern standards (though I choose to believe if all the same individuals made this book today, it would be gender-inclusive and celebrate diversity), the creators of *Free to Be You and Me* meant just that. Everyone, regardless of gender, is free to pursue their truth, their authentic selves, and need not be confined by societal gender roles and expectations. In the poem *My Dog is a Plumber,* the poet Dan Greenburg concludes that you can't judge gender by what a person does and that: "Maybe the problem is in trying to tell/Just what someone is by what he does well."

While inspired by many poems, songs, and stories in this collection, I often sang Bruce Hart's lyrics to the title song *Free to Be You and Me* loudly (and badly) both as a child and now as an adult. I especially liked these stanzas:

> *"And you and me*
> *Are free to be*
> *You and me …*
> *Every boy in this land*
> *Grows to be his own man.*
> *In this land, every girl*
> *Grows to be her own woman."*

And while this song doesn't celebrate our modern understanding of gender, it does recognize that in the world the song imagines, every individual would be free to grow to be their own authentic self.

After about six years of re-exploring kink and dominance and submission, my husband collared me in 2016 on our 25th wedding anniversary, becoming my Master. When we transitioned our marriage to a power exchange dynamic, we were really renewing our spiritual relationship quest. We recognized and embraced the fact that we had always been kinky, and we acknowledged that we had previously had an unintentional power exchange. The truth was that our egalitarian relationship had never actually been fully egalitarian. Making this conscious decision for our lives enhanced everything. In the years of our relationship growth, we met many challenges and embraced the notion of an unequal partnership as matching who we were becoming—and in many ways, who we always were.

But as we were developing our dynamic, even though I was happy, I struggled with understanding how to reconcile being a feminist, an identity that went to my core, with power exchange. Every now and again in those early days, I would panic, I would look at my Master with eyes open wide and declare: "How can I submit to the authority of someone else in my personal life and call myself a feminist? What are we doing?" And he would hold me and help me breathe to stop my mind from racing, and in those quiet moments I would look at what we were creating together. Our dynamic core value is personal growth and dynamic growth. To strive each day to be a better version of ourselves as individuals: a Master, a slave, and in our dynamic. I recognized that my Master taking ownership, and my surrendering into our power exchange, had strengthened our already strong relationship. It had allowed each of us to live more fully as our authentic selves.

We talked a lot back then, and even today, about what feminism means to me. Who I am in the world as a woman, what I value. By that time the feminism of my childhood, as my parents and *Free to Be You and Me* taught it to me, seemed to have altered into a focus on a valuation of a woman based on her career and how far up the corporate ladder she has climbed. For me, the only thing I've ever wanted to do was write for myself and write for people I care about. I never necessarily cared if I got published, I just wanted to write. (And I have, and I do.) But I had never chosen the professional career trajectory, which the media for quite a long time now has espoused as a path of feminist epic-ness. I chose to be an at-home mom and found it to be a fun, challenging and rewarding job that afforded me as much personal growth as it did my children—while personally fulfilling myself with my writing and in a myriad of other ways. Likewise, my greatest role model, my mother, had also been genuinely happy as an at-home mom, fulfilling her sense of individuality with her art.

And so, in my moments of panic and self-doubt and fear that I was failing all womankind by being a slave, I listened to my heart, to my soul. I honored the life of my greatest role model, my mother. Since early childhood I have known that I am not a naturally independent personality, and I have always respected my interdependent nature, which is gentle and quiet. If you know me as a talkative person full of opinions and stories, that means I trust you. I am silent until I feel safe. I am strong, and interdependent, and these two qualities do not contradict each other. I am a submissive who submits to the authority of only one person: my Master, whom I have judged to be trustworthy. And the thing is, my childhood feminism never said I had to climb a corporate ladder or be any particular way to be a "true feminist". In fact, I distinctly remember being told in another poem, *Don't Dress Your Cat in an Apron* by Dan Greenburg from the *Free To Be You and Me* collection: "A person should do what she likes to–A person's a person that way." And what I would like to do is follow the lead of my Master—a Master who is also a feminist.

My Master/slave dynamic has allowed me to grow so much as a person, to be so much more thoroughly who I truly am in the deepest parts of my soul. And I think, though I still wrestle sometimes, that is all that truly matters. I live my authentic truth. And though I struggled, in the end I realize that being in a Master slave relationship with my beloved husband/Master is living my authentic feminist truth, living out my truest identity as a human being. My dynamic allows me to be the best version of myself and to live more proudly, strongly, and freely in the world.

The irony is not lost on me that the greatest expression of my feminism comes from being on the right side of the slash in a Master/slave dynamic—and yet it does. I don't subscribe to a feminism that tells women who and what they should and must be, and I no longer allow that version of feminism to undermine me and cause me self-doubt. I subscribe to my childhood version of feminism that says I am free to be exactly who I actually am, strive to be more of who I want to be, and show up in the world as my most authentic self.

My slavery is my personal best expression of feminism. I am a feminist woman, making the conscious choice to be true to my inner core, allowing my authentic self to shine in the context of my M/s dynamic, being fully authentic in partnership with my Master who has my personal growth and best interests at heart. The women's rights movement of my childhood championed equal rights, opportunities, and greater personal freedom for women. I am equal in my humanity to all people, including my Master, with whom I am in an Unequal

Partnership. I have had so many wonderful opportunities afforded me since pursuing our dynamic and entering the larger BDSM and power exchange community, and my slavery is a beautiful expression of my personal freedom.

Living my authentic life in a power exchange dynamic: I am Rocking Feminism.

dee tealover is the loving pleasure slave of Master Jim, and does her best to be a gentle support to him and their family. The are both members of MAsT Massachusetts.

Surrendering Mind, Body, and Heart

Joshua Tenpenny

It's not uncommon for me to hear s-types worry about not having the "right attitude", or even a "good enough" attitude. I've talked a lot about how I see attitude as the cornerstone of submission, cultivating an attitude of willing surrender, accepting whatever outcome, adapting to whatever is required of you. It isn't part of all power relationships, but it is common. The specifics of what is considered the "right attitude" vary, and different people are going to focus on different aspects, depending on what pleases or annoys the M-type, and what comes naturally to the s-type.

Some components of that "right attitude" are likely ones that are commonly sought in many contexts in the outside world, and there is endless advice on how to cultivate them. Others are more specific to our types of power relationships. The main one for me is *surrender*. There are certain religious contexts that discuss various aspects of surrender, but for many of us, those are not especially relevant or applicable to our power relationship. (While the Benedictine Rule may address what situations it is appropriate to beat someone for disobedience, it really isn't the same thing.)

When I am working to understand something that is hard for me to grasp or put into words, my first inclination is to divide it up into more manageable pieces. (My categories might not fit your experiences, but thinking about the ways that your own experiences do and *don't* fit a given framework can provide valuable insights.) I break down "right attitude" into pieces, and one of those is surrender. Then I break down "surrender" into pieces. What do I mean by surrender? What gives me that feeling of surrender? What aspects of surrender do I struggle with? What types of surrender am I not interested in giving? I come down to three basic categories: Surrender in the mind, surrender in the body, and surrender in the heart.

We surrender in our minds when we agree to be bound by their rules and restrictions, even when we struggle to obey. We surrender in our minds when we give over authority, telling them they have the right to make decisions over this or that. We surrender in our minds when we defer to their judgment, despite disagreements. We surrender in our minds when we choose to make their desires a priority for us.

We surrender our bodies when we do the tasks and protocols required of us, regardless of how we feel. It is easy to underestimate the emotional value to our partner in simply knowing they can rely on us to do what we are told. We surrender when we allow our partner access to our bodies, when they can touch and handle us without restriction, when they can inflict pain or pleasure as they choose. We surrender when we give them sovereignty over our bodies, letting them choose how we dress, and how to alter our appearance. We surrender when we are simply physically present somewhere they know they can find us if they want something.

We surrender in our hearts when we willingly yield to their authority, becoming an extension of their will. When our own desires seem irrelevant compared to theirs. When we yearn for their approval and praise. When we eagerly fulfill their wishes. When we take satisfaction in unpleasant tasks, knowing it is done for them. When we remain open to them despite the risks.

This surrender in your heart features heavily in many of the most alluring depictions of M/s type relationships. It is often what draws us to these relationships, when we have had or desire to have these experiences of deep surrender. But unlike the surrender of the mind of body, it is almost entirely out of our control. Like falling asleep or having an orgasm, all we can do is create the right circumstances for it to occur, remove what obstacles we can remove, and let it happen. Or not happen. For some it happens naturally and reliably, with no struggle. For some, the conditions must be just right, and the smallest thing can interfere. For some, it seems entirely random and unpredictable, fine one day and impossible the next. Even when we get very deep into these relationships, this headspace can be elusive, despite our best efforts.

Some of these acts of surrender are likely things that come easy to you. Some are perhaps ways you have no intention of ever surrendering. Finding what works for you is part of this journey.

Sometimes we wind up going further than we ever thought we would—and sometimes we find that a level of surrender that seemed so wonderful actually takes us away from where we need to be.

I am in no way saying that you *ought* to strive for any specific type of surrender, or that your growth as an s-type should center on finding a deeper level of surrender. It is genuinely OK to only surrender only as far as comes naturally to you, and there are certainly situations when too much surrender is a problem. But what if you do want to increase your capacity for surrender? What if you are frustrated by your inability to surrender in a certain area? How do you get better at surrender?

Surrender Can Be Learned

The first part is to fully accept that there is no shame in struggling with surrender. It is OK if obedience doesn't come easy to you. It is especially OK if you can't maintain the "right headspace" as much as you would like. That struggle is entirely normal, but it does need to be handled well, to maintain a mutually fulfilling relationship.

It is easy to get caught in a vicious cycle of feeling bad about feeling bad, so interrupting that pattern is the first step. Any type of mindfulness practice can help here; it is just about being able to observe that you are in a bad place, without making the situation worse by adding unnecessary blame and shame.

As an s-type, it is easy to believe a "real slave" (or whatever) *ought to* feel awful about even minor transgressions, which can lead to a perhaps subtle feeling that it is more "slavey" to have an emotional meltdown over trivial corrections. It is natural to be extremely emotionally invested in "doing it right", especially in the beginning of a relationship, but try to focus that energy into changing your behavior rather than beating yourself up. If you go into hysterics each time you forget to refill your Master's coffee cup, they've got no coffee *and* a crying slave.

The second part is practice. Just doing all the acts of surrender you *can* do, over a period of time, will generally wear down your resistance to the more difficult acts. (This is effective in sleazy situations too, so be careful about establishing a pattern of compliance with people you don't trust, even when their requests are reasonable.) If the things you are struggling with aren't essential to the dynamic, it can be best to just not worry about them for a while and see what happens. This is largely up to the M-type, but it is an effective approach for a whole lot of things. Certainly, for the first year, there is no reason to really push any difficult issues unless they are total deal-breakers.

One of the big obstacles I see in new s-types is getting so hung up on the areas where they struggle that it sabotages everything else. This is especially true with attitude. When they are struggling with surrender of the heart, they may feel like they need to drop everything until they can "submit genuinely". But if you can just keep doing the other acts of surrender, it sustains the relationship and supports your work in surrendering your heart.

My master, who is a parent, compared this to parenting a child. It's important to act in a loving way toward your children, even when you're not feeling especially loving and their antics are making you grind your teeth. However, not feeling it in the moment doesn't mean that you don't love them. *Acting* consistently loving toward them, regardless of your emotional reaction to their behavior, is a genuine expression of love in and of itself. Similarly, in M/s, consistently doing the *actions* of obedience and surrender, when done toward the M-type you actively desire to surrender to, is a genuine expression no matter what your current emotional state may be.

No Resentments

You don't have to always be "feeling it" to be obedient. You don't have to have every aspect of surrender perfect all the time, and it is OK to struggle with any of these. You do, however, have to be able to do these actions without stockpiling resentment towards your M-type. Frustration is OK (and understandable), and a small amount of guilt won't ruin everything, but you can't be harboring a growing fund of bitterness, built on the idea that you are being treated unfairly, and/or that you've been wronged, and/or that your M-type is inconsiderate or failing at their job. If you realistically believe that you are being seriously mistreated, that's a different problem and you must decide what you're going to do about it. I'm not talking about that. I'm talking about when we get upset over things we've already agreed that the M-type has a right to ask of us.

At one point, I was really upset about something, and I challenged my master over it. After hearing me out, he asked me, "Do you want to have the kind of relationship where I'm not allowed to make decisions you don't agree with?" No, obviously not. That wasn't the relationship I wanted to be in at all. If he couldn't ask me to do anything I didn't want to do, then we weren't master and slave. He'd established this wasn't harming me. It was just pissing me off, and he's allowed to piss me off. But being able to bring this to him, and have him take me seriously, really helped clear the air.

For myself, the reasons I feel bad about doing challenging things generally have little or nothing to do with my master. Usually, it's that I want to believe I'm better at something than I really am, and this struggle is demonstrating that I'm not. That can be humiliating, but it's not my master's failure. It's important that I face down the real emotional reasons, and head all resentment off at the pass.

You Don't Always Have To Be Into It

When struggling with surrender of the heart, my general advice is to lean hard into the other two. Really throw yourself into other aspects of surrender, to the best of your ability. Keep at it for at least a month, and see how you feel afterwards. You can try to pick apart what is going on with you during this time, talk it out with your master, or a therapist, or a friend, but putting the relationship on hold while you try to talk it out is risky.

For this to work, the M-type should first make it clear which activities just seem pointless or unappealing to them if the s-type is reluctant and unenthusiastic. The next step is for the s-type to make it clear which activities are, in themselves, unpleasant to the point of serious distress, causing lasting resentment, or otherwise undermining their willingness to surrender. (It's better for the M-type to go first here, so that the s-type doesn't go on about activities that the M-type would rule out anyway.) If you've already talked about these issues, keep this to a straightforward list of specific protocols and activities.

With those out of the way, the s-type can bring up the next layer of struggles—the things routinely expected of them which are difficult but not terrible—making it clear that they are definitely *willing* to do them. This is a starting point for discussion about how they are to respond when they are not "into it". You might want to talk about what "into it" looks like to your M-type, and which aspects of seeming "into it" are actually important to them.

Some s-types may find that they've set the bar much higher for themselves than their M-types realize. The M-type may be assuming that you are saying that doing a certain activity is miserable or emotionally damaging to you, when it's more that you feel guilty about not doing it perfectly, and you want to give them better than imperfect work … so you end up giving them nothing. Regardless, the point is to work together to figure out a way of responding that works for the M-type and isn't too terrible for the s-type.

These conversations should ideally be infrequent—not a continual revisiting of the same issues over and over. They also should not generally be an in-the-moment response to an order, or the M-type may end up feeling reluctant to give orders, because they don't have the energy for the continual processing. You can revisit things that aren't working, but try to focus instead on doing the things that *are* working.

Finding an acceptable response

In many cases, just acting naturally is fine. If you aren't enthusiastic about changing the cat box, no big deal. But if you are trying to cultivate an attitude of surrender, you should be mindful of how you respond to orders or protocols that you dislike.

The simplest approach is to just do it as cheerfully and respectfully as you can manage. Your M-type will probably be able to tell that you aren't thrilled by it, but they should also be able to tell that you're trying. Some s-types, however, may be concerned that this is moving into the arena of deception, or at least miscommunication; and some M-types might be worried about their ability to pick up subtle cues. If a straightforward report feels like whining, there are a variety of ways to acknowledge the s-type's feelings more explicitly, including:

❖ **The high protocol way.** We know quite a few s-types who have three set responses to any order: "Yes, Sir/Ma'am." "If it pleases you, Sir/Ma'am." "*Only* if it pleases you, Sir/Ma'am." There are variations, but all emphasize the s-type's willingness to do whatever-it-is, while providing a way of communicating that you have some degree of concern. Under high protocol, "if it pleases you" might be used for any time you have additional information you suspect the M-type is not aware of, with "only if it pleases you" indicating you believe the information to be critical. In a lower protocol context, any high protocol phrase can be used to indicate that you fear this act of obedience will be difficult for you. You do need to establish how it is handled.

❖ *The overexaggerated pouting way.* "But I don't wanna!" Usually said with a fair amount of humor, to show that this is sincere but not a critical objection. My master's response to this one is usually to say in an only-slightly-mocking tone of equally overexaggerated false sympathy, "That's OK. You don't have to want to. You just have to do it."

❖ *The humorous grumble way.* "It's a damn good thing I'm your slave, you know that?" Met with a grin and "Yup, it's a damn good thing." Again, this shows willingness to do it along with a clear heads-up about the difficulty.

❖ *The bratty way.* For those who have this in their dynamic. "You can't make me!" "Oh, yes, I can!"

I'm sure you can all think of others as well. Find something that suits your dynamic. You do want to take care if either has a history of a partner (or parent) swallowing resentment for years and then exploding, or a passive-aggressive partner (or parent), or currently has a day job where they must smile for inept assholes. In any of those cases, you want to set responses that clearly differentiate the power dynamic from those other established patterns. Having a set response for the M-type is less common, but it can be very helpful, to reassure the s-type that they are heard and understood, which is equally important. These behaviors can feel awkward or unnatural at first, but give it time. Anything can be awkward until you get used to it.

And Then There's Sex

Of all the exceptions to the "You don't always have to be into it" rule, the most complex can be sexual and intimate services. Some M-types are fine with sex (or certain sexual activities, at least) when the s-type is not enthusiastic, and a few may even find it hot. After all, there's a lot of that in porn. However, many M-types—possibly even most of them—don't truly enjoy having sex with a disinterested partner. Some may be down with a struggle, in the right context, but not boredom or the s-type acting like they'd rather be anywhere else right now.

Similarly, some s-types are down with a relationship where their partner can just take them, even when they aren't into it. However, many s-types only find it hot in fantasy or in a very specific pre-arranged context. When the M-type wants the s-type to be available for sexual activities when they aren't aroused, but the s-type is at all reluctant (or even just inexperienced), it is something that needs to be worked with extremely carefully, with open and honest communication.

The more common situation is where the s-type generally enjoys sex, and really wants to be enthusiastically available whenever reasonable, but can't reliably get there on demand. For many s-types, it is usually sufficient to routinely practice taking fifteen minutes or a half hour alone, doing whatever activities get you in the mood. As with meditation, if your mind tries to wander off to other thoughts and activities, bring it back to that idea. Set everything else aside. Some people may find this more effective with their partner, but practicing it alone helps reduce any performance anxiety, and it means you can practice when there is no pressure to succeed. Whether or not you can get physically aroused is much less relevant than getting into a headspace where you are interested and willing.

Talking It Out

My master and I have a very high-communication approach to relationships, and we generally advise as much explicit communication as you can tolerate. But there are obstacles to talking things out with your partner.

For some s-types, open discussion of their struggles comes easy, but for some it is very difficult to open up. These types are often very invested in showing that they have it all under control, that they can do it all without help. These relationships often push us to explore the edges of our comfort zone, whichever side we are on, and it is not uncommon for a power dynamic relationship to push a person past the point their existing coping mechanisms can handle, so they might not have much skill in conveying their inner struggles in words.

Some M-types really want to hear it all. They feel like they need to know everything that is going on in your head in order to master you properly. This is in many ways the safest approach, provided the M-type has decent emotional and interpersonal skills, as well as sufficient time and energy to devote to this work. If things go wrong, at least you both know where you stand.

The risk here is that all the emotional processing can weigh down the relationship with frequent unpleasant discussions that go in circles and resolve nothing. It can make the power dynamic seem like it is just too much work for not enough reward. It can leave the s-type feeling like their failures are always taking center stage. It can leave the M-type reluctant to give any order that might trigger yet another round of processing, and an M-type with poor interpersonal skills may just stir up a bunch of emotions that neither person knows how to handle.

The "Fake It Till You Make It" Approach

Some M-types just expect you to work through the internal stuff out on your own. They expect you to consistently behave *as if* you are in the right mindset, whatever that mindset is, to the best of your ability. You are expected to treat them with respect (or reverence, or adoration, or whatever) from day one. They know that you won't always actually be in that headspace, but they trust that consistently doing the right behaviors will eventually lead you there. They don't want to hear your complaints or criticisms unless they specifically ask for it. They may even see it as whiny or disrespectful for the s-type to talk about not wanting to do this or that.

It's tempting to think this approach is far less effort for the M than our high-communication "teamwork" approach, but in real life, the Masters who I have seen make this work are continually observing the s-type's reactions, noting subtle indicators of resistance, and carefully shaping their orders to guide their partner to develop the desired mindset and behavior. Most of them had some kind of mentorship, or were themselves trained under similar methods. It is a much higher-risk approach, much easier to do poorly, and much harder to know that things are going poorly until it reaches a crisis.

For people who can make it work, it can be extremely rewarding. It does rely on having very compatible expectations about the relationship, as there is generally a lot that goes unsaid. In practice, it often relies on a supportive community that can provide the direct emotional support and guidance that M-type and s-type are not providing each other. (Also, exceedingly few M-types will be able to figure out how to do this on their own without years of painful trial and error, so advice from more experienced people is invaluable.) Most s-types will need *someone* they can talk to about their struggles, perhaps another s-type. In a more formal relationship, it is common to use a journal (which the M-type reads) or periodic check-ins where the s-type can speak freely. It is also common to use heavy SM as a cathartic release of the emotional tensions that can build up in this approach, and some consider it an essential component.

This approach works well for folks who have already had positive experiences with strict formal discipline, whether from their parents, in their education, in their career, or some other setting. If you have seen good results come from an authoritarian approach, you can make the leap of faith required to trust the process. Also, you likely understand of the various ways it can go badly, and may be able to recognize when someone is fundamentally unsuited to this approach.

This approach is very appealing to some s-types, and horrifying to others. If you know it is absolutely not your thing, good for you for figuring that out about yourself. There are plenty of M-types who aren't like that.

For the s-types whom this appeals to, be aware that if you haven't had any actual experience under strict formal discipline, do not be surprised if you find it isn't for you. The fantasy is often far more appealing. It requires the s-type to have or quickly develop certain emotional skills and strengths, and can push an unsuited person into unhealthy coping mechanisms.

If you have had experience under strict discipline, but have mixed feelings about it, proceed with caution. This approach can be rough on a person, especially if your experiences are from childhood, or combat. It isn't uncommon to have some serious emotional issues from it, even if the overall experience was positive. However, even some folks who have had very negative experiences of strict discipline, or outright abuse in the context of discipline, find that they thrive under the mindful approach to strict discipline in a mutually fulfilling context, and it is a way for them to work through those emotional issues. Others with issues from past discipline might be initially drawn to this approach, but then find it just feeds into their issues, reinforcing their trauma.

The Baby Steps Approach

When you are struggling with surrender of the mind, it may be effective to focus on surrender of the body instead. If you want to turn over more authority but aren't quite willing yet, it can help to have a period where you can try out doing the thing, without commitment. You might spend a few months where the M-type simply lets you know what they would choose for you in a certain area, and if you are willing, you can explore what it feels like to do it. From there, you might let them make those decisions by default, but you can veto them if you really object. Whether or not you decide to go forward from there, you will both be clearer about what it would be like.

The reverse method can also work, but it can be tricky. It is common for people to start a power exchange relationship giving extremely broad authority to the M-type, long before they have established enough trust to be able to effectively use it. The M-type knows on some level that if they ordered their s-type to do many of the things they agreed to, the s-type would refuse, or walk. I don't advise this approach, because in most cases, the M-type feels they can't talk to the s-type about what they think the s-type's actual limits are. It would spoil the illusion of absolute authority that both people are very invested in. However, some folks do well with giving the M-type total authority over something, with the explicit understanding that the s-type is not quite ready to do it, and the M-type has promised not to push them into things they are not ready for.

If I was to lay this process out step by step, it would look like this:

❖ In the first step along this path, the s-type retains control over assessing their own readiness for the thing. They agree that they are willing in theory, but they are confident they are not able do it without real risk of severe emotional consequences.

❖ The second step is the s-type making a commitment to diligently work towards getting okay with the thing, with the assistance of the M-type.

❖ The third step is turning over control of that work, and the assessment of readiness, to the M-type, but requiring thoughtful discussion with the s-type before each part of the work. They promise they will not move forward on it until they have worked through it with you, heard you out, and they have decided you are ready.

❖ The fourth step is turning over that assessment over without qualification. The M-type probably will discuss it, but they aren't obligated to. It is an act of trust, but in many cases, this happens without any real risk of the thing actually happening.

❖ Finally, while it is hot in fantasy, it is exceedingly rare for a mutually fulfilling relationship to include actual application of a fifth step with the M-type doing things that are likely to be devastating for the s-type, without regard for their emotional welfare. Some more extreme relationships have forays into that region between fourth and fifth step, where both people are willing to let the M-type take real risks regarding assessing the s-type's emotional readiness, with an s-type who is personally driven to pursue extreme psychological ordeal. But it is much more common for the M-type to make a show of completely disregarding the s-type's well-being, while actually being extremely cautious to push only hard enough to get the desired response.

You Are Enough

The most important thing in learning to surrender is knowing that we surrender ourselves as we are. If you feel like in order to surrender you need to be better somehow, to be more this and less that, or to get rid of parts of yourself, you are missing the point. So often we want to present a perfect polished image of surrender, but that isn't us.

We come into these relationships as imperfect beings, and we surrender our imperfect selves to other imperfect beings. So much of what holds us back from surrender comes down to not feeling worthy. I hope that this book has helped you see that there are so many different ways to give yourself to another person, and that all sorts of people can and do find fulfillment in these roles.

Further Reading

1. Gates, Aisha-Sky. *Unequal Partnership*. Selenite Press, 2017.
2. James, Andrew. *The Way of the Pleasure Slave*. Alfred Press, 2019.
3. Kaldera, Raven. *Negotiating Your Power Dynamic Relationship*. Alfred Press, 2020.
4. Kaldera, Raven, and Joshua Tenpenny. *Dear Raven and Joshua: Questions and Answers About Master/Slave Relationships*. Alfred Press 2009.
5. Kaldera, Raven. *Paradigms of Power: Styles of Master/Slave Relationships*. Alfred Press, 2014.
6. Kaldera, Raven. *Polyamory In a Power Dynamic*. Alfred Press, 2010.
7. Kaldera, Raven, and Joshua Tenpenny. *Building the Team: Cooperative Power Dynamic Relationships*. Alfred Press, 2013.
8. Kaldera, Raven. *Sacred Power, Holy Surrender: Living A Spiritual Power Dynamic*. Alfred Press, 2011.
9. Kaldera, Raven. *Hell On Wheels: Disabled Dominants* and *Kneeling In Spirit: Disabled Submissives*. Alfred Press, 2013.
10. Kaldera, Raven. *Broken Toys: Submissives with Mental Illness or Neurological Dysfunction,* and *Mastering Mind: Dominants with Mental Illness or Neurological Dysfunction*. Alfred Press, 2014.
11. Kaldera, Raven. *Unequal By Design: Counseling Power Dynamic Relationships*. Alfred Press, 2014.
12. Parker, Christine. *Where I am Led: A Service Exploration Workbook*. Alfred Press, 2009.
13. Ms. Rika. *Uniquely Dominant: Being the Dominant in a D/S Relationship*. Lulu.com, 2019.
14. Rubel, Robert J. *Master/slave Relations: Handbook of Theory and Practice*. The Nazca Plains Corporation, 2006.
15. Tenpenny, Joshua, and Raven Kaldera. *Real Service*. Alfred Press, 2011.
16. Tenpenny, Joshua. *The Service Notebook*. Alfred Press, 2012.
17. Williams, Dan and dawn. *Living M/s: A Book for Masters, Slaves, and Their Relationships*. The Nazca Plains Corporation, 2011.

www.ingramcontent.com/pod-product-compliance
Lightning Source LLC
Chambersburg PA
CBHW031504270326
41930CB00006B/246